THE WRITINGS OF
WILL ROGERS
V-2

SPONSORED BY

The Will Rogers Memorial Commission
and Oklahoma State University

THE WRITINGS OF WILL ROGERS

Will Rogers

More
Letters
of a
Self-Made
Diplomat

STEVEN K. GRAGERT, *Editor*

OKLAHOMA STATE UNIVERSITY PRESS
Stillwater, Oklahoma
1982

Printed in the United States of America
Library of Congress Catalog Card Number 82-80504
International Standard Book Number 0-914596-22-1

CONTENTS

INTRODUCTION

Will Rogers rarely opened his popular weekly newspaper articles without the familiar "All I know is just what I read in the papers," words that clearly reveal his reliance on daily newspapers and the topical origin of much of his humor. Newspapers, however, were not Rogers' only source of information and inspiration; he derived as much from the people he met, the events he witnessed, and the places he visited during his frequent travels. Indeed, his trips throughout the United States and beyond its borders provided the Oklahoman with a constantly fresh perspective of the world around him, even prompting him, when he ventured beyond his home grounds, to alter slightly his opening remarks: "All I know is what I read in the papers, and what I see as I prowl hither and thither."

Travel—be it to Miami or Moscow, to Juneau or Johannesburg, to Bakersfield or Buenos Aires, or to any one of hundreds of smaller or larger cities in between—must surely have ranked as one of Will's greatest passions. Not only did he crisscross the United States dozens of times during his fifty-five years, he also sailed, flew, or by other means journeyed around the world three times, in addition to numerous other trips abroad of shorter duration and distance. While his unquenched thirst for travel, the venture beyond his own environment, provided him with a more cosmopolitan, informed viewpoint than that enjoyed by most of his fellow Americans, it also led him to his death, for his longing to see a land he had never seen before prompted him to take the fatal flight with Wiley Post in 1935 to the barren tundra of Arctic Alaska.

One of Rogers' most famous journeys, however, occurred nine years before that last airplane trip. In May of 1926 he embarked on an extensive five-month tour of Europe, during which he visited most of the major cities on the continent, met many of its leading citizens, and made a first-hand appraisal of post-war developments. At the suggestion of the editor of the *Saturday Evening Post,* he sent the magazine records of his travels in the form of letters to then President Calvin Coolidge. While Rogers was still in Europe the *Post* began publishing the articles under the title "Letters of a Self-Made Diplomat to His President." Immensely and immediately popular, the *Post* articles were combined in the fall of 1926 with several of Rogers' early "Daily Telegrams," a newspaper series that also arose from the European tour, into book form, the book bearing the same title as the magazine pieces.

The magazine series and the book established Rogers' reputation as a keenly insightful analyzer of foreign affairs and as the country's foremost "ambassador without portfolio." In succeeding years he made other trips outside the country—to Canada in 1926, Cuba in 1928, England in 1930, Central America and Mexico in 1931, Europe and South America in 1932, and around the world in 1934—and during each he reinforced his position as the unofficial good-will diplomat of the United States.

Perhaps, two of his more well-known excursions occurred in December of 1927 when he visited Mexico and in the winter 1931-1932 when he traveled through the Far East. After each of these trips he again wrote a series of articles for the *Saturday Evening Post* that closely paralleled in style, format, substance, and even title the original "Letters of a Self-Made Diplomat to His President." These latter-day "Letters," in addition to an earlier "Letter" of January of 1927, comprise this the nineteenth volume of *The Writings of Will Rogers*, a cooperative effort of Oklahoma State University and the Will Rogers Memorial Commission of the State of Oklahoma to publish the definitive collection of the works of a most remarkable American.

The present volume opens with "A Letter from a Self-Made Diplomat to His Constituents," wherein Rogers describes his unprecedented two-day stay at the White House in September of 1926 following his return from Europe. When he had landed in New York City he had sent President Coolidge a telegram and was invited to the White House to make a "report." Rogers' subsequent article for the *Saturday Evening Post* provided Americans in the 1920s, and allows readers today, a rare look into the very private world of a president renowned for his reserved nature.

As he did with his "Letters" from Europe, Rogers again used Coolidge as the addressee of his— Rogers'—"Letters" from Mexico, which comprise the second section of the present volume. The primary difference, however, was that the latter group of "Letters," unlike the former, did not appear in the *Post* until several months after the trip had been made. Nevertheless, the style in which they were written suggests that Rogers wrote them during the visit and not afterwards.

The Mexican trip stemmed from an invitation extended by the recently appointed ambassador to that country, Dwight W. Morrow. The banker-turned-diplomat, hopeful at improving the sorry state of Mexican-United States relations, had invited both Rogers and Charles A. Lindbergh to visit Mexico on a good-will mission. The move could not have been more inspired. Both men, heroes abroad as well as at home, received outstanding welcomes from the Mexican public. And on the northern side of the border, Rogers' daily dispatches and his articles in the *Post* provided Americans with a warmly-humorous, but acutely perceptive view of society and politics in post-revolutionary Mexico.

The third series of "Letters" in this volume derived from a trip that

Rogers made around the world in 1931-1932. The major part of that journey took him through Japan, Manchuria, and China and became the focus of "Letters of a Self-Made Diplomat to Senator Borah" and the closely-related "A Letter to the Philippines." Rogers concentrated his time in the Orient because of a long simmering, oftentimes boiling dispute between the Japanese and Chinese over territorial rights to resource-rich Manchuria. The conflict, which would not be resolved for many years, offered Rogers an opportunity to view an area of the world he had never seen, and one which he found blessed with physical beauty but tormented by human avarice. Nevertheless, in the Orient, as during all of his travels, Rogers found much humor in the human condition, a poignant humor that is perhaps nowhere better exhibited than in this collection of travel memoirs.

In editing *More Letters of a Self-Made Diplomat*, we have generally followed the methodology established in earlier volumes of our collection. Because original manuscripts of the articles are not available—if indeed, they still exist—we took Rogers' texts, verbatim and virtually untouched, from the text given in the *Saturday Evening Post*. Following the style adopted in earlier volumes, we have included annotations of persons and events that may be unfamiliar to present-day readers. At no time and in no way did we attempt to interpret Rogers' text in the notes.

Several persons have lent assistance to the production of this and other volumes of *The Writings of Will Rogers*. Prominent among them has been Dr. Reba N. Collins, director of the Will Rogers Memorial, and the members of her staff, especially Mr. Gregory Malak, curator. The staff at the memorial has given freely of its expertise and time in proofreading the manuscript of this volume, researching many obscurities otherwise hidden from our own staff, and loaning us many of the documents and photographs necessary for us to complete our work.

Gratitude is also expressed for the work and active support of several individuals and groups at Oklahoma State University. In this connection I wish to thank Dr. Lawrence L. Boger, president, and Dr. Robert B. Kamm, the immediate past president, who have endorsed and encouraged the project fully. Especially helpful to our work has been the steady guidance of the Will Rogers Advisory Committee, chaired for many years by Dr. George A. Gries and presently headed by Dr. W. David Baird. Appreciation is also extended to Dr. Smith L. Holt, dean of the College of Arts and Sciences, and to the faculty of the Department of History. The capable staff of Edmon Low Library, in particular the resourceful members of the Inter-Library Loan Department, has provided key assistance. Additional, and no less significant support has come from the regents of the unversity and other members of the administration, faculty, and staff.

Funding for the editorial work of the project has been provided in large part by the State of Oklahoma with the cooperation of the Oklahoma Historical Society. Over the years Mrs. T. S. Loffland, Mr. Sylvan Goldman, the Kerr-McGee Foundation, Phillips Petroleum Corporation, and the late Mr. and Mrs. Robert W. Love have also made supremely worthy contributions to the financial and research needs of the project. To all who have made it possible, we are grateful.

The last mentioned are not necessarily the least appreciated; in this case they are among the most. Ms. Marina C. Pepper, the sole secretary for the project, has managed to juggle the typing of three separate manuscripts—with all their different drafts and redrafts—and has done so with neither a whimper nor a hitch. With similar dedication and skill, Ms. Judy G. Buchholz, the publications specialist at Oklahoma State University Press, has single-handedly guided this volume through the publishing maze, while all the time striving for the highest quality possible. To both of these fellow workers, I am forever thankful.

Steven K. Gragert,
Editor

A Letter From
A Self-Made Diplomat
To His Constituents

A Letter From a Self-Made Diplomat to His Constituents

ON BOARD ROYAL JOKER TRAIN, TOURING AMERICA
WITH OBJECT OF POSSIBLE LOAN TO OKLAHOMA.

MY DEAR CONSTITUENCY: Having nothing but your welfare at heart, I feel that I should make a report to you personally on the matter that I have just investigated. All my other work has been carried on, as you know, practically private, for just the exclusive knowledge of President Coolidge, and naturally I wouldent blab any of that out to you.[1] What I found out for him in Europe, and what I am to find out in America for him is none of your business.[2] But what I found out about the President is some of your business. So, you see, while I am working for him I am also really taking care of your interests.

Now we only possess, with all of our wealth, one residence belonging exclusively to the complaining taxpayers and I thought it would be a good idea to let you know how it is, what shape it is in and what kind of a renter we got in there. You see, there has never been any detailed report on just how our lone residential asset was making out.

The United States owns outright 8,867,221 buildings, but the White House is the only one with a bed in it. The United States has some 30,000,000 employees—or people on salary, rather. But where they sleep is none of our concern. The Senate and the House of Representatives is the only help we have that we know where they sleep. We can read some of their bills and tell where they slept. But the President is the only help we furnish linen and silverware to. Rent is the one thing I can think of that the President don't have to worry about. Now you, as delinquent Taxpayers, have a right to want to know, Is the renter taking care of the place, and what kind of a man is in there?

Well, you see, the way it really is, the White House is supposed to belong to the Government. But the Republicans have it leased for an indefinite period, and they sublet it out to a family called Coolidge. I had just arrived back home from Europe with 850,000 other half-wits

---

Saturday Evening Post, January 8, 1927. Reprinted with permission.

who think that a summer not spent among the decay and mortification of the Old World is a summer squandered.

Americans have one particular trait that they need never have any fear of some other Nation copping, and that is, we are the only people that will go where we know we are absolutely not wanted. Americans spent $700,000,000 to be insulted in Europe last summer, and they could have got it done for half the money here.

I had just landed and finished paying duty on all the linens Mrs. Rogers had bought in Dublin.[3] She had tried all the way over to find someone on the boat that dident have their $100 allowance worth and slip them a few sheets and doilies. She had to be very careful. A lot would have taken them, but they dident want to put up any security that they would hand them back after they arrived.

All passengers started in at Cherbourg, France, with more packages and baggage than I ever saw in my life. We were on the Leviathan, an American boat. But do you know they drank up their baggage before we landed? That is, most of it; and the night before coming ashore they had the most terrible time packing, trying to make bottles look like dirty clothes. On landing I had to go down to Washington on the usual business, to see about the 1922 income tax—that's the year we all had trouble. A Jewish lawyer friend of mine had told me it would go through; I had told him at the time we couldent get away with it. We dident.

So I wired Everett Sanders, Mr. Coolidge's very genial and likeable secretary, that I was coming down to Washington the next day and I would like to drop in and say hello to our President.[4] I had had a couple of very friendly chats with him before departing on this missionary work. But I had not heard from him all summer.

Well, sir, do you know it wasent more than an hour before I got a wire back: "Let us know what train you arrive on. A White House car will meet you at the station, and you are to be the guest of Mr. and Mrs. Coolidge at the White House while here."[5]

My Lord, I couldent believe it! I kept looking at it, and wondering what the catch was—if some one was kidding me or what. So I wired back to Mr. Sanders, as I was still leery about it: "I am stopping to have lunch with the editor of THE POST tomorrow, and if you-all are kidding me about the White House visit, you better head me off in Philadelphia." I dident want to go dragging up to the White House with my old telescope and have two plain-clothes men step out from behind those pillars and say, "Just a minute. Where are you headed for?"

Well, at lunch time in Philadelphia I dident get any word to turn back, so I told the editor of THE POST, and he said, "Why, it may be on the level. I made it on the old Government Tug Mayflower myself once."[6]

Well, that gave me encouragement when I heard the President was getting plain enough to recognize Editors. But I also knew that there was a lot of people that might get an invite on the Yacht that couldent come in through the kitchen to the White House. You see how that is. Mr. Coolidge is a pretty good Sailor—I guess about the best Sailor from Vermont—and, you know, it gets pretty rough down there off those Democratic states shores, even when election is not on. And they tell me Mr. Coolidge takes a kind of a fiendish pride in taking alleged friends down there and watching them hunt the rail. So you don't want to take the importance of a Mayflower invitation too serious.

I sent Mr. Sanders a wire telling him the hour of arrival, and that I sure did feel proud to know that I was to sleep in the White House, even if they had to put a cot in the Blue Room. I put that little gag in there for a reason. I was afraid that after dinner they might send me out to some annex or dormitory or outbuilding to sleep, and I wanted them to know in advance that I wanted to be under the main roof, even if I dident sleep any.

Mr. Sanders met me at the train himself, and we drove in a White House limousine—name deleted by me myself, until same make car arrives at my home gratis, when due notice will be given publically. We got to the White House, and Mr. Sanders went on to his home and I went in, was met by Mr. Hoover—not the one that took our sugar away from us that time, but an awful friendly kind of a bird that is equerry, or night-and-day club host to the White House.[7] Well he took me in, and there sit Mr. and Mrs. Coolidge. My train was late. I knew I should have taken the other line.

Now there was the President of a Country a third as big as Russia and more than half as big as China. He and the Leading Lady of our land, waiting dinner on a Lowbrow Comedian. Now if any Nation can offer any more of a demonstration of Democracy than that, I would like to hear of it. It only shows that with all of our going Cuckoo over anything from abroad that is branded with an affliction of Royalty, why, we still have one home in America that is able to retain its democracy. It wasent because I happened to be the one. But I felt that the common people were being honored. I had heard so much in Politics about them going to do something for the common people and this was the first practical demonstration I had ever witnessed of it. Not only did I feel that he was paying a tribute to just a taxpayer but I felt that Illiteracy was finally coming into its own.

Mr. Coolidge met me very cordially. He was accompanied by

5

another gentleman that I couldent see well enough to recognize. He was called "The White House Spokesman." Now if you don't know what one of those are I will tell you. Well he is some friend of the President's that Mr. Coolidge conceived the idea of sorter having around handy in case he wanted to say anything for publication; or in case he said anything that was not for publication, why it is better to let it be said by The White House Spokesman. You see Mr. Coolidge don't say much anyway himself, and for publication he don't say anything. He brings in his double. Now that is one thing the Republican Administration will always have to be thankful to Will Hays for.[8] I always knew Bill went in those movies for some kind of political reasons; now it crops out. Through the movies Will conceived the idea of the President having a double, and having everything he said that he dident know just how it was going to sound in print said by the double. You can't hardly tell this spokesman or double from the President. I have seen lots of doubles in the pictures while I was out there; in fact a movie actor is no better than his double. But this one the President has is the best one I ever saw. When he is just there not doing anything, you would swear it was Coolidge. But the minute it says anything why you know it's the double.

So it's only in the voice that you can tell the difference. If Mr. Coolidge don't say anything that you want to publish why the double may not be even around at all.

Well, Mr. Coolidge, as I said before, when he walked up to me he held out his hand, opened his lips and as he did, "The White House Spokesman" said "Hello, Will," Well for a minute I dident know which one of them was talking to me. I hadent met this spokesman and I dident see where he come in to be so familiar as to say "Hello Will" without an introduction; in fact, I wasent right sure it was him said it. Then I happened to think a minute and decide that I wanted to use the remark, "Hello Will," in my report back to the Claremore Progress, so I knew it was the White House Double that had spoken to me. But I certainly appreciated Mr. Coolidge shaking hands with me so cordially, even if he dident say a word himself.

Then he pulled a remark that I want all of you that think he or his spokesman neither have any humor, to listen too.

It was the spokesman and he said, "Well, Will, you made a typical American diplomat; you made us all laugh." Now beat that for real humor, either with or without a spokesman. I wish I had a spokesman that could think of as good and truthful things as that. I rate that about 99 per cent among political humor.

Mr. Coolidge then introduced me to Mrs. Coolidge, whom I had never met. He did that himself without any double or spokesman at all. As I dident care to quote his introduction in a book or pamphlet, there was no use using up the spokesman more than we needed.

Now listen, Ladies, if you have never met Mrs. Coolidge, you certainly have missed a rare treat. We have been particularly blessed with the types of Ladies who have graced our Executive Mansion. But this one there now has the reputation, given her by everyone who has met her, of being the most friendly and having the most charming personality of any one of them all. She is chuck plumb full of magnetism, and you feel right at home from the minute you get near her. She has a great sense of humor, and is live and right up and pleasant every minute, and Calvin is just setting there kinder sizing everything up.

Mind you, nothing is getting by him. He is taking in everything, but he ain't just what you would call bubbling over. A joke don't excite him any more than a Republican Senatorial defeat. He takes everything sorter docile. But with it all he is mighty friendly and nice, and talks a whole lot when he is with somebody that he feels can't tell him anything.

Now it was reported at the time through the papers that the night I stayed at the White House he went to sleep on me. Well, I dident deny it at the time, though it was a kind of a slam against me. I had had some pretty good audiences go to sleep on me, and I knew it wouldent do any harm to have him added to my list. But here is the joke of it, which I have never told before: Not only did he not go to sleep on me but I am the one that like to went to sleep on him. I had been asking him a lot of questions about various public things of interest, and naturally his answers would be rather technical or involved, and I would catch myself sorter blinking.

When I have the good fortune to be able to talk to some big man, I don't spend the whole time by spouting off a mess of my jokes. I am there to learn something from him. It's his ideas I want to get, not to try out any of my own on him.

We are sitting there at the table, just the three of us, chatting away about a little of everything, and here is something I want any of you children to know: If you have a dog and your mother won't let you feed it at the table, and says, "Don't feed that dog in here. What if company should come? Get him out of here." Say, go right on and feed your dog, Kids; it's being done in one of our best homes.

The Coolidges have a couple of flea hounds and they was handing out things to them all the time. One of them would come to Mr. Coolidge's place and one to hers, and they seemed to think an awful lot of those two dogs, and the dogs certainly were crazy about them. Well, they was feeding the Dogs so much that at one time it looked to me like the dogs was getting more than I was.

Now I don't want this last remark to get out. I wouldent make it if I thought it would get around up in the Maple Sirup Belt. But at any rate the dogs were not as nervous about the quantity as I was. One old pup come around to me and I just looked at him and told him: "Listen, my rations won't permit me splitting with you. You are here every day, I am only here once." He went on back to the President. The colored Butler was so slow bringing in one course that I come pretty near getting down on my all fours and barking to see if business wouldent pick up with me.

These mutts sure were pretty and fat. They are white Collies. But Lord, I would be fat and fairly pretty myself if I dident have anything to do but hang around that big Dining room and ride up and down on the elevator and lay on nice cushions and sofas.

I saw the colored boy that takes care of the Dogs and I remembered him as being the one that used to keep Laddie Boy for President Harding.[9] I said to Mr. Coolidge, "You still got the same Master of the Hounds."

The President's spokesman whom I hadent noticed even having dinner with us at all, up and took the following words right out of Mr. Coolidge's mouth, "Thats back door Sam; we have a front door Sam and a back door Sam."

Now, you know, the Coolidges palling around with these dogs there like that, it showed a mighty human trait. It ain't everybody that a mutt will take up with. They can read character better than a Politician. It showed the plain side of the family. They fed their dogs up in Vermont and they feed these down here. The White House don't make any change in their life. I bet the night the Queen eat there the old Kioodles got their hand-outs just the same. Entertaining the Queen dident make Cal break out in any lather.[10]

In New York and all other Cities they had to have some Englishman come in and coach the Mayors and Reception Committees what to wear and what to say when they met her. It took two weeks in some places to train them from acting like Americans. I bet Cal dident even consult Ex-Ambassador George Harvey over the phone about what to wear or what to say.[11] You know, when you have to be told what to say when you meet anyone, you are not the one to meet them.

Wanting to find out for you what shape the House was in, I said to Mrs. Coolidge, "I hear you had the whole House gone over and overhauled this summer." I had read something about it, and I imagine you had too.

But she replied, "Why, no, it is to be done later on this winter; but they did a little work here—put in an Ice plant, and did some work on the Kitchen. They are going to put a new roof on and do it all over, but we will have to move out for that."

8

I asked her if they would go to a Hotel and live while it was being done, as I remember when they used to live at the Willard when he was Vice President. She told me no, they thought they would take another House. Mrs. Coolidge asked me if in my travels around over in Europe I had met Queen Marie—she was just landing in this country the following week. I told her no, I couldent find her country. She said that she was to be their guest for dinner when she came, and I remarked about what a charming lady I had heard her to be.

They asked me about Charley Hughes.[12] He and I had just come over on the boat together. You know, Charley used to work for Calvin. He had him there in his faculty for quite a while. Finally Charley worked himself up till he was able to go in business for himself. They are still very good friends, and Mr. and Mrs. Hughes were coming down to go on the boat for the next week-end with them.[13] I guess that's why Mr. Hughes had been practicing going back and forth across the ocean. He will just about fool Calvin and not get sick. I told them to give the Hugheses my best regards for they are mighty fine folks, and how common he was when you really knew him. Mr. Coolidge had read in the papers about Mr. Hughes and me blasting $42,000 out of the Passengers for the Florida relief fund.[14] That was from returning passengers, which would have meant a million going the other way.

Now what will Europe say when they hear there was $42,000 that they dident get?

I asked them about what kind of a summer they had up at that Camp in New York State, and they said they had a fine summer. Mr. Coolidge said he enjoyed the fishing. You can, however, always get the truth out of the Ladies about just how things go at some new place.

Mrs. Coolidge said to me rather confidentially that the mosquitoes bothered her. I asked her how about the President, and she said, "Funny thing, they dident bother him at all."

Now this might be betraying a confidence in telling that, for they might want to get some other customer up there next summer; but I am telling you what Mrs. Coolidge told me, and I sure do believe her; and if my telling this knocks the Coolidges out of getting back next summer, the old farm at Claremore, Oklahoma, has just put in some good screens, and there is Mosquito netting over every bed.

That Mosquito business up there is some of Al Smith's doing.[15] He just about had every Democrat catch every one he could off himself and sent them up there and turned them loose. Al about said, "If I can't beat you, I will worry you."

We had fish that night for dinner. Well, I never paid much attention to the fish. I paid enough attention to it to eat it, but I never gave it any more thought. But the next day at lunch—get this! The next day at lunch—I was still there at lunch the next day! I suppose by all the laws of etiquette and the constitution of Emily Post, that I should have gone away the next morning, but I was still there.[16] When the lunch bell rang I was the first one in to the table. I had been there so long by then that I knew my place; I knew just what chair to pull back.

Well, during the lunch the Butler come to Mr. Coolidge with a platter of something that resembled some kind of hash. The White House spokesman looked at it and asked, "Same old fish?" Well, that sure did sound homelike. I had forgot about the fish the night before, but he hadent. To hear the family discussing the rehash brought me right back among the mortals. I had eaten Turkey hash for generally about a week after holidays and Weddings. Chicken hash generally runs about two days. I had partaken of Beef hash, and I have eaten hash that nobody knows what the contents were. But when you get down to eating fish hash you are flirting with Economy. This old thing of saying he preaches economy but he don't practice any of it is the bunk.

The old Collie Pups were still prowling around there during lunch, and I was mighty glad, for it made me feel more at home. But this fish hash at lunch has put me ahead of my story. I got to get back to the night before. I was saying that I was going to fly back to New York the next afternoon, that I had done a lot of flying in Europe and that it is the only way to travel; and that we over here should do more to foster commercial aviation, give the companies a government subsidy so they can exist.

The White House spokesman said, "We have more than anybody now. We have flown more miles." I told him: "Yes, you are counting in all that the Air Service is flying. We are carrying a lot of letters and advertising circulars, but we ain't carrying any people. We must get our people used to travel by air."

He said, "We are laying out quite a few routes now and there is a passenger line from Norfolk to Philadelphia that stops at Washington." I knew about that one, for that was the one I was going on—and then have to engage a special plane, as there was no regular service to get into New York, our biggest city. But I dident want to get in any argument. You always have to treat your Host with consideration. Mrs. Coolidge remarked during the heat of the debate that she dident know there was a regular passenger line to Philadelphia from Washington.

"Does anybody ride on it?" she asked.

The White House spokesman replied, "I don't know. I don't."

But by the way, they did have the line during the Sesqui-Centennial, and it was run on the exact lines and system that they have in Europe.[17] They had lovely big inclosed planes that seated about ten passengers, with double engines on them. I had a fine trip to Philadelphia; and then

Old Casey Jones, the famous flyer that hauled Tunney down to the fight , picked me up there and breezed me to New York in a little double-seater.[18]

But I am like a moving picture now—I am wandering off from my original story, I got to get back to the night before. When we had finished the meal, why, we went upstairs. Mr. Coolidge and I went into a kind of a den, or study, of his, where we were supposed to smoke. He got out a box of Cigars and offered me one. I refused with thanks, as I dident smoke.

He took one, then said, "Well, take one for Luck." I did, and placed it very careful in an inside pocket. I thought if that's what brought him all his, I will not only take it but I will try to smoke it if it nearly kills me.

Well, while we are sitting there in that little room, I would ask him questions, and he had his feet up on his desk and was leaning back, and he talked all the time. The Philippine situation was very timely then. Carmi Thompson was over there at the time trying to discover some Iron Ore.[19]

I want to get out of everywhere but America, and not let Americans even get out of here. I had heard that one end of the Philippines had wanted Independence and that the other dident. I told him I had heard that they had Oil on one of these ends and now Carmi had struck Iron Ore on the other, so that meant good-by to Independence for both ends. I thought that was a pretty good Gag, but it dident get what I would designate as a Guffaw.

I asked him what all our Gunboats was doing in China and I told him it was pretty tough on a country when they couldent have their own civil wars without us and England butting in.

I wanted to tell him to round up all them Gunboats of ours in that Yang-tse River and bring 'em home and trade 'em to some nation for some Aeroplanes. But I dident feel like giving him too much advice. I was there to listen, not to advise. Lord, gunboats will be as old-fashioned in the next war as a Whip socket. I told him that I had attended the first week of the preliminary Disarmament Conference in Geneva, that they had held the conference to see if they could hold a conference if they decided to hold a conference.[20] It dident seem to be any disappointment to him to know that it had got nowhere. The World Court—it dident take the White House spokesman long to tell me about that: "If they accept all our Reservations as laid out by the Senate, we will go in; but we will accept no alterations."[21]

Between you and me, I think they were kinder hoping that Europe would turn the proposition down. It would give them a chance to duck out gracefully, where they had sorter pulled a bonehead.

While we was talking about the Debts I told him I was in England when the Daily Mail had discovered all at once that they had been

11

paying us three years, and finally happened to think of it and earmarked us as Shylocks. He said in a characteristic sentence: "Well, England's got a right to holler—they are paying."

I want to tell you one thing: Any time you think the White House spokesman don't know about everything that is going on all over the World you are Cuckoo. I had just been to Russia for three weeks, and I felt kinder cocky and says to myself, "Here is where I give our President some late dope on Russia." Say, he had forgot more about Russia than Lenin and Trotzky and I ever knew.[22] I would start in telling him about the farmers over there not selling their stuff because they dident get enough for it. Why, he knew the amount they each raised, and even knew the farmers' names.

Mr. Goodrich, ex-governor of Indiana and an old friend of the Coolidges, was there later on in the evening, and he had been quite a lot in Russia and knew all about it.[23] But even the both of us combined was not getting any new ideas over that he dident know. Now we have no representatives over there, and how he finds all this out is more than I know. I believe he is taking a Correspondence course in Detective work. Mr. Goodrich and I, however, did certainly get Mrs. Coolidge interested. He was telling how they christened the babies, and I horned in with my experience of seeing the men and women bathing together in the Moscow River, with not even a pair of trunks in Russia. Mrs. Coolidge was all interested in it, and more so when Mr. Goodrich bore me out in it, and proved that it was not one of my jokes.

Mr. Coolidge dident seem to get het up any over this negligee custom. However, it was the only thing about Russia we brought up that he dident explain more to us than we knew ourselves. He certainly would have had a hard time improving on my knowledge of that bathing. If you can't learn anything after standing for three weeks and looking at it, you are pretty dumb.

Before we went into the main living room to join Mrs. Coolidge, and where, as I said before, Mr. Goodrich joined us, why, while I was asking the questions, and for once in my life had enough sense to keep my mouth shut, something come up about the hardships and amount of work connected with the presidency, and he remarked that the office of Chief Executive exacts a great deal from its incumbent.

I told him, "Why, you seem to have solved it better than any one of our Presidents I know of. You don't worry so much."

The White House spokesman said, "No, I never get mixed up in any of the big questions. I just let the people do a little thinking for themselves. I have found they'd rather do that." Say, that about solves up the whole thing.

Well, we then went in and joined Mrs. Coolidge. She was a-knitting, and a-smiling. I wish I could tell you Ladies what kind of dress she had on. I guess it was chiffon over organdie—that's about what it looked like to me. It was mighty becoming, anyhow. She dresses in awful good taste. Well, that suit of his is in good taste itself. So I certainly got nothing to criticize about their clothes. The old Collie was right there. One was at Mrs. Coolidge's suède pumps and the other one was lying up on a big lounge with his head in Mr. Coolidge's lap and he was a-scratching him back of the ear.

These dogs come from Wisconsin, and I think the reason Cal likes them so much is that they are the only two things ever come from there that wasent Insurgents. They just look like they are ready to vote anything with the Party. All they crave is meat and harmony.

Mrs. Coolidge and I got to chatting then about Lady Astor, who was to be there right away, and she was asking me about her.[24] She was very anxious to meet her. I was telling her she had a treat in store for her, for Nancy sho was a live one; and Mrs. Coolidge was interested in my telling what a great family woman Lady Astor was in addition to all her political duties, and how I had almost boarded there while in England. Her and Lady Astor in lots of ways remind me of each other. 'Course, Mrs. Coolidge is more reserved. But they both got humor, and they are in for anything to get a good laugh out of.

Mr. Coolidge asked me about being part Indian, and if I dident come from Oklahoma.[25] I was telling him yes, and why I had to leave there, and was just on the verge of asking for Executive clemency, when he up and said, "I am part Indian. My Folks had Indian blood."[26] Well, I commenced asking right away about the tribe, and where did they come from. He said he dident know the exact tribe, but he knew that away back his Ancestors had Indian blood.

I wanted to kinder drag him in with our Cherokees. I could see an appropriation for an Indian Hospital at Claremore, Oklahoma, the Home of the only water in the world that will cure you by smell only. Then he told me it was some tribe up in New England. Well, that let him out of our tribe. I knew it wasent the Cherokees. If my tribe ever settled in New England with all the rest of North America to pick from, they certainly wouldent be known today as the most highly civilized tribe in America. That's the bunch of Indians up there that let the Pilgrims land. That showed right there they dident know anything. Why, it took the Pilgrims 300 years of constant education before we let them land in Oklahoma with us, and then we made one of our only mistakes. But he really, away back, is some kind of Indian, he told me.

Well, we are sitting there apparently what I would call going along pretty good. Mr. Goodrich had left and I was all set to start in on some inquiries on Farmers Relief, as I knew the Farmers to be raising more yells than corn. Then, too, Mrs. Coolidge and I were what I thought having some very pleasant chatter, When Mr. Coolidge says, "Grace, where is Will going to sleep?" Well, Lord, Will hadent thought of sleeping anywhere for quite a while yet. This remark of his struck me like what the writers call a Bolt from the Blue. I was just getting into the shank of the evening and Mrs. Coolidge was just getting right down into the heel of that old sock. It was either a sock or a sweater or a neck scarf—a Newby we used to call 'em. I don't know whether Mrs. Coolidge knew which it would be till it was finished. That, as I have always noticed, is the principal joy of knitting—guessing on what it will turn out to be.

Well, I saw that I wasent going to be able to report any relief to the Farmers that night; that the only thing I could see in sight for them was, if the worst come to the worst, they would have to go to work instead of town every day.

Well, I dident relish this being shunted off to the hay this early in the evening. But for the good of the party I dident say anything.

Mrs. Coolidge said, "Will will sleep in the State Room."

I thought, "My goodness, am I back on a Steamer again?"

I bid Mrs. Coolidge good night. She said they had breakfast in their room and that I would be served in my room at any hour I desired. Well, these breakfasts is what I had heard about. But I find they only hold them publicly when there is a Campaign on, or when he has some particular policy to put over. He has the fellows come for breakfast and does his dictating between the pancakes. He walked down toward my room with me, which was the big southeast corner room.

Just then an old Darky that had been a snoozing out there somewhere bobbed up, and Mr. Coolidge bid me good night and turned me over to him. He took me in a room that was big enough you could have roped a steer in it. Great big bedstead with four big mahogany-looking pillars and a covered-wagon effect across the top. It was built up on a sort of an altar. It was the biggest, widest bed I ever saw, a regular Brigham Young affair.[27]

I knew that evidently a great many famous people had slept in there at various times, and I knew I had no business even in the house, much less in that bed—I wouldent have felt right. Right off it was a little kind of an anteroom with a small bed, and I went in there and turned down the covers and slept in there. You remember the Queen—Queen Marie the Roaming Rumanian—was to have stayed at the White House. Well, this big room was to have been her room, and this little side room I stole into would have been where the Old King would have slept if he had been with the troupe.

The old Darky was mighty friendly and I could see he was willing to do some trick and fancy chatting if just given any encouragement.

I asked him, "How long you been here?"

"Oh, I come with Mr. Roosevelt."[28]

"Mr. Roosevelt, eh? You been here quite a while. You have seen several of them come and go. All of them different, I guess—no two of them alike?"

"Yes, sir; yes, sir; that's right. Dey all sho is different."

"This one you got here now is sort of a queer one, ain't he?"

"Well, sir, Mr. Rogers, he is and then agin he ain't. I tell you 'bout Mr. Coolidge. He don't bother nobody and he don't want nobody to bother him."

Now get all your statesmen and all your Newspaper Editors to define President Coolidge, and if they beat that definition of him for accuracy, I will join Aimee McPherson's church.[29] He wanted to know what time I wanted breakfast served and what did I want. He told me Mr. Coolidge eat breakfast in his room pretty early. Then if there was any kind of special breakfast on, he eat again later with them. He said Mr. Coolidge went out for a walk every morning very early.

Well, I got up and got out what I thought was pretty early, but I met the President just getting off the Elevator. He had already been out for his walk. It wasent eight o'clock yet and he was already to start Vetoing bills by then. I saw Mrs. Coolidge and had a chat with her. She was as live and cheerful early in the morning as at dinner.

Mr. Hoover come up and wanted to know where I wanted to go—said that a White House car was at my disposal. I asked Mrs. Coolidge if she was going to use the car that morning. She laughingly said she would just walk where she was going. As Miss Alice was in New York, where I had seen her a day or so before, I told them I wanted to go out and see my other political accomplice, Mrs. Ned McLean, out at Friendship.[30]

Things were pretty dull around the old Town Politically. Had a chat with Secretary of Labor Davis.[31] He was leaving for Oklahoma to see if he could implore any of them to do any work down there. Went over to the office building and saw Mr. Sanders, and when I got back from Friendship it was time for Lunch—the one I was telling you about where the homelike Episode of the Fish Hash took place.

The President receives a line of callers every day around 12:30, and I had noticed quite a long line over there at the office, and also the cabinet had had their weekly meeting that morning to lay out their next week's plans against us.

So at the Lunch Table that day I said to Mr. Coolidge, "I see you had a lot of Visitors today." And to get in a little bit of my bum comedy I asked him, "What Notables and horse thieves did you have call today?"

As quick as a flash, and without the least semblance of a smile, the White House Spokesman replied, "The Cabinet."

15

Well, that one got such a laugh with us that he followed it up with: "And Senator Butler."[32]

Mrs. Coolidge then asked, "Who else was over, Papa?" She calls Mr. Coolidge that. You see, they were just in the usual family conversation now. I had been there so long I was one of the family.

The White House Spokesman said, "Burton, from Ohio."[33]

Mrs. Coolidge said, "What did he want?"

He replied, "Wanted me to go to Cleveland and make a speech."

She asked, "Are you going?"

"No, I ain't. Made two speeches there already and they don't know it yet."

It don't take him long to give an answer on anything. One time up in Massachusetts, when he was Governor, a Newspaper wanted to get out a big story on what everyone would do if they only had thirty minutes to live. They were very anxious to see what Governor Coolidge would say. They were supposed to write it in. Most of them had said they would pray or that they would give all they had to some Charity. When they opened his it said: "Wouldent do anything! What would be the use?"

But it was now getting late along in the lunch and I was leaving, and thought to myself they can't do anything but shoot me for trying, so I am going to ask him. He has been very good about telling me about all the things that are agitating us now. So I just up and said: "Mr. President, I know it is sorter impertinent, but it's not for publication, and I just want to know for myself, so in after years I can say to my friends, 'I knew it all the time.' Tell me and I will give you my word it will never be mentioned, How about 1928? Are you going to run?"

Well, Mrs. Coolidge started to laughing and I asked her, "What are you laughing about, Mrs. Coolidge? It's just what everybody wants to know and I won't tell it."

She said, "I was laughing because I want to know the same thing you do." So I said to him, "Come on, Mr. Coolidge, tell Mrs. Coolidge and I. You know she won't tell and I swear to you both I won't." She insisted too, "Tell us, papa."

The White House Spokesman said, "I got enough troubles now without looking forward that far."

Now that's what he told me. But I can tell you if he is going to run or not. I am not going to, but I can. I can tell you whether Russia is going to be recognized by us, and about the World Court, Debts, Philippines, Disarmament—I know what he is going to do on every one of these. And then they tell you that Coolidge don't talk! That's why these old Congressmen and Senators can't ever get anything out of him—they are so busy trying to tell him something and asking for something that he don't get a chance to talk.

16

Now about the humor part of it. He has a great sense of humor, but the trouble about the Coolidge humor is that it is wasted on most of the people that he comes in contact with. Most people can't get a joke unless someone says, "Come here, boys, get this one. Here is a new one; just heard it last night." In other words, they have to have it announced to them before what to expect.

Cal just sits there and pulls 'em without any warning on the old vote grabbers and they don't get him. I wish I had a dollar for every good Gag he has pulled that has gone over some Politician's bean. I would give anything to just be able to be hid somewhere and hear every one he pulls. I would have me some act. He pulls 'em—if you don't get 'em, that's your fault. He bid me good-by very cordially. He and Mrs. Coolidge asked me back again—it might have been her that did—and they sent me away to the Aero field to go back to New York. I had had a very pleasant visit.

Now you want to know what kind of a Renter we got in there. Well, I will tell you. He is a nice man when you know him, and He don't bother nobody and he don't want nobody to bother him.

And I can tell you whether he is going to run again, but I promised him. Now what more talking do you want a man's spokesman to do?

More Letters From
A Self-Made Diplomat
To His President

Will Rogers on the steps of the United States Embassy in Mexico City.

20

More Letters From a Self-Made Diplomat to His President

M Y DEAR CALVIN: Well, I just got down here as you suggested me doing. You said I ought to go somewhere, so I figured it was Mexico. I kinder kept waiting for my transportation and expense money, but as it dident come I just figured that with Congress there watching you, and you talking so much Economy, that it would naturally look kinder bad for you to be raiding the Treasury just to send another Ambassador where we already had one. I took a receipt for the fare and will put in a claim, and by the time it goes through all the various departments it will mean a nice little nest egg for my grandchildren.

Well, it's been quite a while since I carried on a correspondence with you, and you might have forgotten the old handwriting. But we will just take up where we left off, although a lot of things have happened since then. You sent me over to see about the debts and disarmament and Mussolini and Russia and a lot of other knickknacks.[1] Well, it's just about as I told you then. Them that ain't paid ain't going to pay, and them that has paid is sore because they did.

I notice Mellon goes over every once in a while thinking that he could do better than I could.[2] But he never brings anything back in his grip only what he takes over. They are just going to let 'em drag along till another couple of wars, and the first thing we know we will be so many wars behind with our collections that we will forget what war we are trying to collect for. Personally I would like to see Andy get something out of 'em. For he has made a good showing here at home with what little resources he had to work with, and a nice chunk paid in over from France would have just about put him in the Alexander Hamilton class.

You know, Alexander and Andrew both took over our Treasury when it dident have anything in it. A war against England had just put us in the red when Aleck quit dueling around one day and built the thing up into a going concern. Well, Andy took it over after we had just had a war on England's side, and we were broke flatter than we was when we

Saturday Evening Post, May 12, 1928. Reprinted with permission.

fought against her. It's cost us more to fight with her than it did against her. So Andy has done mighty well. He has built up a surplus that calls for a Congressional raid. This is the first time the boys have met in years when they really had something to divide up.

Well, that, as I say, settles the debt question as well as it will be settled. Now that brings us to Disarmament. Summer before last I wrote you about that. I told you then that the Washington Conference was a success because we did the sinking, and that the Geneva Conference would be the same success under the same conditions.[3] But as we had nothing to sink, the party fell flat. Where we made our mistake was in not building something in the meantime to sink. It's a mistake to say that disarmament is not possible. It is possible as long as we are the hosts and provide the sinking. Well, I am glad we found that out as quick as we did.

And don't overlook that little fellow Hugh Gibson and Admiral Hilary Jones.[4] We thought when the conference was called that they wasent hardly big enough; that we should have some better known and bigger names to represent us. I know the two Kids. I was with 'em on the boat for a week and with 'em in Geneva a week. They wasent very big, but they were the only men we ever sent to a conference in our lives that got wise that we were supposed to furnish the drinks for the house. We have had bigger men go to conferences, but we never lost as little as we did at this one. So if the time ever comes before you choose to get out of there, if you can throw anything those two boys' way, why I wish you would do it. They come nearer being Diplomats that anything we have had at a conference in fifty years.

Now the other things you sent me for was Mussolini and Russia. Well, at the time, you remember, everybody was saying that Mussolini would plunge Europe into war any day. Well, if you will have one of the help there look back over the files of our correspondence you will find where I reported to you that Mussolini dident want to fight any more than I wanted to punch Dempsey in the jaw; that he would fight when the time come, when he would have to get more territory for his people; but that he knew that he was not ready yet, and that he did these things to keep France and these other Nations scared and make 'em think he was going to fight.

Our Friends to the South

Now that has been a year and a half ago, and he hasent plunged anything into war yet, and he is not going to; he is too smart; and he is not going to plunge for the next couple or four years, for he knows the plunging is not good. But he has got something that France and all Europe is jealous of, and that is the breeding system. They are raising five hundred thousand boys a year; and you can have all the advanced war methods you want, but, after all, nobody has ever invented a war that you dident have to have somebody in the guise of Soldiers to stop the bullets. So you see, he knows that every year he will be more ready than the year before.

You see, Boss, with all of our Diplomacy and advancement and education, Nations have never become civilized enough to sell another Nation a piece of ground when they absolutely needed it for their overflow. Some Nations own big dominions that are sparsely settled, but do you think they would sell them to some nation who would settle and develop them? No, sir! It would be a breach of honor if they ever let anything go they got their clutches on. They don't mind losing it in a war, but they don't want to have to sell it; that would be too commercial. So Muss knows at some time, if he lives long enough and Italy's markmanship don't improve, that he will have to go out hunting and bring in some more land where his people have room to live.

Now that brings us down to Russia. Russia just thrives on propaganda. She does love propaganda. Instead of taking the money and improving her country, why, she sends it out to try and buy propaganda. If she spent that much money at home, then invited people in too see how well she was doing, why she wouldent need any propaganda. So Russia just remains poor, just to show the World they are right. They call each other Comrades, but they don't call each other to dinner very regular.

Poland has got independence, and they want to do something to celebrate their independence, and they figure that taking Lithuania would be just about the fitting climax to a proper celebration.

Ireland quieted down, just as I told you it would. You see, they found out in a war with each other that somebody got hurt, so why shoot each other for no good at all? So Ireland is going fine.

China, while you dident send me over with our Marines, has had a war. It was the usual modern war. Nobody knows who won.

Now the reason I am taking all these things up is just like you did in your message to Congress. You drag in a kind of a rehash of all that has happened since you last lectured the boys before. So you will pardon me for mentioning all the foregoing. But I want to show you that I am earning every nickel I get out of the job, and like yours or any presidential Message, I am trying to prove to you that I am the best man for the job. So it stood to reason that when clouds begin to gather in another direction that I was the one to make a weather report. So we started in to pay some attention to our neighbors on the south. Up to now our calling card to Mexico or Central America has been a gunboat or a bunch of Violets shaped like Marines. We could never understand why Mexico wasent just crazy about us; for we had always had their good-will, and Oil and coffee and minerals, at heart.

So when our punitive expeditions —— Whenever we lose a foreign military argument we call it Punitive.[5] Well, when the punitive smoke had cleared away we couldent figure out why they dident appreciate the fact that they had been shot in the most cordial manner possible; that we were only doing it for their own good. We couldent realize their attitude in not falling on our necks and blessing us for giving them the assistance of our superior knowledge of government.

Well, to show you that they couldent take a joke and were utterly lacking in humor, they resented it instead of thanking us. We got to counting up and taking census, and we found that our last Southern friend geographically was located at Brownsville, Texas, and Key West, Florida. Well, that dident make us lose any sleep. But the first thing we knew these people were buying things, and we looked close and they dident have our trade-mark on 'em. In fact they was getting things in other countries and not from us. They was going away over to Europe to do it.

And then they got to passing laws, what they could do with their own lands and their own Natural resources, and here they wasent asking us anything about 'em. Well, that was a fine come-off! What right did they have to pass a law telling us what we were to do with their resources in their country? And the funny part the rascals got away with it! Can you imagine the nerve of some little upstart Nation telling an American Oil Millionaire that he could dig Oil only fifty years more before taking out another lease. Or some other little Pup-Tent Nation still further south electing a President that we hadent Vessayed? Here they were taking themselves seriously. That wasent so bad, but it was interfering with our trade, our Oil and our Bananas.

Well, we just got out the old typewriter, loaded her up with ammunition and commenced to shooting the Notes to 'em. We would show 'em! We would keep 'em so busy reading they wouldent have time to pass laws. But the rascals wouldent even go to the trouble of having the notes translated. We tried Diplomats on 'em, but they wouldent dip. So we begin to realize that we better find some way to fix this up. It's all right to lose a friend; but when you lose a friend that spends money with you it's beginning to get serious.

The Bright Boy of the Class

Of course, as you know up there, Mr. President, some were just for going down and taking Mexico over. Where did this country down there, with no great chains of Commercial Clubs, and Chambers of Commerce and Junior and Freshman Chamber of Commerces, and Rotararys, and

24

Kiwanis and Lions and Tigers Clubs, and No golf pants, and no advertising Radio programs—where did a Nation like that come in to have Oil, anyhow? It was a kind of an imposition on their part to even have us go to the trouble of going down and taking their country over. But we would go ahead and do it and have it over with; we should have taken the whole thing before when we took the parts we did.

But our wiser heads got to thinking, "Well, we picked up the Philippines and now we got no place to lay it down." Then some that had studied History says, "Look at England! They took everything that wasent nailed down and now look at 'em!" Then somebody got to figuring out: "We better find some other way."

Now I don't know if it was you, Calvin, or not. I kinder give you credit for doping it out. 'Cause when those balance sheets commenced coming in from down there, and they was slowly slipping into the Red, why, that was kinder cutting into one of your pet schemes, and I can just see you looking around for something that wasent a Diplomat and saying:

"I will take one last chance, as it's business we want and as it's business we are arguing over. I believe just for a last resort I will send a business man."

And as the football season was on and being the only time of year when Colleges ever came into anybody's mind, why, you happened to think of your old preparatory School of Amherst. It was still up there around Northampton to furnish dancing partners for Smith Girls till they could get over in a big town and pick up something permanent. Well, when your thoughts went to Amherst you couldent hardly help thinking of the old Graduating class, and of the fellow that they practically had the graduation for. Amherst had practically existed for four years just to advance the qualities of a student called Morrow.[6] They voted at the end of the graduation as to what boy in the class would be apt to accomplish things that would make people doubt he come from Amherst. Well, Morrow got every vote in the class but two, and you got those two.

Now Morrow voted for you, but there has always been a traditional suspicion that you dident vote for Morrow. In fact the first vote you ever cast is suspected of being a kind of a family affair. Now I am not saying it's so. It's only hearsay with me. I got the story from Morrow. Well, anyhow you showed yourself a good fellow by not holding against him the fact that the rest of the class outside yourself considered him the brightest boy.

In the meantime he was drifting along from bad to worse, till he had finally landed in the Morgan manger.[7] Well, it seems like at heart you had always liked this fellow. While you had never been able to exactly help him, you always felt sorry for him, for you knew that given a chance he was really above his surroundings. Morgan's had kinder picked him up to add a little tone of respectability to their Klan at a time when they needed character more than interest.

So you decided that here was a chance to pull him out of this bog hole of Bonds, this stench of Stocks, this incense of Interest, this lather of Loans, and redeem him back to us where addition of figures is still in its infancy. You even decided to get him out of this sordid financial state and send him to Mexico. Well, asking a man to go to Mexico at that time in the interests of the United States was just like saying, "Your tumbler of Carbolic acid is ready, Sir. Would you like water with it?"

Well, everybody thought when they read you had asked him to go that you were still sore at him for getting all those votes that time. But understanding you like Butler and I do, why, I knew about how you figured it.

You just said: "I wonder if we tried using kindness and common sense would it do any good, or would it be such a novelty that Mexico would think we were kidding 'em?"

That's when I think your thoughts hit on Morrow. You thought here is a fellow that will understand a race of people even if they all don't wear knee breeches and talk of their Golf scores. Well, I am not kidding you when I tell you you was inspired. You hit on him when nobody else was thinking about him, and here there was a couple of hundred so-called Diplomats laying off that would have even been willing to go to Haiti. We knew, as I said before, about him being with Morgan. We also knew that Amherst had just whetted his appetite for an education.

Well, if you remember, when you appointed him he gave up his job with Morgan. Well, that made a hit with everybody, for it showed that he didn't have the least inkling of a Politician in him. For it's not necessary or even customary to give up a side line when taking on any kind of Government work. It's generally understood that you won't do enough for the Government that it will interfere with any regular employment you have. But then he showed that he was going to take this business serious, and give up some important money to do it. He left Morgan flat, when Morgan had nothing but a secured mortgage on the World at 7 per cent.

The Fateful Summons

But I must get back to myself and tell you how I got down there. I was sitting around Beverly Hills waiting for another screen wedding between old-timers when your mental message of telepathy come. So I just lit right out. I went down to the Mexican Consul to get a passport, for I remembered what a time I had had getting out of this country the other time. You remember they like to held me up because nobody was with me that had witnessed my birth. Well, my birth was not of such international importance to the Mexican Government, and they also dident charge me for the passport. England and France and us too—we all charge ten dollars or more to give you the privilege of seeing them or us. That's more than you would pay to see Ziegfeld's girls.[8]

Well, you see, Mexico don't charge you to go see their country. There is just lots of little things like this I will tell you about as I go along where they are primitive. I went around by the way of Laredo, Texas, for I had heard Morrow went that way, and what was good enough for one of J.P.'s Boys was good enough for me.

Well, of course, on account of the friendly way our Newspapers have of mentioning all the robberies and banditry that they can hear of in Mexico, on account of being nothing of that nature here at home, why, I thought it wouldent be official for a train to go in there unless everyone on it was killed and robbed at least once. So I begin to get leery the night I left San Antonio for Laredo, where I was to arrive the next morning, staying on this same car and going straight through to Mexico City. Well, I was dreaming about bandits and ransoms and backs up to walls and all that, and finally I heard a pounding at my drawing-room door.

I says to myself, "Well, that's them and they got me." I was scared about stiff. I heard some fellows talking Spanish outside my window. They kept knocking on the door, and finally I heard my name: "Is Rogers in here?"

I thought, "My Lord, they even know the name! I am a goner!"

The Ranger Gets His Man

I was afraid if I dident open it they would shoot it open, so I did. Well, there stood some pretty tough-looking Hombres, but they spoke English, or what they thought was. They wanted to know if I was Will Rogers— that they were after me. I could see the wife trying to raise the ransom money. I had always said a man had no business in another country if he dident take his own chances going there, and that he shouldent put up a holler for his government to protect him.

So I says, "Here is where you are going to need some protection yourself."

I turned on the lights, and they looked worse in the light than they had sounded in the dark. It was still dark outside, and I had no idea what time of night it was.

I thought, "Well, I have always read they don't shoot 'em till daylight, anyway."

The nearest one had on a big belt and silver-mounted pistols: "We are looking for you."

27

"I thought you must be, to have found me away down here in Mexico."

I had read and answered questions about what books to take with you if you were going on a desert Island all alone. But I had never read any instructions what to do if you have got only perhaps an hour to live. Books and things always instruct you in the wrong things. I had read that they died mighty brave in Mexico. But I wasent a native. I started to dress, but I was stepping into my shirt and trying to pull my pants on over my head.

Then one of them thought they better announce who they were: "This is the mayor of Laredo, Texas, and a bunch of the town's prominent citizens, including the Captain of the Texas Rangers." [He was the Guy I had seen with the big gun.] "We come down to take you to breakfast."[9]

Well, readers, if ever the Governor sent a man with a reprieve, he did so with that announcement. If they had been Mexican Bandits they would never have had to shoot me. I would have just died of fright right on their hands and saved them any homicidal trouble.

I said, "Well, how did you fellows get into Mexico?"

"Mexico! This is Texas. You haven't gone into Mexico yet. Your train don't leave from over the river on the Mexican side till eleven o'clock. It's only six now."

Well, I didn't know whether they were or not. I knew they were Americans, but I wasent sure about them being prominent Citizens. I have watched these Committees that meet trains to welcome guests and they are generally the ones chosen because they have silk hats and striped pants. These dident have on the regulation regalia. They were just a bunch that had stayed up all night in a poker game and happened to be going home when the train come in. There was a Mayor and some bankers among 'em, but that meant nothing as far as social standing went.

Well, they were a fine bunch, even if they were masking under an assumed name. We went down to a nice up-to-date Hotel, had a good breakfast, talked a lot of politics. They seemed tickled when I told 'em that the Democrats had finally decided to have another go at the cup. They were like Sir Thomas Lipton—they believed if they got a good wind they could some day cruise in.[10] I nominated Dan Moody for Vice President.[11]

Well, soon as we eat all they would bring, and got the two parties straightened out, why, we pulled the old Rotary stunt of going out in a machine to see the town. I thought at first that I could have stood where I was and looked at it. But after I got out a ways, why, I saw that I was wrong.

The town of Laredo is a real thriving up-to-date little city. The only

28

thing I was disappointed in was the river. I had seen the Rio Grande further up, and I looked for it to be pretty big down there. But the further it went it looked like the smaller it got. I found out afterward what made it. It's the Americans taking all the water out of it. It's a good thing the Mexicans don't want to use their share, for if they did they would have to cross the river to get it.

Laredo on the Mexican side was a mighty good-looking town itself. There was about a four or five story brewery on their bank of the river that give them just about as envious a looking sky line as a town could wish. Then they had a place on our side where they used to watch the Revolutionary battles across the river, when some overambitious bandit would decide he would like to have the brewery. Then the Americans would rush down to the river to see the battle, watch them shoot each other, then go home and condemn the Mexicans for being so cruel-hearted as to sit and watch a Bullfight.

Then we drove down the river, and do you know what the rascals had the nerve to show a Californian? Why, orange trees—miles and miles of 'em! Where did this cattle and Burro raising State come in to be butting in on our National commodity?

The Border Towns

Then what do you think they had—hundreds of acres of them? Onions! I am not kidding you. There was enough in one field to change the breath of North America. I never had any idea that anyone took Onion raising serious. I just thought when everybody got through planting their garden, if they had more room left over they put in some Onions. I had no idea anybody made it a business. But with this Laredo the odor of a growing Onion was fragrance to their nostrils. It's what Machine-gun fire is to a Chicagoan; what Tom Heflin's voice is to a Klan sheet and pillow slip.[12]

But here was the great Southwest Texas, where if a man dident come in to the ranch at night dragging a lobo wolf or a mountain lion on the end of his lariat, we had always been led to believe he was a sissy. Here they was out day-herding onions! You can never tell what a great State will come to.

Well, like all Mexican-border towns, they get along great with the other side. Both sides of the line, or river, understand each other and get on fine. Our only trouble with Mexico is caused by people that never saw it. Laredo, Nogales, El Paso, Brownsville and all the rest of them, they could go along forever and never have a word's difference. It's always the guy from New York or Chicago that has the grievance. And here's a tip for you, Calvin: When you are appointing one of these commissions some time to deal with them over some problem, appoint some of these fellows on the border that knows both sides' angle.

Well, this Mayor and these Bankers, that was still disguised as prominent Citizens, took me over on the Mexico side, where I was to catch my train again. The Mexican customs are very nice, and don't want to put you to any more trouble than is possible. But they are very strict about Liquor. They used to, before Prohibition in this country, have no trouble, because both sides of the river had practically the same stuff. But now we are making corn liquor of which nobody don't seem to be able to get ahold of the recipe but us, and it's what they have to keep out of Mexico. It's the stuff that causes all the uprisings. They have a native drink there called Mescal, or Tequila, that they use to think was pretty Bravo; but since we got to smuggling in our concoction, why, they just use these two Mexican drinks as a chaser. Our Bootleggers guarantee a Revolution in every bottle. A half case will make you a General and a whole case you believe you are President.

A Great Disappointment

But when I told them I dident have any, why, they dident search me at all. They are the funniest custom officers. They seem to believe you. They are not a bit like some of ours in New York. These take it for granted that you are not smuggling in anything, while the N.Y. ones believe everybody is, until they find that you are not; and that makes 'em think they have made a mistake and they start all over again.

It is a very nice train—has a couple of Pullmans that go clear through from San Antonio to Mexico City. They are regular Pullman sleepers leased from the Pullman Company. There is a Club and Buffet car, where you get your meals. The waiters speak English, so there is no need to start trying your Spanish yet. You leave Laredo at eleven that day and reach Mexico City the next night at eight o'clock. You are on a day and a half and one night. There is not much to see after you leave. It's mostly level and nothing but mesquite brush. Nature so provided that the worst part of Mexico joins us. If it hadent been, we would have taken any good part long ago. That night I don't know what kind of country we passed through, but I suppose it was the most beautiful part of Mexico, for if you ever talk with a native of any country where you have spent a night and day on the train, he will always say, "Oh, it's too bad. It was during the night that you passed through the loveliest country. What you saw in the day was our poorest." So I guess we hit some pretty stuff that night. I dident look out much. I was still leery of the Bandits. I knew how sore a bandit got when he held anyone up and they dident have enough to suit him. Every time the train stopped I would wait for the shots and groans.

I had made my will and looked over the insurance papers to see if they covered foreign countries. All this was due to the bandit tales you read in our papers. If they are short of a couple of local murders and a robbery at home that morning, they can always fill in the three columns with some imaginary holdup in Mexico. Or if it's a California paper they can put in a Frost in Florida Kills all the Citrus, or if it's in Florida, they can get a couple of columns with Snow in California Freezes Tourist to death.

Well, I was kinder disappointed when daylight come and nobody had robbed the train. I felt like suing the American Newspapers for advertising something that I dident get.

While I am just sitting here looking out the window, I just wonder what you-all are doing up around the old Capitol. I can see the Senators and Congressmen with their knapsacks, ready to carry out Andy's hard-earned savings. I understand he told them he had saved 225 million for 'em, and they think he is holding out on 'em. They want to split 300 million. So it looks like a fellow don't get much credit for saving anything, for the more he saves, the more they think he ought to save.

But I can't be studying about you and that gang. I got to tell you about this sister Republic of ours. You see a lot of Ox teams, only they have the yoke fastened onto the horns; we fasten them onto the necks.

I can just hear Americans coming down here say, "Oh, isn't this a primitive country! Look at them still working oxen! You would think they would have a tractor."

Well, it might strike them as being sorter primitive. But to you and me, Cal, it ain't so primitive. The last oxen I remember seeing was right up there in the edge of Plymouth, Vermont, last summer—in fact on your farm. So Oxen don't seem to have been any great drawback when we needed a President and an Attorney General; for ain't Sargent right out of that Gee-and-Haw neighborhood too?[13]

Burros—lots of Burros. You don't see many horses along here. Everybody is either riding or driving a Burro. (You know what a Burro is, don't you? It's a little old kind of a mule; it's not a piece of furniture. That's spelled Beaureaux.) And the loads they can carry! Here is one with two big baskets, one swung on either side. I bet you could put a full-grown barrel in either basket. Then the man is riding up on top of that. His feet stick straight out along the Burro's neck. Here is a whole pack train of them, packed with mesquite roots for wood. It looks like a cord of wood on each one.

Oh, get this! Here is a street car come to meet the train. It runs on a track and has mules, not Burros, hitched to it. They are taking them off one end and hitching them on the other. They don't have to turn the car around, and the driver conducts, when he is not conducting the Mules. The people are getting in the little street car to go up to the Pueblo. It

Rogers in Plymouth, Vermont, the birthplace of President Calvin Coolidge.

hasent been so long since we had 'em, and I always wanted to drive one, only we used horses.

Ten Minutes for Refreshments

Got out just now and walked up along the station platform along by the day coaches. They are just packed. It looks like half of Mexico is in those coaches and the other half come to the train to sell 'em something to eat. They must just wait till they get on a train to start eating. They have every kind of eatable in the world to sell. All kinds of candies and sweets, and at this particular town they have a kind of a candy that is like a very thick sirup. It's in boxes and is considered quite a delicacy all over Mexico.

Here is a bunch of soldiers going to get on the train. A lot of them have a stick with green-looking lemons stuck on it like a string of fish. Sucking on a green lemon would just about make me want to get into the heat of a good revolution. Here's little carved wood furniture and little wooden dolls to sell.

A great thing that seems to sell pretty pronto is just sticks of sugar cane that they just eat like a long stick of candy. Every station has an old deformed-legged beggar, a meek-looking old man that drags himself along. Every one looks like they are over a hundred years old.

Men meet and embrace like women. They don't kiss, but they give what is called the Embrazo—a term of great affection. They embrace and pat each other's backs. With us, if one fellow pats us on our back, our chest is stuck out so far we couldent reach out and pat him on his.

Here is a young girl whipping her dog. He run under the train and she thought he was going to get run over. She sure is working on him.

Every town, no matter how little, has one or more big churches, their steeples rising high above the other buildings.

We are winding our way down along a stream, with big old Cottonwood and Pepper trees around the little Dobie—sod—houses. Pretty near every man you see has his blanket over his arm. They don't have to go to a whole lot of trouble to go to bed.

Here they are plowing with forked sticks as plows, like Bible days. Then we run into a town and there is up-to-date American Autos, and the young girls all with bobbed hair and lips painted.

It's a great country of contrasts. Goats—you see lots and lots of Goats. They use them for the milk. Every little hut has a goat staked out in the grass some place near. Here is a big band of them herded by a little boy. He has a stick. It looks like a staff, and one of those early Biblical pictures of the shepherd boy.

Quaint Mexicana

The thing that strikes me is that we go away over to Europe and prowl all around hunting for odd and different things, and here they are at our very doorstep. I was all around Spain and Italy, Russia, Holland, Switzerland, and all of them, and there is more quaintness and different things to see here than I saw in the whole of Europe. They are building roads now, too, so when the American Tourists do start they won't have room to put 'em.

Every Mexican woman has a shawl over her head, and if it's early in the morning, when it's kinder chilly, why, the men have theirs wrapped all around their head. They seem to figure if they can just keep their heads warm it don't matter about the rest of them.

Here is another big band of goats and a woman is herding them. She is standing up. If a man was herding them he would be sitting down in the shade of a mesquite bush. They have more odd-colored goats—every color in the rainbow, striped ones, spotted ones.

Here is a pack train of burros with big rocks weighing a hundred or more pounds each—and some of them have several on them. Oh, I savvy now! It's from the mines. It's Ore being brought down to a smelter to be melted up. There must be fifty of them. A Burro and a Ford is two things you can't seem to overload.

Cactus—some of the oddest shapes you ever saw. The fences are all made of rock or of cactus that is planted in a row. Every woman looks like she is leading or carrying a baby, some of them Indian-fashion on their backs.

All the women seem to wear black. There can't be that much mourning in the country for dead husbands. Why, even up home, if women wore mourning for divorced husbands there wouldent be this much black.

Here is the women down at the creek washing clothes on the rocks. They look like they make a kind of picnic out of it. They all got their families, and you can't hardly tell whether it's a washing or a camp meeting. The bushes are all full of clothes drying.

Oh, here goes an old-time stagecoach pulled by four mules! It's not quite as big as our old ones, but it sure is just like them.

Here is a couple of kids got a goat roped and the woman is trying to milk it. That old goat sure is wild.

Here is the town of Quaretario, or something like that. Anyhow, it's the town where they killed Maximilian.[14] He is the fellow that Napoleon III sent over to rule this country. He couldent come himself. I guess him picking somebody to send over here is kinder like your job, Mr. President, trying to pick somebody to go and run the Philipe. I thought we was going to give 'em up soon as they was ready for independence. How

34

can you tell when anybody is ready for independence? Can't judge by us.

Here they are trying to sell Opals. The Opal mines are near here somewhere, so the Porter says. I get all my news from him. He is my Massachusetts Butler; he digs up all the news for me.

After I left home I got a wire from Mr. Robinson, President Calles' American son-in-law, asking me to join the President's special train that is coming back up this way on a tour.[15] I told him I sure would join him. So I guess I won't any more than get into Mexico City tonight than I will have to go right out. Morrow is going with him too. So I will see that Morrow looks after our interests on the trip.

We are climbing now, because Mexico City is away up on a kind of a high Plateau. I always thought the place must be hot. But they say it is cool the year round. It's getting late in the evening, and we see the women or little boys driving the cattle or goats home at night. They pen them in corrals near the houses. There is a little bit of boy with his dog driving in some big old oxen. What a cow-puncher he will be if they ever give him a horse! Here is a very pretty woman riding a burro and sitting sidewise.

We are passing over a bridge with a stream and some women are bathing. Oh, you Russia! But these are very modest about it.

Here is another Station. Oh, what beautiful drawn work the women are selling! They do make beautiful things down here. It's getting dark. We can't see anything else till we get into the city. I am awful anxious to see this Presidential train. You know, I never saw one in my life. I read a lot about yours when you was going to the Black Hills to pacify the farmer last summer, but I dident get to see it. I remember about you taking Rebecca the pet Coon out there. I just got to thinking, mebbe that's what I will be on this trip.

Yours for information you can't get through a Diplomat,   WILL.

P.S. Don't worry about me down here. I have already announced publically to the World that I am not a Candidate for a thing. Don't let the boys take everything that Mellon has saved.

More Letters From a Self-Made Diplomat to His President

SOMEWHERE IN MEXICO ON THE PRESIDENTIAL TRAIN

MY DEAR CALVIN: I havent had time to write you for several days. I dont know whether you have heard from Morrow or not. I told him when it looked to me like I dident have time to write for him to do it, and then when it looked to me like he was too busy with something else, why, I would do the writing.

First I will tell you about the train and how we started out. I got in there the other night and was met at the train by Mr. Robinson and his wife, the President's daughter. They took me bag and baggage right over onto the adjoining track, where stood the Presidential train. It was to go out in about an hour or so. There was bands playing and soldiers' bugles blowing and swell-dressed Presidential guards. I never saw so much excitement in my life as was going on around the depot.

Now I don't want to discourage you, but you talk about a train, this Mexico has a Presidential train. It is brand-new, only delivered by the Pullman Company to them a short time ago. If you ever was in this you would actually be ashamed to get into one of those things the B. &. O. and the Pennsylvania haul you around in. Now you know Dwight Morrow has seen some pretty good trains in his time. Being with Morgan, he naturally mixed up with about the best we got. But I wish you could have seen his eyes when he got on this one. I really felt ashamed of his embarrassment. He was just rubbering around and couldent speak. It was humiliating to me. I had let on like the Iron Mountain had had one running through Claremore, Oklahoma, like this all my life. But Morrow's rubiness made it look like I was the only American that had ever been used to things.

Just Like Home

Of course the President's car is last, and it has a great big sitting or living room in the back end, or what I would call a parlor. There's where we would all meet and swap Diplomacy when we wasent eating. Then the President's own room adjoins this. Then the diner is a great big room in the next car, with a big long table running through the center, just like a regular home dining room. It's all very finely paneled wood of some kind; I guess mahogany—as that's the only fine wood I know the name

---

Saturday Evening Post, May 19, 1928. Reprinted with permission.

of. The chairs and couches were great big comfortable affairs. There was draperies and cords and tassels; and, oh, I must tell you, some of these tassels and cords were missing. When the train was shipped from the Pullman factory to Mexico, it stopped in several American towns and the people were allowed to go through and see it. Well, that's when they lost the fancy knickknacks. They had to quit showing it in the states or the people would have taken the wheels and the running gears off it. That is a trait that I don't believe any other people in the world have developed it to the extent that our folks have. It's almost impossible to show the American folks something that if you turn your head they won't try to carry it home. The new train never lost a thing after it got into Mexico, as that Progress and Go-Get-'Em Spirit had not penetrated that far south.

There is about eight cars in the train, all made to go together. All compartment cars except the two or three baggage and automobile cars. The President's Autos were all carried and unloaded almost as quick as we stopped and were going some place. They were unloaded just like circus wagons down a runway. The cooks were right from his Palace at Chapultepec, and the eats sure were good.

There was four Presidential guards stationed on each vestibule between the cars. I never could find out when they eat or drank or was changed, for I spied on 'em and I never could catch 'em doing any of these. But they stuck the trip out and finished in good shape.

As I say, I got in at eight o'clock, and we were to leave out again at ten. We were having a great time around the station. The Mayor of Mexico City come down to welcome me.[1] He dident know that I was President of the Ex-Mayors Association. You know there is an organization that will grow. The only thing I am afraid Jimmy Walker will supplant me as head of it some day.[2]

The Ambassadors Meet

Morrow was the first to show up. I had never met him. But he sure did win me right from the jump. I thought mebbe on account of being such a friend of yours that he would be kinder like you. What I mean by that, he would be kinder stingy with his chatter. But, say, he is the most pleasant fellow I ever saw. He is little, but five foot six of solid personality. We talked about you and he asked me how you was doing, and I made out that you was doing all right.

There wasent any use letting him know that certain little things wasent breaking just right. I just kinder let on like you had relieved the Farmers and fixed the Dikes on the Mississippi and Had Mussel Shoals going and Boulder Dam started, and had taxes cut down, and had done all those little annoying things that have been coming up. He seemed

37

tickled to death; said he always had confidence in you; even when you was elected Vice President, he never lost faith.

We was to have several Americans on the trip with us, men from a construction company of New York City.[3] They are doing some tremendous big public works for Mexico in the way of Dams and irrigation works, and those are the things principally that the President was going out on this trip to inspect, and Mr. Morrow was to go with him—incidentally the first time that an American Ambassador had ever accompanied a Mexican President on a tour of the Country.

You know, this Morrow does a lot of things that I imagine are not in the book that tells what Diplomats should do. You know, he kinder figures out that if Calles is the man that he was sent there to deal with, that Calles is the man that he should know and understand. Diplomats, when they get to a Country, they figure they must first meet the rich people of their own Country who are living there, and then the rich ones who belong in the Country. But as far as the Government officials are concerned, why, they will perhaps know them at some time through the exchange of official visits.

You know yourself, Calvin, that there is lots of men high in official life in every country that socially couldent make a swell drawing-room with a letter of recommendation from an archbishop. Take our own country. We got men that have drawn every Government Salary that is in the gift of the Common people, yet a policeman wouldent let them on Park Avenue. Why, there is homes in New York that a Congressman would have to disguise as a waiter to get into. It's nothing agin you-all. You are just a branch of people that havent been housebroke to their ways. A Politician couldent pour a cup of tea into a washtub without wasting half of it on some Hostess' bare knees. If an Official in public life does happen to crash the gate of a swell dinner party, he is there in about the same capacity as an Actor, a Prize Fighter or a Channel Swimmer—just to be looked at at close range and not through any degree of equality.

But these regular Diplomats, they kinder run in that Social class. They are the buffers between Officeholders and Society. They come from the Social set, but have to cultivate friendship with Politicians in order to get the appointment. When they have to go to Washington to kinder stir around with the Home State Senators and Congressmen, why, they feel like they are slumming. So, naturally, when they get their appointment to represent us at some other country, why, they know the class of men who are running that country won't be of any higher social standing than the ones at home. So they naturally hunt up and flock with people who are Butler-broke and Footman-wise.

You know, there is one thing that an outsider can't do, I don't care how much money he may have suddenly made. He can't get used to doing

Ambassador Dwight W. Morrow and President Plutarco Elías Calles.

anything in a house without knowing in his own heart that the Servants know he is doing it wrong. Culture, after all, is nothing but studied indifference. A high-toned Diplomat has about the same disdain for a Politician that a young College graduate has for the people who never went to grammar school, but who he has to go and ask for a job.

A Fair Share for Everyone

But this Bird Morrow dident pull that. In fact, I doubt if he ever was much on Drawing-room stuff even at home. He could get into that set, but he was too smart to do it. In fact, I think running with you had kinder kept him pretty common. He wasent in Mexico to follow suit of our other Diplomats and try and bat three hundred in the Dinner-Table League. He had no daughters that he wanted to palm off on some unsuspecting young Don, and what his charming wife lacked in the usual Diplomatic social ambitions she made up in real down-to-earth common sense.[4] He just figured the men running this Government may not know a Demmi-tasse from a Hors D'œuvre. Their Dress suits might be made by Sears Roebuck and they might wear scabbards on their table knives to keep from cutting their mouth. But they were the ones that his Government had sent him here to deal with.

He was down here to do business with Mexico and not lead a Cotillion in a charity fête, got up by some of the oldest families in aid of the starving Golf Players of Scotland. It dident matter to him if some of the Mexicans officials could show more bullet holes than Diplomas. He just forgot his Emily Post and wiped out the memories of nights spent on the Corsair and he commenced to hunting out the men whose names were not on the Social register, but whose names had to be signed on the perforated line before you could walk away with a Government appointment.

He just figures: "I don't know how they got in office, or where they got in office from, or what their previous condition of servitude was. They are the ones that are on bases now. I don't know if they got on with a base hit, a walk, a Revolution or one of those Coupe-De-Tays. I only know they are in, and they are the Babies Cal sent me down here to play marbles with."

So that is one of the main things I base his success on in Mexico. If he gets away with this, it's liable to change the whole business of Embassy-ing. He is just liable to change it into a human job. You see, heretofore an Ambassador liked to judge his results by how successful his dinners turned out. Well, Morrow would rather have the oil situation turn out successful even if his guests showed up with their dinner Jackets on backward.

He is trying to get down to earth and say to the Mexican authorities:

"Let's see if we can't split this oil thing so we can both make a little money out of it. You got the oil and we got the market, so the quicker we get together, the quicker we will all be making some Jack."

The Latin races are proud and temperamental, but at that they are not different from the neighbors on the north. They are business men. They feel that they own the resources, no matter what they might be, and if we come in and develop them, that's all right, but that we shouldent want to get away with all of it. After all, the fellow that furnished the resources ought to have a fair divvy of the loot, and Morrow feels they should have it.

You know, sometimes the fellow who is putting in his money feels that he ought to have the big end. But, after all, when he gets through he has got his profit and his Investment out. But the one with nothing but the resources, when they are gone, his original investment is blowed up. Nature only put so many resources in the ground, and when you happen to own some of 'em, why, you got to nurse your investment along.

Well, just before the train was supposed to pull out, along come President Calles—pronounced Ki-us. Had all his family with him. It looked like the Roosevelts rolling out for Oyster Bay in the early day, only Calles' children run more to daughters. There was daughters of pretty near any age you wanted, all pretty, as most Mexican Girls are. But these were exceptionally so. They had all come down to bid him good-by. This was to be an all-male trip we were making.

Calles is a big pleasant fellow, a regular big two-fisted He Man, big, square-built, broad-shouldered, hair slightly graying; must be a man in his early fifties. Got a corking sense of humor. In fact, all the Mexicans have. They are not near as serious as people think. They get a laugh out of everything. In fact, I couldent find anything they did take serious but a Bum Bull. You let a cowardly Bull come into the ring, and they certainly were serious and meant it when they would demand of the Judges or Referees to take him out. That's the only time I saw Mexicans serious. Why, the Latin-American Cartoonists and Characturists are the greatest in the World. They have some marvelous humor just in a few strokes of the pen.

Secondhand Conversation

Calles don't speak English, but I think he understands a whole lot more of it than he lets on. Now ordinarily when you can't talk to a man or him to you, why, the whole thing is spoiled. You can't do anything through an Interpreter. Neither party's personality or meaning gets over. It's kinder like talking over the radio—by the time it gets to the other party it's not you saying it.

But let me tell you about the break I got in Mexico. There is a lot of Ex-

American brothers there names Smithers.[5] They are in business there and are old friends of the President. Well, this one that was with us is the best Interpreter IN THE WORLD. He is the only man that can interpret humor from one language to the other, and not only not lose any of it but gain some additional in the exchange. The reason he is so good is because it's not his business, and he don't think he is a Interpreter. Regular interpreters interpret every word literally, and when it gets in the other languages it don't mean anything. But this Guy gets the real kick or meaning to it, and then puts it over in the other language just like it was meant in the first language. He could get more laughs out of my stuff with the Mexicans than I could out of the Americans present when I was first telling it to him. 'Course part of that was due to the Mexicans having perhaps more humor than the Americans on the trip. But I doubt it, for we had a keen bunch, and Morrow has always got his ears cocked for a gag and nothing escapes him. Well, that made it a great trip. This old Smithers got so he could imitate me pulling a Gag, and when I would tell one on you, Mr. President, he got so he could do you in Mexican. Can you imagine a Vermont Mexican?

Well, we finally started out. It must have been a good deal like your train when you-all lit out for the Black Hills last summer. It was the first Presidential train I had ever been on. I felt like Rebecca the Coon.[6] I knew I was out of place, but I just said, well, I will try to act like I belong. We had three United States Correspondents with us.

Oh, say, there is another thing I want to tell you about. This fellow Morrow calls himself Ambassador from the United States, not America. You know Mexico feels—and with some slight justification—that they are in America too. They don't feel that America ends at the Rio Grande river. Of course they may be wrong, but they are just childish enough to feel that way. But we always speak of ourselves down there as being From America, as though they were in Asia. But Morrow don't make that mistake and they appreciate it.

These three U. S. newspaper Boys were great, and there was three Mexican Newspaper Boys with us. All spoke English and were a fine bunch of boys. One Mexican was named Tim Healy—Señor Don Tim Healy.[7] There is a great Old Mexican name. Well, you know Obregón— the next President's real name is O'Brien.[8] These Irish, you got to watch 'em or they will take these Countries. There is a few of 'em sneaked into Oklahoma and got mixed up with the Rogerses and the Cherokees, and I am a sort of an offshoot—an Irish Indian. Well, this Healy is a bright newspaper boy in any man's country. The President's Military Staff officers were a fine bunch of young fellows, graduates of the Military school.

A General Joke

The President's Doctor, a noted Physician and surgeon, was along on the train. He and I kinder threw in together and always rode in the same car out to the various places, and when he wasent explaining to me to be careful what I said in my Spanish in Seven Days, that I thought I was saying one word but that it meant another, and that I seemed to have a knack of trying to say a word that sounded like some Naughty word. Well, if he wasent coaching me, we would be talking operations. I had had one, so naturally I knew more about it than he did, and he had taken bullets out of two-thirds of Mexico. He is the fellow that took off Obregón's arm, in the battle with old Poncho Villa.[9] We was in the town where the battle was and he showed the place. Obregón licked Villa in that battle.

You know, this Obregón is a really great General, and a real Comedian and full of jokes. He is either leading an army or telling a joke all the time. He is the fellow that the Sculptoress wanted to make a bust of him after he had lost his arm and he said, "No, they were liable to mistake it for Venus De Milo."

I had dinner up to his house in Mexico City one night. I must tell you about that. But what I am trying to tell you now is about this trip. Calles used to be a General too. The biggest laugh I got in my entire trip to Mexico was unconscious, and for a minute I had no idea what made it, or what it was about. There was a big bunch of Mexican officials and Generals, and newspaper fellows and a little of everybody, just sitting talking about the elections and Revolutions and Presidents and all those little details, and I made the following what I thought to be wise observation:

"Why don't some man who is not a General, or not connected with the Army in any way—say, some well-thought-of business man—why don't someone like that go out for President?"

Find the Civilian

Well, now offhand that don't sound like a funny remark. But I am not exaggerating to you when I tell you it knocked everyone in the room right off their seats. I never remember getting such a guffaw. They pulled themselves together after the merriment had somewhat subsided and then looked at me in abject pity. That had been the funniest and most unique suggestion that had ever been offered in the history of Mexican Politics. A Civilian NOT connected with the Army offering himself as President! Well, after I had had it explained to me, and the entire history of Candidates for all time put before me, I could then realize why I had unknowingly pulled the biggest laugh in Mexico. So they gave me the problem of finding a Civilian to run. I am not betraying any secrets when

I tell you that this is much later and there has been no one applied. They afterward related that story to the President, and he said it was by far the best one I had pulled in Mexico.

There was a fellow on our train that had charge, from the Government angle, of all these irrigation works which we saw. He was a very high-class type of man. His name was—well, I always called him Marharajah —it sounded like that.[10] He has dealt with all our various water Commissions over Colorado and Rio Grande water rights. He is a very able man—spoke such good English that it embarrassed me. You know, we keep on talking and arguing over what we are going to do with Boulder Dam and all the Colorado water, as though we owned the whole thing, and would perhaps leave Mexico nothing but the bed of the river for a sand pit.

Suppose some river run out of Canada down our way, and they took it all out and drank it up or watered their lawns with all of it before we got a crack at it. Say, you would have a conference up there so quick and so strong that you would have even Chas. Evans Hughes heading it, would-ent you, Cal? You remember, Chicago dug a drainage canal out of Lake Michigan. They just wanted to float some garbage and odor down toward the Mississippi, and you remember Canada stopped 'em muy Pronto. Still, when we talk about what all we are going to do with our rivers we never give Mexico a tumble. But there is an old International law that kinder makes you let water alone and let it go where it wants to, and most of our water seems to want to go to Mexico if left to follow the dictates of its own conscience.

Well, I got to close. I will tell you a lot more about the trip in a later letter. Morrow, from what I can see of him, don't look like he is doing anything toward keeping you posted. If J. P. Morgan could see him eat Chili con carne and Hot tamales now, he wouldent know him. I will tell you about the Industrial schools and the big Irrigation projects and—oh, yes, a big ranch we went to and spent Sunday, where they raise fine bulls for the Bull ring, and they had a private show and fight in their own ring. It was great; no horses or Bulls killed at all. Don't let me forget to tell you about it.

How's everything going up there? We read in the papers down here about the boys all coming to this Congress with their loot bags to carry back what poor Andy had skimped to save. I see where you tell 'em the swag is only a couple of hundred million, but they feel that you and Andy are holding out on 'em. They think you can stand more of a touch than you say.

I don't see why you dident just send each fellow his share and it would have saved 'em holding this Congress at all.

How's Dawes getting along with his troop?[11] Looks like he has just got himself some ear muffs and hardened himself to it and just let the Senate do their worst.

Well, must stop; got to be there for dinner. You know, the other night on the train I was late for dinner, and when I come into the diner, the President had Mr. Smithers say to me very sternly and with much gravity:

"Mr. Rogers, you are late to dinner. I don't know if you know it or not, but that is a very grave breach of etiquette. In fact, it is an insult to the President for you not to be here to sit down with him when he arrives. What have you to say?"

In Right With the Right People

"Well, I just want to tell the President that I am sorry. I was up in the front cars with some of the soldiers. I have only been in Mexico one week, but you tell him I have learned that it's better to stand in with the Soldiers of Mexico than the President."

Well, he got quite a kick out of that, and to show you he was there with a Nifty, he said, "You tell Mr. Rogers that that was very smart of him to find that out, but that I found it out years before he did—that's why I am President."

Say this fellow Morrow though, pulled a worse one than I did. He was hungry one morning for breakfast and wouldent wait, and he sit down before the President come in, in fact he was most through when the President come in—he would have been if he hadent been so hungry. Then he tried to lay it onto me—said I coaxed him to sit down. That really was an insult sitting down before he got there. I told Morrow it was bad. But it being his first Diplomatic post, why I think the President kinder overlooked it. But after that, when I got tired waiting on him, I would go in the kitchen and eat something beforehand, and pretty near every time I would catch Morrow in there drinking Coffee, and he Dunked his bread in it too.

Do you ever Dunk your bread in your Coffee when there ain't any Senators there for breakfast? What do you feed all those Guys for anyhow? You are the only President that ever made a Cafeteria out of the White House. They will promise you anything while they are eating off you, and the minute they get out from there they will vote against your measures. Get wise to 'em. They been kidding every President like that for years, and the ones in your own Party is the worst. Well, must stop.

Yours faithfully,

WILL.

Mr. Calvin Coolidge,
  White House, Washington, D. C.

My Dear Mr. Coolidge: I went to Mexico to make friends. I think it's a great Country. I like it. I like Ireland and Mexico better than any other Countries. They both got humor, and while they both think they take life serious, they don't. They will joke with you, sing with you, drink with you, and, if you want, fight with you—or against you, whichever you want—and I think if they like you well enough they would die with you.

Now if I had gone in to Mexico looking for bad things, I wouldent have had to do a lot of looking. If those are the things it would have pleased me to find, I would have soon been tickled to death. It all depends on how you want to find a country. I dident go down there with what the Guy that is always wanting to snoop into somebody else's business calls An Open Mind. His mind is not open. If it was he wouldent have to announce it. It's because his mind is narrow that he suspicions that someone won't think it's open unless he announces it. It's like a man getting up and proclaiming "I am a Gentleman." He knows that he has kept it so well concealed up to then that no one has suspected it, and he is beginning to have a growing doubt himself. So he announces it to allay his own fears. So always be leery of these Babies with Open Minds. They are—they are open at both ends.

Taking Them at Face Value

I dident go in with an Open mind at all. I went in to enjoy the people and the Country and get some Real Chili Con Carne and Tamales, see the Mexican Ropers—the best in the world—see the Señoritas dance, and mebbe, if fortunate, see 'em shoot a Presidential Candidate. For there is a system I think which has much merit, and could be adopted without serious loss to almost any country. So you might say that I went in with No mind at all.

Now I know it's hard for anyone that is vitally interested in one side to see much good in the other. It's the same with Politics. Some people can't possibly understand how you can like one side when you vote the other. Well, what's that got to do with it? And that's the way I feel about Mexico. I want to write and talk and describe the people as they struck me. Now what they had done and what they had been responsible for, whether they was right, whether they was wrong, whether they thought they was right or just did it out of pure cussedness, why, I don't know.

I don't think I can rightly be criticized for not settling controversies that have been problems in the Country for a hundred years. Those things should always be left to Editorial Writers at home who have never

46

been down there. They always settle them to their own satisfaction. In fact, Mr. President, I dident go down there to worry much about all their vexing problems. I just kinder took their Country like you do ours. I just thought I would let them fight their own battles. Even their trivial affairs such as Politics, I couldent work up much of an interest in. I wanted to see how they bred and raised the young Bulls that they use in the Bull Ring. It may not be showing proper respect for a neighboring Republic's Politics, but a good young Bull interests me more than any Politician I ever saw in any Country. I had never seen a Cockfight, and I personally don't approve of it—this thing of having one Chicken with sharp knives on its legs, immediately and instantaneously sever the jugular vein of its opponent, who also has on similar knives and has an equal chance of doing some severing itself.

You will never get any high-class Civilization, like Bootlegging and road houses and filling-Station holdups and Interior Bank Robberies, in a Nation that persists in cock fighting until they adopt our humane method of dealing with a chicken. I don't look for that Country ever to become civilized enough to put on an up-to-date Oil Scandal. Look at the difference in the way we deal with a Shanghai Rooster. We chase him around the barnyard, throw a few sticks of stove wood at him, and if we can't wound him enough to have him surrender, why, we keep after him till we hem him up in a corner and then catch him. Then you get a good hand holt on his neck and start wringing it. It's about the same physical contortions that you go through in cranking a Ford. I have seen women who have their dues paid up to the Humane Society, but are none too strong physically, wring for five minutes on some roughneck old Rooster, and finally have to give it up and leave him half conscious while they went to hunt a hatchet to do what they had been unable to accomplish, human against Chicken. Mind you the Rooster had no knives or hatchets where he had an equal break.

So instead of witnessing a debate in the Chamber of Deputies, I wanted to see just one Cockfight and I must say the Birds displayed more physical courage than you would find in a whole political Campaign carried on by humans.

Even the Revolutions dident Intrigue me as they should. I was interested more in the well "reigned" Horses, of which Mexico is the past master in training. They put a reign on 'em that it makes 'em a joy to watch 'em work.

I also have no humorous cracks about Mexico being Lazy. If they are any lazier than us, which I doubt, but if they are, and can make a living at it, why, then I give them credit of being the smartest Nation on earth. For our own educational system is to teach our youth to learn something

47

so that he will feel assured he won't have to do any manual labor through life. So if Mexicans can abstain from physical work without having to go to school 12 or 14 years to learn how not to work, then I claim that's a national asset.

Yours, WILL.

More Letters From a Self-Made Diplomat to His President

SOMEWHERE AWAY OUT IN MEXICO.
*[If I knew the Town I couldent spell
it, and if I did spell it you or Everett
Sanders either couldent pronounce it.]*

MR. CALVIN COOLIDGE,
PRESIDENT OF THE UNITED STATES AND VICEROY OF
CHICAGO.

M Y DEAR CALVIN: I call you Calvin because I hear Dwight do it so much here on the trip. In fact we have all become so familiar that we call each other by our first names. President Calles' first name is Plutarco, and we speak of him as Pluto for short, and the Mexicans don't know why we always kinder smile when we say it. When we say it our thoughts ramble back to a resort in Indiana, and Ballard and Tom Taggart and all the old Gang.[1]

Guess Indiana hasent been much of an inspiration to you lately, has it?[2] If I was you I would do all I could to let it go over to the Democratic side, if you can fool them into taking it. It does you more harm than what little Senate support you get out of it.

But I must get back to International relations. I can't be telling you about all the States that are eligible for a sanity Clinic. If I did I would have to drag in my commonwealth of Oklahoma. She received statehood before she was ready for a Solo flight. She went up alone, but she has had bumpy air ever since she took off. She is bucking a head wind that looks like it gets worse every administration. She is either on the ground with a missing Engine or in the air with an incompetent pilot who has pulled it into a stall, and she is now in a tail spin.

Dairy-Made Diplomacy

But if I keep on talking these things the first thing I know I will have a letter that will look like it's from a National Committeeman and of course will be thrown in the wastebasket and answered in the regulation style with Form Number 432. But it's Mexico that I am trying to give you

---

Saturday Evening Post, May 26, 1928. Reprinted with permission.

the dope on. You want to keep your eye on this Country. There is some pretty slick people here. They can have more political Campaigns and dig up more money for 'em—according to the wealth of the country—which leads me to predict if we annex them they would be Republicans. They just got the earmarks and traits of Republicans—that is, the smarter ones. Of course the Peons are just natural Democrats. So you would have to educate them up to where they would be ambitious to live off the Government, and they would all be Republicans.

We been out on this trip several days now on this Presidential train. Morrow is getting kinder used to it now, and don't gaze around so wild-eyed as he did when he first saw it. 'Course it looks like kind of extravagance for a President to have a whole private train. But everything in pretty near all countries equals up in the long run. He hasent got a Yacht.

The first place we visited was a big Industrial School. This President is greatly interested in Schools. He used to be a school-teacher up in his State of Sonora, and a Man when he gets into office will naturally kinder favor helping out the thing that he used to work at or be more interested in private life. Now take, for instance, your business when a young fellow. It was officeholding. Well, you see, having been connected with that all your life, your thoughts and sympathies, even as President, are always with your old profession. You have always kept in touch with the people in that line of business. You have never got so big and so busy that you dident have time to see an Officeholder, and have always done all you could to help him.

Well, that's the way with this fellow Calles. He was a school-teacher and he will always do all he can for the School-Teacher. He likes to help along schools, and try to build up more of them, and make schools the outstanding thing of the Republic. Perhaps if he had been a Banker, he would have tried to make Banks the outstanding thing; or if a Sailor, perhaps tried to make Mexican commerce strong on the sea. It's as I say, no matter who you are, you revert to type; and where he has centered on Schools, you have naturally centered on Politics, and that's why you have made the big success you have out of it. There is nothing you won't do for the officeholder, and try and help build up his profession, and there is nothing that he won't do for you—as long as he knows you are for him. Well, this fellow has built up the schools over Mexico—not as much as your business of officeholding is built up, but it's showing great improvement.

This school looks like it is based a good deal on our big Agricultural Schools at home, like Ames, Iowa, and Oklahoma A. and M. Of course not so big and elaborate, but they have all the things there—regular school-room course, farming, dairying, fine stock, workshops, and a great fine-looking bunch of Boys. They have a marvelous dairy. You know, that's another one of Calles' hobbies. He has a fine dairy ranch just outside Mexico City. That's the ranch that he and Morrow go to that you read about. There is where they settled the oil problem, was in a dairy. Mebbe you ought to take up some old heifers and start a sort of make-believe dairy up there in Rock Creek Park, and mebbe get some of these Foreign Ambassadors out there and get 'em so interested in Butter fat that they might loosen up and promise to pay us something on account.

A Little Inside Dope

This fellow Morrow looked these Holsteins in the face a few times and he settled the vexing Oil problem to the satisfaction of Mexico—and ours—so it might not be bad to get a few old Guernseys and serve a little breakfast out there among the milk buckets, and let the ambassadors see these old Cows. You know, there ain't nothing that is as sympathetic as a cow. She could just look at those Dignitaries with those Legion of Honor ribbons across their chest, and I'll bet you that they would feel so sorry for those old Bossys that they would start a Debt settlement before the end cow had given up her last drop.

It would be mighty nice if you could give Mellon some little outside aid. Up to now we have only received skimmed milk from them. If you could just collect something from over there it would make the next Congress worth while for all the boys. As it is, it looks like it is going to be kinder slim, with most of 'em just after going through a Campaign. And here is a little inside dope for you: The Boys are going to be a little leery about slipping the old Liberty Bonds around so promiscuously. You are liable to get John D. collections of a Dime.[3] So it kinder looks like a lot of guys are going to have to run for office just on their merits—and that will ruin 'em.

I believe this cow thing would work out, because I know even when we was going through this school dairy, Morrow said, "Let's go from here and have a drink. I would like to treat." So it's worth trying. Borah is out there in the Park on his horse riding every day, and you could get him to help round up the cows for the breakfast. But don't let the foreign Diplomats see Borah, for it would make 'em so mad they might not even eat with you, much less pay you something.[4] You know, they thought till they got over here that Borah was Prime Minister. Of course we don't have any Prime Minister, but Borah occupies the same position here that one does in Europe. And they have heard about him being more for America than he is for Europe. They feel that if it wasent for him they never would have had to stop borrowing. Now Borah will go in with you on this scheme, for nothing would please him better than to get something out of somebody from the other side. But keep him hid in the hayloft till they go away, for they know that he is the Mussolini of the U. S.

Just Between Farmers

These boys played a fine game of baseball for us, and basket ball as good as any school teams up home could. There was an old Bull there, but nobody offered to fight him. I felt awful disappointed. I thought every time a Mexican met a bull he sold tickets and then fought the bull. They tend and irrigate hundreds of acres on this big farm of the school, and they teach each boy farming according to the part of the country he comes from.

We drove back into a town and then went to a Cooperative store that was owned by the farmers and ranchers. They sell and handle the farmers' grain, and sell him his farming tools at wholesale cost, plus the cost of handling. There was a lot of old real farmers, and they gathered around the President and they was talking not like farmer to President, but farmer to farmer. There was no kotowing. They was just a-telling him where it was working out and where it wasent, and what they could do to improve it.

That made a big hit with Mr. Morrow the way they met the President and put their problems up to him—not the President of the Farmers Guild, or Secretary of the Chamber of Commerce of Corncob, Iowa, or the Editor of some Farmer's Weekly—but the real old fellows, the ones that had plowed till the train come in and then was there meeting the President man to man. These dident have a single resolution to present. All the organization they represented was some Oxen, Burros and a plow. But he spent more time with them, and gave them more consideration, and seemed better pleased while with them, than he did all the Officials and Governors of the various States we passed through that come to the train to see him. These old Farmers had their own Bank. This Coöperative owned the whole thing and they owned the coöperative. They sold their own grain, bought their own machinery, loaned themselves their own money, and in fact if somebody made a profit, they was tickled to death, because it was them.

I wish you would meet some Farmers some time before you get out. You would really be surprised. They are mighty fine folks, hard-working, sound-thinking. They only got one thing against 'em, and that's the people who represent 'em. I wish you had passed a rule while you was in there—— Well, it ain't to late yet. You can do it this summer—and mebbe next summer. How 'bout it, Calvin?

But here is the rule that if you had used it you would have understood the Farmer's problem and would have been able to help him out: When a man showed up to see you about Farm relief, make him show Everett his hands, and if he dident have some calluses on 'em and some marks of a plow and grubbing-hoe handle, why, just have Everett tell him you wasent home.

You are a plain kind of a fellow at heart, and you would like these farmers if you ever met any of them. The ones you meet are Luncheon Club Farmers. The ones I am talking about, the wives bring their Lunch to the field.

Why, do you suppose a busy farmer could sit and listen for an hour at a lot of Guys singing some silly songs, and shake hands with the fellow next to you—and then go out and try to undersell him on a deal? That's not the Farmer's stuff. He eats with his mules, where he knows there will be no speeches. If there is, a Mule will make it because he will be hungry, and will at least know what he is hollering for, and it will be appropriate to the occasion. The Mule can at least think of something to say besides "The Trouble with us farmers is"—now mebbe he is an Automobile dealer, or handles Radios—"our trouble is, we buy on a protected market and sell on an open market." Then everybody will applaud, as though he has said something new. He heard his great-grandfather say the same thing. All that is necessary to make a Farm Relief speech is to memorize that above statement. What's going to be done about it? Nothing.

Why ain't there going to be anything done about it? Because there is more people eat what the farmers raise than raise what the people eat. The minute there is any Bill to raise the price of what you eat, the people know that it is making them pay more for it, so they are Agin it; and as there is, as I just told you, more eating than there is raising, why, your Bill won't get far.

Then why don't they cut down the tariff on what he has to buy? Because the Republicans don't want to. Why don't the Democrats then cut down the tariff? Because they never get enough votes to get into Office; and if they did, they can't get enough votes to cut down the tariff.

Do all the farmers vote for the Democrats, so they can get in and cut down the tariff and get cheaper manufactured things? No; just a few in the South that don't raise anything but cotton, and don't have enough to buy anything even if the tariff was cut down. Well, why don't the big farming States of the Middle and Northwest vote for the party that wants to lower the tariff? Because they are Republicans. Well, why are they Republicans? Because they were against slavery. When was they against slavery? In 1861. Well, ain't the war over? Yes, but the North don't know it. Well, ain't slavery over? Yes, it's over for everybody but the Farmer. Well, ain't a Farmer's problem, whether he be in Maine, Georgia, South Dakota, Michigan or Arizona—ain't it the same? Yes. Well, then why don't they all vote together at least, either on one side or the other? Because their fathers dident vote that way, and it's against Tradition.

What is Tradition? It's the thing we laugh at the English for having, and we beat them practicing it.

Well, what is the Farmer's solution? There is no solution. It will just be forty years' argument, the same as Prohibition. But the two things will always furnish a Campaign measure and give us something to argue over, and as long as we got something steady to argue over, why, we can always stop long enough to laugh at Mexico and Ireland for not settling their problems quicker. Now I imagine by the time this gets to you, with No Air Mail, that Mary McHaughen Bill will be looking you in the face again.[5] Those Congressmen and Senators that will pass it up to you know that it won't work, but it saves their face with the Go Devil and Gang Plow Boys back home.

Me and Morrow been talking this thing over. 'Course he comes from Wall Street and ain't supposed to know much about farming, but he does. You know, when you have worked on the J. P. M. range, why, you just about got to know everything. You never know what end of the country a loan might come up from, and you got to know what the collateral is.

Reclaiming Barren Land

Well, we all went back to the train, run the Automobiles up the runways into the special baggage cars and all went in for a big dinner in the diner. The next place we visited was a great Dam that was to irrigate thousands and thousands of acres. I forgot the exact figures, but it was a bigger project by far for them than the Boulder Dam would be for us—of course I mean compared to the resources of the two Countries. It looked mighty good out there at this tremendous big works, seeing all these old American Engineer Boys. Met their families and all. They are having a fine time, have good quarters and are all learning the language; kids going to school there. They will be a couple of years on some of these works.

Lots of fine young Mexicans too that spoke English and that have responsible positions under the American Contractors. One Dam we visited there, the American Newspaper boys dug up American Engineers from nineteen different Colleges up home. Lots of them you have heard of in Football. Naturally you would have to hear of a College man in football if you heard of him at all, for he could be the best Student in the World and never crash a Sunday Supplement.

You sure was proud of those big strapping old boys in their Overalls and high boots, away out there in a barren Country, putting over a big Engineering feat that would attract tremendous publicity if done near one of our big Cities. And when you think that this same big Company has 'em working like that on big projects in Egypt, Russia, South Africa,

South America and all over the World—it sure makes you proud of your Country when you see 'em away off that way, and when you think they are there for a real constructive purpose, doing work that in ten years they can go back and see dozens of little towns and thousands of prosperous little farmers, all thriving and making a living, where, when these Boys first went there, it was nothing but desert.

That's the way to get to understand all our neighbors on the south—do it with Engineers and Road builders and our fine Doctors.

I am not a-hinting anything, but I would like to see you get the Boys out of Nicaragua by July Fourth. I know it's kinder hard to turn around —we got in so far and the road keeps getting narrower and rougher. But I do wish you would figure some way of backing out. Who was the Guy that figured out the way for us to go in there in the first place? Get him; he must be kinder original. So see if he can't think of some unique excuse to get us out like he did to get us in.

Not Cowardice But Justice

I think Nations talk too much about their Moral rights, when, as a matter of fact, I don't think they have got any, any of them. Nations are always yapping about their Honor, when, if you just read an unbiased history of all their carryings on since they first started, they just ain't got much honor, and it's because they know it at heart is why they are so jealous about protecting what little they have got. Did you ever notice the fellow in a party who is always getting insulted the quickest and oftenest, is really, if you know him, a Guy that it wouldent be possible to insult?

What causes trouble with Nations is they are too conceited to admit they are ever wrong. If Nations ever arrive at that stage where they are as Big as individuals, and can acknowledge they are sometimes in the wrong—not have to have it arbitrated and ask the other side to give in something so it won't look so bad for you—but just come right out and admit: "Boys, we made the wrong move. It ain't cowardice that is making us apologize; it's just Justice." Big men can do it, but big Nations, "Got their Honor to protect," and just because they don't do big things is just the reason I say they havent got any Honor.

Now I am not a-hinting that we are wrong in this particular case. But when we start out trying to make everybody have "Moral" elections, why, it just don't look like we going to have Marines enough to go round. 'Course we don't need 'em here at home. We got our elections going along on a pretty good basis. We don't regulate 'em by morals; we regulate 'em by supply and demand. Now this year I think will be a good year. I think votes ought to bring more than they ever did.

But I do hope if the boys have to stay there, that they will have a good honest square election—no caucuses, no Campaign funds, no trading Delegates; just a real election, where everybody walks up and votes for who he wants to. I hope the Marines will have some Cameras there and takes pictures of it, and bring them back up here and show 'em all over, and then their trip might not have been in vain. Only thing, we are liable to take the picture for a comedy. Now about this Sardino that we're trying to can.[6] Now I don't know if you know it or not, but they, in these Countries, don't always look on a fellow that is out in the hills fighting, as a bandit.

Now take right here in Mexico, and old Poncho Villa. You can get just about as many or mebbe more that will tell you he was really on the level, and that he was a Patriot and wanted to do his country a real service. They claim at heart, if he liked you, that he wasent a bad Hombre. Now if you remember that far back, we dident have a whole lot of luck trapping him, and he was right here in the next country joining us, where we was right next to all our supplies and equipment. We had him surrounded one time in a town called Las Quas Ka Jasbo, but we couldent find anybody who knew where Las Quas Ka Jasbo was.

Now if you can get people in a country who think that Villa was on the level, and was doing what he was for the good of his country, what must be the feeling in Nicaragua about this Sardino, who, they tell me, a whole lot of the Nicaraguans look on as a real Patriot? He wants us to get out of there, and he will then come in and behave himself.

Of course if we don't catch him, we can come out and always refer to it as an "Expeditionary Excursion." That's what the Government calls a thing when they don't get away with it. If they are a success, why, they are referred to as War, but if not, why, we try to laugh it off as an "Expeditionary Force." I guess that's what the Democrats call most of their elections. It's not elections; it's "An Expeditionary Excursion momentarily in politics."

The one bad part about these Razzees we are always making into somebody else's territory is they make our Soldiers look bad. They go into a Country where they havent got a Ghost of an equal chance with the fellow they are after. He is among friends, with the whole country to live off of, and it makes it look like a great big nation can't even capture some fellow with one-hundredth part of their military strength. It's not fair to our Marines and Soldiers. 'Course the elections that they are in there to cauterize don't come off till October, so as soon as that election is over, why, I would have planes and special boats right ready to jump them out of there and make Chicago by November fourth.

It's a good thing Nicaragua arranged their election so that our troops would have time for the jump to Chicago by November. Of course that's liable to bring on some International complications, that sending of

America Marines to Chicago. You know, a short time ago the American Government sent some Prohibition officers into that Country and Chicago made a holler about it. They were going to take it up with the League of Nations, till they found that England was a member of the League. They claimed an outside Government had no right to send in prohibition Agents to capture booze and then undersell the local enforcement ones.

Old Models Exchanged

But if I was you I wouldn't let 'em bluff me. I would go on in there with the Marines. We took 'em into Mexico, Haiti and Nicaragua, and let's don't make any exception with Chicago just because it's bigger. The first thing you know people will be saying, "Well, America won't supervise and purify elections in big Countries; they only pick on the little ones and make them be good."

If I can get a Passport Vessayed and arranged, I am going into Chicago after I leave this Country. I met a fellow here in Mexico, he is going there too. He has been negotiating with President Thompson of Chicago in regard to a big ammunition contract.[7] This fellow is from the Krupps' in Germany.[8] Other firms have had the contracts in Chicago, but on account of elections coming on, they just couldent supply the demand. These firms seem to have give pretty good satisfaction in the old days when they was shooting just Pistols; and even when they remodeled, and made everybody bring in their Pistols and exchange 'em for Machine Guns, why, these Ammunition firms speeded up production and seemed to keep up with the demand.

But when this new edict come out for everybody to bring in their Machine Guns, and exchange 'em for Bombs or Pineapples, the firms just couldn't keep up with that, and so that is why this Krupp man is here on his way there. His firm is going to not only supply the scrapnel for these Bombs but he has an idea that he can get Chicago to make another change and go from the Bombs to the Big Berthas and the Tanks. He has a plan whereby you can exchange in your Bombs and they will give you a liberal allowance on a Tank. They have 'em that will go in your Garage, and anybody that can run a car can fire one. He tells me that he can make delivery on 'em by November, in time for elections.

I am anxious to be there and see that election. I am covering it for a bunch of European Dailies. 'Course, down here in these Foreign Countries they are all pulling for King George to make a good showing.[9] But George is going up against a pretty tough fellow when he matches it with this present President of Chicago. I don't know whether you know it or not, Calvin, but it's an old personal animosity between the two men.

They fell out over wearing apparel. George sent word to Bill Thompson that if he ever come to England he would receive him, but that he would have to wear Knee Breeches. Well, Bill said that "Any Country where they wore Knee Breeches for no apparent reason whatever was cuckoo." And George went haywire when he heard that, and sent word back to Bill "That any country where a man in a City wore a Cowboy hat, sitting in an office all day, was Hooey."

Unnecessary Precautions

So that's the whole low down on this Chicago-English Feud. They are split over knee breeches and Cowboy hats. I imagine in a controversy of that kind you would string with the Cowboy-hat Guy. I saw your Picture all last summer with those on, but I never have caught you in the Rompers yet. I forgot to tell you I am going up to Chicago with this Krupp fellow, for he speaks the language and can act as Interpreter for me.

And, say, talking about Guns and Soldiers, why, we got a peek at some today. We are in a part of the Country where she is very much Chicago. There is a lot of Bandit bands around here. The Americans working on the Big dam at this place watched a battle over a few miles in the valley the other day between two rival Gangs. Only these poor Devils are so primitive down here they are still shooting with Rifles and Pistols. It only shows you what little Progress Banditry and Gangs have made here.

We had to drive out about twenty-five miles from the little Station where our Special train was sidetracked, to get to the dam. Well, the authorities of that State had made every precaution to protect our party, in case they were liable to get over-ambitious and try and raid our Gang. I think the bandits used splendid judgment in not doing so. Not on account of the danger, but on account of having their raid for nothing. For while we had a President and an Ambassador and a lot of Big Engineers and Mexican Officials, I don't honestly believe there was $200 in the entire Party.

Well, all along the tops of the hills you would see mebbe seventy-five or a hundred Soldiers on little Mexican Ponies standing up there guarding the road, and all scattered along in various places there was dozens of troops of them.

They sure was a mighty picturesque-looking lot. There was quite a contrast between these Presidential Guards we had on our train and all of our Staff Officers, compared to these troops that are really operating out in the field.

These old Lads out here in the Cactus was a-riding anything they could get their Mcguays on—every kind of Pony and Mule and all kinds of saddles and uniforms. Well, they had on everything in the way of a uniform that ever was wore in any country's army, with the possible exception of a Red Cross Nurse's Middy and Skirt. A Masquerade ball couldent have showed any greater variety. They just carry a blanket, or Serapah, and when night comes there ain't any Taps at the Barracks. These old Boys just find some cactus where the thorns are all running one way and spread their Serapah down, kinder dust the rattlesnakes over to one side, find a soft top rock for a pillow and stake their pony to a Yucca. Mebbe they have got a little sack of Freeholys—beans—and some Tortillas—biscuits shaped like a pancake. Their commissary Department is generally tied behind their saddles. If you run a little short of grub, why, you just borrow the makings of a another Cigarette.

There is no Cooking vans and Tents and Pneumatic pillows and beds move with these Babies. When a Mexican soldier rides up and gets off, there ain't any use of him waiting for the Cooks and Pie wagons to show up, for they ain't coming. He rides through a field and breaks off a few Sugar cane stalks and he is set for that whole campaign. You know, that's why us and England can never catch these kind of Indian Skirmish warfare band of opponents. Down in South Africa, where I was one time, they never could get this old De Wet, the Boer General.[10] The Boers traveled and eat and slept just like the Mexicans. When they was hungry, they just reached back and untied the leg of a sheep and eat their breakfast, lunch and Dinner while they kept moving. Every time the English would get close to him why it would be Tea time and they would all have to stop to pour. And it's the same with us, or any regular big high-powered, big-time Army.

That's why we won't get this Sardino. He will be thriving on Bananas and Coconuts and Pineapples and sugar cane while our old Marines are used to those Navy beans and Salt Pork and a lot of steaks and Biscuits and Light bread. A Banana is all right with us, but it's got to be in a Banana Split, with some ice Cream spread over it. Pineapple is all right for a Sundae, but for a diet to pursue a Nicaraguan on, why, it just ain't being used in the best Armies. Sugar cane is all right, but it 's got to be rendered up into a liquid and have some nice Buckwheat cakes to sprinkle it on. You see, we feed our Soldiers, and all those Armies down there pay theirs so much a day and he feeds himself. So if there is any kicking at the grub down there, he has to take up the complaint with himself.

Just Call Him General

That's how these Generals down here sometimes get such a stand-in with their men. It's the way they look after them and dig up places and stuff where the men have a chance to get something. That's where a lot of the loyalty to some of these Generals starts. If he looks after his men well, he soon has him a big Army and a lot of influence.

Now there is an awful lot of Generals down here. Somtimes it don't look like there was enough Privates to go around. I believe—I won't be sure, but I think they told me there was around six hundred in their Army compared to, I think, less than a Hundred in ours. I might be wrong, but I doubt it. Anyhow, I do know that that was the ratio; it was six to one more than us. Of course, all their Governors and big—what we would call Political officeholders are all Generals.

But the Generals they don't come in much contact with the Soldiers. The Generals are mostly around the Cities. The Soldiers are out in the Country, with mebbe one General watching them in a certain Territory. But the Generals are mostly stationed around the Cafés, especially in Mexico City. You can walk into a big Café in Mexico City at night and holler, "Hello, General," and it's like hollering "Hello, Abe" in the lobby of a New York Hotel. You will have everybody in the place answering you. I don't know why they all want to be Generals down there. It's just a kind of little racial weakness that they can't help. All races have something that we can't account for.

They like to put on their Uniforms and strut around. It's a pride with 'em, just like Americans gets all diked up in his Golf Breeches and sweater, and struts. Now mebbe he couldent coax a steel ball into a hole with a Magnetic needle, but he just likes to get those clothes on. You take the costume away from Golf and the thing wouldent last twenty-four hours. And it's the same with a Mexican General on military and Feast days. There is hundreds of those Generals in Mexico that couldent lead a Regiment in a battle any more than some of these Men we have in Humorous costumes could lead an opponent to the eighteenth green.

Scaring Away the Enemy

But don't get the idea that they are all that way. Say, they got some real two-fisted Generals down there. There is one little guy I must tell you about him sometime. It's General Amaro.[11] He is Secretary of War. He would be a Military man in any man's country. And General Escobar and General Lemone and Almasans and Cruze and Obregón—don't overlook him as General outside his political record.[12] There is some great Characters among these Generals—a lot of humor and some great stories. I got to tell you one before I close. This was told to me by General Obregón at his home one night for dinner. Here's his story:

"I was laying off one time between Revolutions. It was a kinder slack season, so just to keep my hand in, I thought I would form me one of my own till a better one showed up. So I got me a bunch of peons together, drilled 'em all up a little bit and decided to go over the mountains and take another town, where another General held.

"Now this Bird had a couple of small Artillery pieces—in fact that's how he held the town. I got my amateur Army all up and ready to attack the town, when one of these Cannons went off. Well, my soldiers sure took to the Mesquite. They scattered like a covey of quail. It was like a train whistling when you are trying to pen a herd of wild steers.

"Well, I went out and headed off my army and got it all rounded up. You see, it's the first time they had ever heard a cannon. A rifle shot had been about as far as their Revolutionary experience had carried them. They thought, 'Why, here we come over for a nice pleasant sociable revolution, and this other side springs all this big-League stuff on us!' They thought somebody had unconsciously thrown 'em into the middle of the European war.

"Well, I got 'em about ready for another charge, when the enemy Cannon bellowed a second time. Off again! Back to the tall Cactus! They patted Jack rabbits and Coyotes on the back as they passed 'em. Well, I got 'em all assembled again and ready for another race as soon as the starting cannon fired, when a Captain come up to me—I had made him Captain, as he had shoes. If he had had boots, he would have been a General.

"This Captain says, 'General, those cannons are not as bad, I don't think, as they are supposed to be. I thought when a Cannon shot, everybody got killed. But here they have shot twice and nobody has been hit. You know what I think they are for? I think they are just made to scare a lot of PENDAHOS.' "

Now the word "Pendahos" means halfwit, bonehead, Dumb. In fact we havent a word in our language that covers as much ground as this word "Pendaho." Obregón listened to him—this Obregón has a lot of humor—get this remark—and then said:

"Yes, they are made to scare Pendahos, and that's what makes it very dangerous for our Army."

That fellow that told me that is the next President, and so you are going to have to brush up on your humor to keep up with that bird. I must tell you the next time about us going to the big Ranch to spend the day, and how they put on the private Bullfight in their own ring, and how the President went right in himself and fought 'em.

Well, here's looking at you!

Yours,
WILL.

More Letters From a Self-Made Diplomat to His President

MY *DEAR MR. PRESIDENT,* White House—with new roof and everything: Well, Dwight and I are still playing a series of one-day stands around the Dams and Irrigation projects and Schools. But yesterday we had the time of the trip. We spent the day at a big Ranch, or Hacienda, with some friends of the President. I think it was just above a town called Aguas Calientes—that means Hot Water. Well, you could name pretty near any place in Mexico Hot Water if things wasent breaking right with you.

Well, the President just had the train moved up to a station right on these people's ranch, and we all got out and was driven down to the big Headquarters. Say, you talk about a place! You know, all these Guys and Committee's coming in there offering you places to go for the summer. So you have naturally seen the pictures of some pretty nice Chateaus. Now I don't want to knock my good friend old Governor Bulow, of South Dakota, and his Black Hills—where they incarcarated you for three months last summer for vetoing the Mary McHaughen Bill.[1]

Did you know Bulow is a Democrat? That's the furtherest North a Democrat ever got, so they made him Governor. The Republicans up there are like they are most places—they are so jealous of each other that they would rather give it to some outsider than to give in to each other.

Did they ever tell you about how they loaded the Creek—Squaw Creek—for you? Well, Sir, he told me about that when I was up in his State relieving the Farmers last winter of $3 for the best seats and $1 where you couldent hear. So I am just as strong advocate of Farmers' Relief as Jim Watson or any of the big dirt Farmers.[2]

But I must tell you about how they Salted the creek on you. The old Governor, being a Democrat, naturally would think of something funny —that's what keeps 'em Democrats. Well, he issued a secret decree all around the State that everybody that could find, search, discover and finally seize or capture a Fish, even if it was necessary to go out of the State to bring him in, that they wasent to eat it, no matter how hungry they were, but were to put it in a bucket and bring it to Squaw Creek and give it its temporary Liberty.

Saturday Evening Post, June 2, 1928. Reprinted with permission.

Well, they put a wire net at the upper and lower end of the creek, along above and below the Lodge, so the fish couldent get out of that territory, and then they started in feedin 'em liver, and the fellow that fed 'em liver they had him made up just like you, Cal. You see, it was to get the Fish used to you; and he would tie the liver on a string and they would eat it off. Then, of course, when you come and put a hook inside the piece of liver which was on the string, why, it just naturally made you look like one of Izaak Walton's original cast.[3] 'Course it don't matter to you how the fish got there, and if you did catch 'em second-handed. But what I am getting at is you want to let the people know this summer where you are going so they will have time to load up the creek before you get there.

But I must get back to this old Mexican Ranch. It looked like a whole town, and had been in the family over 75 years. A Beautiful young married Lady was the heiress and hostess, she and her charming Husband.

Oh, there was some beautiful women there at the party that day, and how they could sing those Mexican songs and play the Guitar! You know, this President Calles is Cuckoo over that. I could take a Guitar and start playing and get him joining in, and I believe I could tole him right off into the Ocean. Well, it was wonderful, sitting around a big Patio full of congenial people. Not a Revenue officer in twenty miles—just like Chicago. We dident know the words to these wonderful tuneful songs, but the old agitated Grape juice a-turning somersets in the glass makes everybody speak the same language. The Americans in the party was a little shy on the words to the songs, but that's the only thing they was delinquent in. It was a real holiday. All the country-side gathered in, rich and poor, the President and the Peon—Real hospitality.

The main part of the house looked about like Westminster Abbey. It was of the old early Spanish type, with a big open court, or Patio, in the center. There is where they had the tables all set and just everybody all together having a great time. I made the speech for the Ambassador. I spoke a little more Spanish than he did.

Well, Morrow was a-chatting and sitting by the Hostess. She spoke splendid English—in fact better than Morrow. There was no Amherst twang to it. Out of all these beautiful Ladies that was looking after all our party, the best I could seem to land was a Peon Ranch Boss—Male—who took a particular shine to me, and right at the height of festivities wanted to escort me out and show me the stables.

And say, we had another American with us that is from up your way some place. His name was Rupee—I think that's the way you spell it.[4] I know that's the way you say it. He was a Guest and an old friend of the Morrows, and was on this trip with us—an awful nice fellow, very tall and very shrewd; dident say anything—worked a good deal along your line. In fact I could never get just what he was doing down there, but of course you know. Well, I just want to tell you, he was on the job. If you sent him there to keep quiet and look, he sure did it. I thought for a while you had sent him down mebbe to watch Dwight. Then sometimes I would think mebbe he was watching me. Well, anyhow, before the day was over at this ranch we had him singing Mexican with a New Hampshire accent.

You know, all these old ranch buildings are all inside one big inclosed wall, and in connection with the House there was a great big Church, with two high towers, or steeples, and all up on there were Soldiers, Guarding against anything that might show up. This was up in kinder the Bandit Country. It sure did look like what the story books called Midevil times with these Soldier lads parked on those high points.

There must have been three hundred people eat there. There was about a hundred from our train. They brought everybody on it—train crew, Soldiers and all. They had two Orchestras playing. That's one thing you never run short on in Mexico is Orchestras or bands. You just can't hardly do anything at all without being accompanied by an Orchestra. And most all I heard could play good too. Well, we had Spanish Dances and songs. The Orchestra Leader dident know how to lead one song and the President took the Baton and really led it. If he had moved his knee I would have thought it was Whiteman doing it.[5]

After lunch everybody piled in cars and on horseback, and out to the Bull ring. This ranch raises fine bulls that they use for the big fights. They have their own ring to try them in. It's the most unique thing, all built out of 'Dobie—mud—walls, and all the corrals are all the same. They had a dandy Grand Stand made up over it, and used a lot of the young bulls, about two-year-olds.

Well, this was a bullfight that I really enjoyed, for there was no bulls to be killed, or horses. And say, what a bunch of amateur Bullfighters we had in our Gang! I thought we had officers and Diplomats and Politicians, but everybody that could grab a cape and get in the ring did so. The first thing I know, I look, and there is the President himself in the ring with the cape, making passes and the bull sailing by him. Can you imagine that? The President, right down there taking a chance! You know, these Bulls dident know that they wasent to be killed and that this wasent a real Bullfight. I thought of you when I saw him down in that ring. I was trying to picture you down in there with that old Bull a-coming head on; a speech on economy wouldent have done much good then.

But say, listen! Don't think I am laughing at what you or anyone else might have done. They all kept hollering, "Where is your American

64

comedian?" Well, to be perfectly frank and honest, the American Comedian was up in one of the most comfortable and highest seats that the arena afforded. That's why he was still a Comedian, because he had never become quite half-witted enough to enter the arena with any man's male Ox. Even if they took the horns off and made a muley out of 'em, that wouldent even tempt me. I'll bet if a bull was charging down on you, Calvin, you could name at least a dozen Senators that you would like to have between you and him.

I tried to get Morrow to go down there. I told him that it dident show the proper respect for an American Ambassador when he was out with the President to not accompany him on all various social pilgrimages.

Morrow said, "Everything in the world is in your contract when you become Ambassador to Mexico but to fight a Bull."

I moved over and entertained the Ladies while the boys was displaying their prowess with these Bovines.

The fighters hollered, "Come on in, Señor Rogers, we are not going to kill the bull."

I said, "That's the reason I am not going in there. If I was in there I would want you to kill him, but on account of my Operation I am not allowed. If it wasent for that ——"

No, sir, I had been butted enough in a branding corral by snorty old calves to know that Clem Rogers' boy Willie of Oologah, Oklahoma, wasent carved out to meet any Bull in combat.[6]

The President slipped and fell once, just as he made a pass and let the Bull go by, and the Bull turned and was on him; but his Chouffer, who out of all our Bunch was really the best one, was right there with his cape and led the Bull away. Now this President evidently hadent been in a ring in years. But it's just kinder like our baseball. I guess we never entirely forget it. I think all Boys that are raised in the Country had learned the first rudiments of it. Of course, not the skilled part of the Killing, but they could all take care of themselves with a cape.

Oh, but I must tell you this: You know they had been kidding me about not associating with their Bull. All at once, when they was all waiting for a new Bull to come out—from the ring you can't see what is coming out—well, out comes the real thing—the Stud Bull, a magnificient animal that they had imported from Spain to breed from. Oh, a great big black powerful animal!

Well, when that door opened and he come charging out there, you never saw as many capes, hats and even shoes left in one arena in your life. A raid on Mellon's Treasury by Congress was nothing to the way Presidents, Generals, privates, Secretarys of State, personal Physicians, vallets, Chapultepec Castle cooks and just Mexicans made for those boards and walls. Men scaled walls that had come to the ring leaning on a cane and went over them like they had been one of these Zuave troops. You see, the ring had got so full, everybody was wanting to fight these smaller Bulls. Some were fighting 'em with their coats and vests, and even red undershirts. There wasent enough capes to go round.

But, Boss, when this Male Toro hit that arena he emptied it with nothing but a glance. No Revolutionist ever cleaned out a place as thoroughly as that Baby did. He emptied it like a speech on the tariff will the Senate Gallery. They dident stop to sit on the top of this wall they had scaled—they just fell on over; and those boards that they are supposed to hide behind, why, there looked like there was half of Mexico tromping on each other behind them. The President was down and two Peons was standing on him. A Skunk in a parlor couldent have more thoroughly disrupted a party than this lone Bull did.

Well, that's when little Willie had his laugh. I had seen this animal in the corrals as we come up, and had admired him, and as I had slipped down to the corral unnoticed during the hilarity, a few Five-Peso Notes scattered around judiciously among the foreman and the Cowboys that was doing the Turning of the Bulls in the Arena had sure bore juicy fruit, and I was a-sitting there enjoying the returns of a spendid investment.

I dident even till now let on that I knew how that Bull got in there. But during his lonely stand in that ring, with not a human within a Niblick's drive of him, I did announce publically and in bad Spanish to the President and all his assembled Subjects that I had heard that Mexicans were Bullfighters, and that there was a Bull that I sincerely believed would accommodate 'em, should they by any chance have such a thing as a Bullfighter in the crowd. Well, that got a laugh, but it dident get any entries. Finally one of the gang who had been Bullfighters up to the time a Bull entered decided to run from one of these hiding places along the wall to another. Well, he was caught trying to steal. This Bull run the width of the arena and caught him between bases. He picked him up on his horns and tossed him over behind the place he had just come from. If he had' thrown him any other place it would have been just too bad.

The President come around up in the stand. He just happened to think of something he had forgotten. The Bull just pawed the ground and knocked two peons off the fence with the gravel. I never saw as many Bullfighters trying to lay a cape down without anyone seeing them do it. If the little Bulls could have seen through the wall what was happening out in the ring, I believe they would have been well repaid for their afternoon. It looked like the Bullfighting was about over that day. When the Bull couldent get the fighters to come in, he turned and challenged the whole stand full of us. A couple of the folks made faces at him, but that was about as far as they went. I winked at him and wanted to thank him for making it a perfect day. They opened the gate and turned in some old steers—Cabresto's. The old Steers glanced around at all of us, and looked disgusted and went on out. The old Bull turned and followed 'em. As he got to the gate he turned and put one forefoot up to his nose and wiggled his toes at all of us and majestically walked on out. But it had been a great afternoon and a very colorful sight—this lone bull ring away out there to itself, on a kind of a hill, where you could see the whole surrounding country.

Taking Him on Faith

We went on to our train, loaded our Automobiles, and all the countryside stood around admiring the beautiful train. Some of the folks went down with us on the train to this large town near. It had been a great day, and had only showed how they all had lived and enjoyed themselves at these big ranches in the old days, before Revolution and banditry and strife upset them. But they are getting it all slowly settled, and they sure do know how to enjoy themselves. Some of the kinfolks of the people that owned the ranch lived in this town—Aguas Calientes—and the women and girls went down on the train with us. That's the first time we had had any She stuff on the train. It was only about an hour's trip.

Well, when we got there, we got out to bid 'em good-by, and there was a public Jitney, a kind of an old rattletrap bus affair standing there, and these folks asked the President, "Come on out to the house a while." Well, he grabs Ambassador Morrow and myself and just the little bunch that was standing there, and we packed into the Jitney like sardines— about 8 or 10 Women and Girls, a few scattering husbands, Presidents, Ambassadors, Comedians, an Associated Press Guy sitting on the radiator; and mind you, there was only one Soldier grabbed that thing and was on there with us, and we bumped and jolted and stalled clear through that town, away out in the suberbs, where these people lived, and all piled out of there, went in and turned on the lights. This time they exchanged the Guitar for a Piano, and they puts on some more singing. I'll bet that's the first time Morrow had ever been in an old Jitney. But he sure was a good Sport.

He whispered to me as we was winding our way down a dark street, "Where are we going, do you know?"

I said, "Lord, I don't know! But this Guy hasent led us wrong yet, so let's stick to the finish."

The thing that was impressing Morrow, I knew, was the nerve of this President, leaving his train, with all its Guards and precautions, and in a town where he had plenty of enemies, and driving right through it in the night. You got to give this Bird credit, whether you are for him or against him. He has certainly got the physical courage.

67

One of the Old Customs

This was a lovely home we were at, and we had a great evening. We piled in the old Jitney and the same Gang all took us back. The train was supposed to have gone right on through there. But what's five or six extra hours in Mexico? You never get where you are going on the day you start—unless you havent got any friends. If you make a date with anybody and don't keep it, why, don't apologize when you meet him. He dident get there, either. It's the land of "Manyana" and you like it. What's the good of meeting anybody up home? They are only going to try to sell you something or you them something. So we would be better off if we dident keep our dates.

The next day we went up through Monterey, a beautiful old City. The President had some kind of a political conference with some local Ward healers, so that give us all a night off. The Ambassador went somewhere to see a fine Picture Exhibit. But the newspaper Gang and I went out hunting some Chili and Tamales, and then down to the main Plaza. Well, sir, I wish you could see it. It was parade, or social, night. The girls all walk one way and the boys walk the other around this Block, or beautiful old square. You just kept strolling, and each one looking the other over as they pass. Of course if you get the proper encouragement, why, you can speak and turn and join some Girl, and that puts you marching with the Girls.

Most of our bunch was pretty good-looking young fellows, outside myself and Constantine, of the New York World.[7] He said this was an old custom and was only carried out in certain towns. Well, it sure was carried out in this one. If all the marching those people did that night had been laid end to end, it would have taken two days to pass a given point. This Guy Pyle, with his Stone Bruise Derby across the country, ought to get some recruits from down here.[8]

We run onto a Mexican Boy that spoke good English and he wanted us to go to his Automobile show room and he would show us something. Well, he did. It was a great big Mexican Lion, just running loose around in this big show room under the cars.

He says to me, "Go on and pet the Lion. He is gentle—he is a Mexican Lion."

I told him I knew he was Mexican and the chances are he dident like Gringos. Well, an idea struck me and I wanted to buy the lion, or borrow him, or rent him, or something. I wanted to take him to the train and turn him into President Calles' stateroom—you know, Calles is called the Lion of Sonora. Well, when he come in that night and opened the door, I wanted to see what would happen. It was an awful cute lion and I don't think he would hurt you.

The train pulled out that night about one o'clock, and the next day we went to another big Irrigation dam and a tremendous canal that run from it that looked as big as the Panama Canal to me. I counted forty big steam shovels at work on this one project, and another bunch of fine grinning American Boys putting the thing over.

Oh, yes, here is one I must tell you that happened after we had been to that ranch. Morrow and Calles were having a kind of confidential and business talk, and they got off onto the Land problem. You know, next to the Oil, the land problem is the big thing. A while back they got a kind of socialistic scheme down here. It was that the Government would take over a part of the big landowners' land and give it out among some of the Peons. Well, they did that; of course, promising to pay something at some time for the land to the big owner. So Morrow happened, in talking to Calles, to ask him if in taking land away from people did he take any away from these Dos Amontes—the ones that had owned the ranch where we spent that day.

Calles dident hesitate, but answered, "I don't remember if we did take any of their land or not, but I doubt if we did. For they are Friends of mine, and if we had, I would have heard from them and remembered it."

Morrow thought that was about as frank an answer as one man had ever given a Diplomat.

We are all sitting back in the train observation room chatting. A Governor of one of the States got on the train. They would generally travel with us during the time we were in their State. He and Calles was sitting there talking, and all at once we were coming into a Tunnel, and Calles got up and excused himself and started to leave, when Morrow said, "I guess the President is afraid to trust one of his Governors in the dark." That was a yell with us all. The next day we met another Governor and I got Constantine to interpret it, and tell it to him, as it had been a big laugh on the train. He told it to this Governor and it laid right where he put it. In other words, it died standing up. It wasent funny to this old Boy.

When you are out on one of these train trips for seven or eight days like we was together, it gets just about like a camping party. I wish you would frame up something of that sort up home—kinder go round and see what all the Country is doing. Course there is places up there that you wouldent need visit, for they ain't doing anything. But it would do you good to kinder prowl around. This fellow keeps right in touch with all these things himself. He don't take any Politician's word. And I have wondered at times if you havent trusted 'em a little too far. Some big public work up home like these are down here that we have been out seeing, they would be great for the unemployed up there.

Work Instead of Wind

Course I know you-all don't want much said about any unemployed till after the election, I see by the papers that we are getting down here. They are keeping unemployment kinder quiet—that is, the Republican press is, and that means about all the press there is, for the poor Democrat he don't read enough to support many papers. Now take that Boulder Dam, that would give a lot of work, and that Mississippi River, that would employ a whole lot of people. It sure will seem good to everybody to read where somebody was actually shoveling some dirt on the Mississippi River instead of us continually reading:

"There has been a Commission appointed to go down and make a report on what is the best plans to work out the flood-relief problem. This Committee is to confer with another Committee, who has been appointed by the House, and they are to confer with the Government Engineers and hand in their report."

If every man of every Committee that has gone to that river to investigate had put in one hour's actual work raising the levee, why, it would have been so high now you couldent have got water out over the edge with a hydraulic pump. So the next Committee you send to that river, give 'em a spade instead of a report sheet. Taxpayers don't mind paying for work, but it's investigations and reports that keeps us broke. I wish I could take you with me on one of those pilgrimages I make around up there every year. Say, you don't know what a Country you are President over till you would follow me around a while.

Well, we are drawing near the close of our trip. I hate to see the old party break up. We have had lots of fun and seen some Country. These people have some great natural resources here that they havent touched yet. You know, I kinder wonder if a Nation ain't just about as well off that has all these natural resources and havent used 'em yet as. one who is just in the middle of or has about used theirs up already.

We are going at top speed, because we are using all ours up just as fast as we can. If we want to build something out of wood, all we got to do is go cut down a tree and build it. We dident have to plant the tree. Nature did that before we come. Suppose we couldent build something out of wood till we found a tree that we had purposely planted for that use. Say, we never would get it built. If we want anything made from steam, all we do is go dig up the coal and make the steam. Suppose we dident have any coal and had to ship it in. If we need any more Gold or Silver; we go out and dig it; want any oil, bore a well and get some. We are certainly setting pretty right now. But when our resources run out, if we can still be ahead of other nations then will be the time to brag; then we can show whether we are really superior.

This Age of High Living

You know, you been President at a mighty fortunate time in our lives. The Lord has sure been good to us. Now what are we doing to warrant that good luck any more than any other Nation?

Now just how long is that going to last? Now the way we are acting, the Lord is liable to turn on us any minute; and even if He don't, our good fortune can't possibly last any longer than our Natural resources. So as I look at Mexico, which hasent even been scratched as far as its natural wealth is concerned, I believe they are better off than us in the long run.

It just ain't in the book for us to have the best of everything all the time. A lot of these other Nations are mighty poor, and things kinder equal up in the long run. If you got more money, the other fellow mebbe has better health; and if another's got something, why, some other will have something else. But we got too big an over-balance of everything and we better kinder start looking ahead and sorter taking stock and seeing where we are headed for.

You know, I think we put too much emphasis and importance and advertising on our so-called High standard of living. I think that "high" is the only word in that phrase that is really correct. We sure are a-living High.

Our children are delivered to schools in Automobiles. But whether that adds to their grades is doubtful. There hasent been a Thomas Jefferson produced in this country since we formed our first Trust. Rail splitting produced an immortal President in Abraham Lincoln; but Golf, with 20 thousand courses, hasent produced even a good A Number-1 Congressman. There hasent been a Patrick Henry showed up since business men quit eating lunch with their families, joined a club and have indijestion from amateur Oratory. Suppose Teddy had took up Putting instead of horseback riding. It's also a question what we can convert these 4 billion filling Stations into in years to come. But it ain't my business to do you folks' worrying for you. I am only tipping you off and you-all are supposed to act on it. Say, did I tell you Lindy was coming down?[9] Yes, he will be in here right soon now. I suppose we will be hearing up home that the State Department, or you, or some of you, sent him down here. Well, here is how it was: Mr. Morrow got pretty well acquainted with him when Lindy was making arrangements to make that tour for the Guggenheim people, and of course any time you are in with Morgan and Co., why, you naturally know all the other operators.[10] I guess Dwight had mebbe O.K.'d a loan for 'em some time. But all these big moneyed people, they are just like the underworld— they all know each other and kinder work together.

Doing His Own Flying

Well, after Morrow had been appointed to come down here, he said to Colonel Lindbergh, "I am going to Mexico. I wish you would come down some time and see me. That would make a great trip for you."

Lindy immediately fell in with the idea and said, "Gee, that would be great! Nobody ever hopped from here to Mexico City. I would like to make that trip."

Now Morrow told me this part illustrating the Own mind of this Boy. He told Lindy, "Oh, don't make it all in one hop. Come to St. Louis, then San Antonio, then Tampico and then in."

Lindy just looked him in the eye and said, "You take care of that end of it, Mr. Morrow, and I will take care of the flying part."

Morrow said that kinder proved to him that this Kid was doing his own planning and his own thinking. Well, we were out on this trip a few days, when Mr. Morrow said, "Lindbergh promised me he would come down and I think it would be good time for him. I think I will wire him, and I will also ask the President and get him to invite him down too." Well, he did it, and the next day he told me, "Say, the President wired Lindy a long personal wire, direct to him, and I sent him one. Now we will see what he says." I asked him then if it was through the State Department, and he said no.

Well, the next day he gets a Cable: "Will be there the first clear day." So Morrow is tickled to death, and all of us just a-waiting. Paris won't have anything on this country for a reception when he lands. I sho' will have something to tell you when Lindy comes. I would like to have you meet Lindy some time, Calvin. He is an awful nice fellow. I will give him a letter to you when he comes. You would like him—he is awful quiet. But Lord knows what you and him would talk about if you was together, 'cause he won't ask you anything, and you are so used to having people tell you all they know without you asking them anything. So I would like to see you and Lindy together. Of course I would rather hear you all together than to see you, but I guess that will never be possible.

Well, we are going to get into Mexico City in the morning off this trip. The Ambassador insists that I come and stay with him at the Embassy. They say we got a mighty nice Embassy down here. Doheny give us the living part of it. If it wasent for a lot of our rich men that have been charitable enough to give a few houses around over the World, our Ambassadors would be living in boarding houses. 'Course there is lots that are rich that wouldent, but those who make it a business of Embassing would.

Post Office and Embassies

Say, there is a thing you might take up some time, Calvin. We got some awful fine Post Offices up home in towns where the trains don't even throw off a mail sack, and I don't see why we can't get at least as nice places in all these various Countries where we do millions of dollars' worth of business, and make it look like we at least take good care of our folks. We are always talking about our Standards of Living. Well, let's enlarge it to take in our foreign help. Chances are the Congressmen wouldent be for it, for it wouldent mean anything to their particular voters. But you try and get them to let us get some real homes for America Consular and Embassy service abroad and we will vote with them on getting their creek widened. You know yourself that about all there is to Politics is trading anyway. That's why Politics is not as good as it was years ago is because they don't have as many old-time horse traders in there. These we got now are just Amateurs. They are crude with their trades. There is really no Finesse—you might not get that; it's a French word and means sneaking it over.

Well, what else do you think this Morrow did? We got the greatest fellow you ever saw on the trip here with us. His name is Colonel Sandy McNabb, and he is the Military Attaché of the Embassy, and he is the one that Mr. Morrow brought on the trip with him.[11] So you see we carry our own American Army with us. This Sandy is quite a Character. He speaks Mexican better than he does English, and is a great friend of all Mexico, especially Ex and Next President Obregón. It seems that Sandy was stationed up at Nogales—a real town, too, by the way, and if you can ever throw them a Government appropriation, why, be sure and do so. It comes nearer being a Western Town than anything we got left in this Country, so remember the name—Nogales, Arizona.

Well, Sandy used to command a regiment there, and he is a great Pistol and rifle shot—in fact instructor to the Army—and he likes to hunt. So he was always wanting to get off to go down into Mexico to hunt. Well, he being an American Colonel, he had to get permission through not only the Military but the State Department to go into a foreign Country. Well, he bothered the State Department to death, either getting in or out of Mexico. He would go down into Sonora and hunt and visit with Obregón, and Obregón is very fond of Sandy—Sandy is a red-headed, tough-looking egg. Well, the Secretary of State has done nothing during his term in office but sign official documents to exit and Entrance Sandy.

Now here is what I am getting at, Calvin: This fellow Morrow—who I think you will remember at Amherst; he is the one that used to help you out at examinations—well, when he found he was going down there, he in some roundabout way heard of Sandy McNabb and how he stood with the Mexicans.

Well, to show you how this Morrow's mind works, he said, "Give me this McNabb person as my Military Attaché."

Then the Embassy employment office says, "Oh, no, Mr. Morrow, you don't want Sandy. Sandy has no more social qualifications than a Billy Goat. We will procure you a man that went through West Point, Harvard and took a post-graduate course with Emily Post."

But this Guy Morrow said, "Listen, I dident ask for this Job in the first place, and if you are going to start trying to run it by telling me who I am to have, you better get you another Boy."

Morrow knew Sandy couldent dance a step, even if he could get somebody to dance with him. But he did know that Sandy knew Mexico, and that's what he wanted. He was going to Mexico to make friends with 'em, not to fight 'em. So Morrow got Sandy. Now Sandy has perhaps drank 200 saucerfuls of tea, tromped on 56 old Señoras' corns; but Sandy is not Advocating intervention with Mexico, and he is Military Attaché yet.

Well, Mr. Morrow appointed Sandy as my Aide. He was—when we got into the City of Mexico off this trip, why, Sandy was to be my personal escort and aide. Well, the last fellow I had that escorted me around had on a cap with Cook and Son and he used to say, "On the right you will see —— " So I told Sandy, "There is to be none of that On-the-right-you-will-see stuff." So I got to tell you later about what a time Sandy and I have. But why I was illustrating to you all this is Morrow's way of doing business. No wonder he is getting somewhere.

Well, I got to close. We will get in early in the morning and I will have some news for you about the great old City of Mexico. If you ever Choose, I wish you would drop me a line.

Yours,
WILL.

More Letters From a Self-Made Diplomat to His President

MEXICO CITY, DATE—ANY TIME YOU
WANT. WHAT'S TIME IN MEXICO?

MY DEAR MR. PRESIDENT,
White House,
Washington, D. C.

Say, what a City this is! She is a cross between New York, Tulsa and Hollywood, with a bit of Old San Antonio and Nogales, Arizona, thrown in. Say, it's clean and well kept too. They got the finest and youngest Police Force you ever saw. All look about like high School basket-ball players. They threw all the old-time whiskered grafting cops out and picked this gang of young kids, and I want to tell you they are a snappy-looking layout. This fellow General Cruise has been responsible for reorganizing all that.

Say, you ought to see Chapultepec Castle, where their President lives. Why, the White House wouldent make their living room! It's on a high hill overlooking the whole city, and there has been some mighty stirring times around it, more than Congressmen and Senators just coming to cadge a breakfast out of it like they do you. And there is a place called Xochimilco—try out some of the old Amherst Latin on that. It's all beautiful Lakes and little rivers and canals, just like Venice. And the funny part—all that in a desert country. You row all around in little boats—it's great. And then the Pyramids—why, they are almost as large as the ones over in Egypt; only there is not as many steamship lines goes to them, so naturally you don't see as many folders of them as we do the ones on the old Nile. These are about forty miles out of Mexico City. And there is some great old towns out around here, one the summer residence of Maximilian when he foolishly thought the country needed an Emperor. The most beautiful grounds you ever saw, and wonderful old Churches.

And say, speaking about Churches, I was fortunate enough to be

---

Saturday Evening Post, June 9, 1928. Reprinted with permission.

The American-owned Mexico City Country Club which Rogers visited during his stay in the Mexican capital in December of 1927.

here the other day on Guadalupe day. That's the greatest day in all Mexico. It's their real Patron Saint's day, and the Church and Shrine is right in the edge of Mexico City. Well, I never saw such a sight in my life—hundreds of thousands of people on the roads in all kinds of conveyances, and walking, and the place packed for a half mile all around the Church. When you remember there was no services held in the Church at all, and then to see those masses of people in there praying and others trying just to get near, it showed what a very religious people they are. On the outside, it was like a great country fair, with everything in the world to sell and everything to eat. All was carried on very quiet and earnest. There was singing in the Church carried on in an impromptu way by various groups, and the Church wonderfully decked with flowers. It was just about the most impressive sight I ever saw in my life, and it made you wish more that the religious troubles might be settled as soon as possible, for it's the poor and devout that suffer.

A Good Time for a Bomb

Col. Sandy McNabb that I told you about sure is a fine Aide; in fact he is the best one I ever had. Sandy knows everything and everybody. He is a great friend of Obregón's, and we went to Obregón's house for dinner last night, and I must tell you a funny thing that happened. You know, they had just thrown a Bomb at Obregón's car a few days before—kinder getting educated up to our Chicago stuff. He told us it cost him over a thousand dollars to send messages thanking people who had wired him congratulating him on his successful escape.

He said, "It would have been cheaper if they had hit me. I couldent afford to be missed again."

He is very funny, this Obregón. He is always telling stories—good ones too. Well, we are out in the living room after dinner, and it's really the front hall, as the big doors were open that lead right out to the outside, and we were all standing talking, and suddenly the lights went out all over the house. Well, that dident look so good to me; and he must have had the same idea, for he come back with the following remark in Spanish which I could understand: "It's a good time now for the Bomb."

Say, he took it as a joke; but I want to tell you that when those lights went on again, I was clear across the room from him. I figured if they saw where he was standing before they cut the lights, why, I certainly don't want to be backstop for any Mexican Pineapple. It was just one of those epidemics of Static that electric lights have down there the same as the Power Trusts have 'em up home. He got a great kick out of seeing me

77

so far away when the lights went on. But if the same play had come up again, I would have done the same thing, only perhaps gone further. He is an awfully jolly fellow, and will be the next President if they keep on missing him.

Oh, we went into their Congress. They call it the Chamber of Deputies, and they wear pistols. They are allowed to wear a Gun the same as an officer. I got a great kick out of that. Can you imagine, if we did that, the damage Jim Reed would have done by now?[1] Jim would have exterminated half—the Republican half—the Senate by now, and would have been shooting most of the Democrats just for practice. Can you picture the late Henry Cabot Lodge directing Republican affairs with a Forty-five as a Baton?[2] And if Dawes had a gun, we would have to draft a new Senate every morning. I kinder like it. I never heard one Deputy call another a Liar all the time I watched 'em operate. But up home it has become so common that it's almost a greeting.

You know, another thing I kinder like down here—everybody, no matter how wealthy, how influential, or how poor and aristocratic, they all refer to themselves as Mexicans. That was so surprising to me after living in California, where there was so many from Mexico lived, who always called themselves Old Spanish Families. I thought there must be something against the Mexicans that they always wanted to be called Old Spanish Families. But in Mexico they are Mexicans, and proud of it. You ask them if they are not really of an old Spanish Family and they will say, "No, I am a Mexican." Well, that sure was a relief, I loved that, to find somebody that would tell the truth.

Dinner at the Embassy

Here is something in the way of news to you that you want to remember: I find after getting down here and circulating around with all of them, that the Americans are the best treated of any race here. They come first, the English second, Germans third. Then it is a question which gets the least consideration from the Government, the Mexicans or the Spaniards. Now that is no joke; that is the absolute truth. They will all tell you, we get the best of everything and the Mexican the worst. You would kinder think the Spaniard would be the big Ace down here, but he don't rate at all. They are great trades people and own all the grocery stores, and when they get a hold of anything they hang onto it, and that's why the Mexicans don't think so much of them.

Mexicans are liberal and great spenders if they got it to spend. I bet there is better Automobiles in Mexico City in accordance with its wealth than any other City in the World. They want the best, those Babies do— Clothes or anything.

Oh, yes, did I tell you about 'em selling Documents and supposedly official papers down here? Well, you can't hardly land down here till somebody comes up to you mysteriously and wants to sell you some Documents. The Hotel Bell boy, instead of like it is up there, wanting to sell you some "Good stuff" before he gets your door unlocked, why, down here he wants to know if you don't want to buy some Papers. You can order any paper you want. You can say, "Yes, I would like to have Maximilian's marriage certificate." Well, he will tell you that he will have it there in 24 hours. You can order the Birth certificates of old President Jasbo's illigitimate children, and name how many you would like them to be, and he will deliver them to you. You can get the conversation between Calles and Morrow at a ranch breakfast if you want to order it, and give 'em time to make it up. It's just one form of organized Graft that we don't seem to have up home.

Well, I must tell you about the dinner. Mr. Morrow give an awful nice dinner to me the other night at the Embassy. He rounded up about fifty —all men—that dident have nowhere to go that night, and we had an awful nice party. I heard the Morrows kinder excited around there one day, and they told me the President had accepted and that he was coming to the dinner. Well, I dident think so much of that concession on his part, as he had been eating with us on the train all that time, and had seemed an awful good fellow. But I come to find out what made all the excitement. It was the first time that a Mexican President had ever been in the American Embassy. That shows you how this Morrow gets along with these people, the ones that he has been sent here to do business with.

Well, we had a great time. Morrow had rounded up a lot of prominent Americans that lived there who had never even met the President. All Calles' Cabinet was there. But there was nothing formal about it. It was all just a good time. Morrow is a Dandy impromptu speechmaker, and I had me an impromptu one that I had only worked on steady for four days. I think I got some notes on it here somewhere, and I will jot it down and let you see that when it comes to mixing with these Diplomats, I was going down, doing the best I could.

'Course I knew that I stood a chance bringing on a war between the two Nations. But I handled it so diplomatically there may never anything come of it. That's the way Diplomats are supposed to do things, ain't it—handle 'em so they will just naturally die off without anything ever being done about 'em. Morrow can write you what he said himself. It was nothing that I can remember now. We had this same interpreter, Jim Smithers. We had there Señor Estrada—he is their Secretary of State.[3] He is the one that has to open the notes from Kellogg every morning—that is, up to the time that Morrow come.[4] Now you don't send any more and that is very smart of you-all.

79

Well, here was my oral note to the President and his Cabinet and our Ambassador and the others:

"Gentlemen of your word, AND Diplomats: Now that we are all here and no note to open, let's be honest with each other and get the low-down on Diplomacy. Everybody wonders what I am doing here. I was originally sent here to step in in case the Senate dident confirm Morrow's appointment. They confirmed him, but they hated to see someone get the job that was not a Politician. Some in the Senate condemned him for working for Morgan and Co, but other more thoughtful heads reminded these Belligerants that we are all working for Morgan and Co. Now about Diplomacy—Diplomacy was invented by a man named Webster, to use up all the words in his Dictionary that dident mean anything.

"A Diplomat is a man that tells you what he don't believe himself, and the man that he is telling it too don't believe it any more than he does. So Diplomacy is always equal. It's like good bookkeeping. He don't believe you and you don't believe him, so it always balances. Diplomats meet and eat, and then rush home and wire their Governments in code that they fooled Secretary of State So-and-So. He dident know what I was eating. That's how slick you Babies are.

"The reason I can speak so freely about Diplomats is because there is none here. America has none, and it's a cinch that you-all down here haven't. They are really an ingredient of Europe's—England and France and all those Countries. They really take 'em serious over there. They breed 'em and raise 'em just for that; and due to having such good ones, they are continually at war over there. We don't have diplomats over in this Western World, and naturally we don't have any wars with each other.

"Diplomats are just as essential to starting a war as Soldiers are for finishing it.

"You take Diplomacy out of war and the thing would fall flat in a week.

"A Diplomat and a stage Magician are the two professions that have to have a high silk hat. All the tricks that either one of them have are in that hat, and are all known to other Diplomats and Magicians.

"Diplomats write Notes, because they wouldent have the nerve to tell the same thing to each other's face.

"A Diplomatic Note is like an annomous letter. You can call a fellow anything you want, for nobody can find out exactly who's name was signed to it.

"England, France and Germany have Diplomats that have had the honor of starting every war they have had in their lifetime. Ours are not so good—they are Amateurs—they have only talked us into one.

"Now about Politicians. The least said about them the best. They havent the social standing of the Diplomats. All their damage is internal. Where the Ambassador generally winds up with a decoration of red ribbon, the Politician generally winds up with an Inditement staring him in the face. Now just here lately it has been reported through the Press, that some of our United States Senators had received some several thousand dollars from Political factions down here. I asked your President here about it the other day, and here was his reply:

" 'You have been down here and had a chance to study most of our leading men. Does it strike you that we are the type that would voluntarily give some other Nation's politicians $300,000?' And then he laughed.

"Well, I agreed with him. I have looked you-all over—in fact that is really what I come down here for was to find out if any of you really were giving money away. I had been sent here by some Senators that had heard that rumor, and I was down to show you where you could place some more. But I find that I am here on a lost cause. No Mexican Politician ever gave anybody anything.

"Politicians are typical in every country. You have the greatest arranged political system in the World down here. Your Constitution says a President can't succeed himself, so Our President here just alternates every four years with Mr. Obregón, and in that way you people know who will be President for the next twenty years, while up home we don't know who will be ours next year." [I dident tell 'em, Cal, that you knew, but that nobody else did.]

What Mexico Needs

"Now I want it distinctly understood that I dident come down here to try and cement good relations between the two Nations, through these so-called cementers that we are always biting at each other's heels. I am not going to tell you that you ought to wake up and be progressive and trade your Burro for a car. The only thing I can see that you need in this Country is more rain, and if Calles here don't give it to you, I would start impeachment.

"Everywhere I go down here somebody invariably asks me for a Cigarette, so if you ask me what this Country needs it's more Cigarettes. [There is a good chance to ring a cigarette add in there, but you notice I dident do it.]

"I come down here to see a lot of the American Colony who are here with us tonight, for I knew there was lot of them that couldent come back home and see us.

"I dident come here to tell you that Mexico needed American Capital. Pass a law to make your rich Mexican invest at least half the money he gets out of his own country back into it again. You have more money in

81

this City invested in French dresses and perfumes than you have in the country in plows. It's not American confidence you are looking for—it's Mexican confidence.

"Make your rich, every time they send a Child to Paris to learn 'em to talk French—make them send one to Sonora to learn to talk Yaqui. They are the ones you have to live and get along with, not the French. You got more imported cars here than you have milk cows.

"I was up and paid a call on our friend here, Mr. Estrada, Secretary of State today, and he got out a wonderful bottle and gave me a swig of what he called Mexican Hospitality. It was Tequila. Then he asked me how I liked Mexico. Why, with one more swig of that a person would have been fond of Siberia.

"The only trouble with this country is, the Verbs have too many endings. I hope Morrow don't get up and tell you that he come here to give you all your Liberty. Why should Mexico be the first Country to have it! It's unusual for a Guest to compliment a Host at a dinner, but I think you will like this little Guy Morrow. You are supposed to be kinder rough babies to deal with, so that's why we sent a fellow down from Wall Street. He looks gentle, but say, you don't raise 'em down here in this cactus any more hard-boiled than we do up there on that little Alley.

"There is no reason why we shouldent get on with this Country. You have lots of things down here that we want, and as long as we get 'em, why, we ought to hit it off great. I want to thank everybody for their hospitality. I just want to find one thing before going home—I want to find what makes every Mexican a Guitar player. Now if I was looking for comedy in Government, I dident have to come here. I could have stayed at home. I come down here to laugh with you and not at you. I dident come here to tell you that we look on you as Brothers. That would be a lot of bunk. We look on you as a lot of Bandits and you look on us as one Big Bandit. So I think we fairly understand each other, without trying to express it. I have nothing in the way of hospitality to offer you when you come to my country, unless you visit me in Hollywood, and I will take you out and let you see the Screen Stars get divorces.

"So we will not drink a toast in Mescal: Por toda mal Mescal, Por toda bien tambien. Viva la Mexico, Viva Estadas Unidas, Bueno Noches, Amigos. Caramba! Yours, Will, Ambassador, without rhyme, reason or Portfolio."

P. S. Say, you and Hughes neither one dident make any better speech than that in Cuba. You spoke on Columbus, I think that was an old speech you had made when you graduated from High School. 'Course those Cubans just eat up anything about Columbus, because they think he landed there. They got him mixed up with Roosevelt. He is the one landed there. But Hughes wasent afraid to speak about Nicaragua. He told 'em that we were in there and were going to stay till every one of them voted Republican.

Ready for Lindbergh

PRESIDENT CALVIN COOLIDGE,
  WHITE HOUSE, WASHINGTON, D. C.

I havent written you in days, for we all been so upset over Lindy's coming. Say, Boss, you don't know what an asset we have got in this Boy Lindbergh till you see him in a Foreign Country. Here's what happened: The Ambassador dug us all out early in the morning. Now Lindy couldent have made it before about noon if he had been on time, but Morrow says, "He might catch a tail wind and get in early." Well, that was a laugh to me. I knew what chance he had catching a tail wind. Wind don't start blowing till you get in the air, then it sees which way you are going to go and it goes around and heads you off.

We got to the field about 7:30, and even as early as that, there was the President and all his Cabinet and staff there already, up on a kind of a stand built over the hangar. And there was over two hundred thousand people on that field. Now they waited there, with not as much as a drink of water, or a sandwitch. The thought never entered their mind to eat. It was anxiety over that Boy that they were living on. You never saw such anxious faces in your life when they begin to realize that he might be lost.

An American audience wouldent have had that patience. When noon come, they would say, "Well, I would like to see the Kid land, but I got to find some hot dogs around here somewhere."

I heard the President tell Mr. Morrow that it would be the greatest calamity that ever befell Mexico if that Boy was lost coming in there; that he was coming just to pay a visit to a people that he had never seen or who meant anything to him, yet he was taking his life in his hands just to come and be friends with them.

He was lost over the clouds and went away off to the Northwest of Mexico City, yet he got his bearings and got in there at 3:45 in the afternoon. But the people were all right there yet. You never saw such rejoicing in your life. You know, those Latins are kinder temperamental anyway, but they went Cuckoo, and the Americans were worse than them. I thought I would have to give up my bed at the Embassy. I told Morrow that morning that I had my things all packed and would go to the hotel.

He said, "Why, you will not!"

Charles Lindbergh, Dwight W. Morrow, and Will Rogers surrounded by members of the staff of the United States Embassy in Mexico City.

I said, "Why, yes. It's been understood that Lindbergh is to have the Guest's room which I am in."

The Boss of the Show

Morrow is an ambassador at heart. This Guy, although he never held a post before, he looked around the room and said, "You will not leave— this room is not good enough for Lindbergh." And he took me and showed me his room that he was giving to Lindy. Well, when I saw his room, this one of mine did look kinder punk. I like to have left then of my own free will.

Here is something I must tell you. When he lands up home, we have to have policemen or Soldiers to guard the plane, for the people will cut the tail off, or fill their pockets with spark plugs, and mebby if they can carry it, stick the engine under their coat. Well, in Mexico the people, instead of trying to tear the plane up for souvenirs, they carried it on their shoulders to the hanger. They are just ignorant that way; they dident know enough to cut it all up. They are the most primitive people that way—no Pep and Progress. And instead of thowing confetti or ticker tape out of the windows as he passed, everybody threw flowers.

They have a queer way of entertaining, and about him going to the Bullfight. They even wired me: "Don't let Lindbergh go to Bullfight." What could I do about Lindbergh going to a Bullfight? I was lucky to shake hands with him, much less telling him where not to go. Then to Morrow they sent a hundred messages: "It will be national disgrace if Lindbergh goes to Bullfight."

I wanted to wire them and tell 'em: "What do you keep worrying about Lindbergh going for? Why don't you stop the Bull from going?"

There is the head man in that show. He come in to breakfast one morning and a screaming headline said: America Protests Lindy Going to Bullfight. He glanced at it, then said, "Well, that settles it. What time is the fight?"

Now he had no idea going at first; it was not on his official program. The Mexicans are very considerate that way. They know Americans don't care for the fights and don't ask you to go. In fact, about 90 per cent of them don't go. It's just a certain bunch that goes; but the ones who do go, go every Sunday. The only time you ever see a vacant seat is when some fan has died during the week. The President says they go thinking some time during their life they will see a good fight.

I dident see Lindy after he saw one, as I left Mexico the afternoon he went. One day I am coming into the embassy and he was going out with his Helmet and Goggles. I asked him where he was going.

He said, "Come on, I will take you up with me. I am going to take up a Mexican Plane." Well, on the way out he said, "Now I won't take you up

85

first, as it wouldent look good to come down here and take up an American first."

Now how's that for diplomacy? Who would have thought of that? One in a hundred would have noticed that he had taken up someone besides a native. But that one in a hundred was the one he was catering to. You know, I wish we could get our Tourists and rich people that go abroad to show one-tenth as much consideration for the feelings of the people of the country where they are visiting as this Kid does. If they did, we would be the most popular people on earth. You know, flying is the least thing we can learn from this Boy.

Well, after I saw 'em lead out one of these Mexican Planes, I was in favor of him taking up all of Mexico before he got to me. You know, they got dandy aviators down here. But it's their Planes that are obsolete. They are the ones that France used in the first of the war. But now we are allowing them to buy up home, so they will have some real ones soon. But they are good flyers. One fellow, Casterhoun, flew me around that Volcano Popocaterpillar, and I want to tell you when he banked that around the edge of that old smoking crater I commenced wondering what my insurance covered.[5] And they got another great little flyer, Carranza.[6] He made a nonstop flight to El Paso and his wing caught fire and he flew over into a rainstorm and the rain put it out. Now that's some Aviating, and thinking, and also some research work, to find a rain in Northern Mexico. Well, Lindy took Casterhoun up, then Carranza, and then he hollered for me. He had to or I wouldent have been there, for the old Plane looked like a weak Sister to me. It's almost sacrilegious to say that you would be afraid with Lindbergh, for my only chance of ever becoming immortal was to have fallen with Lindbergh. But even at that, I was too big a coward to want to fall with him. Going to the Embassy afterward, I asked him about the Plane, and he made the only undiplomatic remark I ever heard him make, and I don't think he would have made that if he had realized who was with him.

He said, "I just wanted to fly that Plane to see if a Plane that old would fly."

Mexican Trick Ropers

They gave a Roping Contest, or Rodeo, for me—the Charro Club— that's an organization of Ex-Cowpunchers and prominent fellows in the City. You know, the Mexicans are just about the best Ropers there is. They have their own arena. Of course when Lindy got in the Country and I had got him to promise to go out there with me to see it, why, it was forgot that it had ever been got up for me. I think he enjoyed it, for there was some fine work done by General Cruise and the Besareil brothers,

Rogers and Mexican army pilot Augustín Castrejón who took Rogers on an air tour of Mexico City on December 13, 1927.

who had just returned from giving Exhibitions in the Bull rings of Spain.[7] They are Mexico's best ropers.

They showed how they Tailed the wild ones down. They run by and wrap the tail under your leg and then go on by, and, brother, it certainly upsets 'em. Then they did a stunt running a loose wild horse around the arena and jumping onto him from your horse. He wouldent have a thing on, not a surcingle or halter—just naked. They wanted me to get in there and rope, but, Lord, I had just as much chance trying to show them something as Jim Watson will have with his two Delegates at K. C.[8]

I was going to leave that Sunday by plane for Tampico and then fly on to Brownsville and San Antonio. I had a very big old bag that I dident know if it would go in the Cockpit of the Plane. So I took the Colonel in to ask him. It was full of Mexican spurs and Silver bits, and a big carved knife that Obregón had given me. Lindy has been joking me about leaving in an old Standard plane. He said if I struck a head wind I would be in Mexico all winter.

So when I showed him this big bag, he said very seriously—for he likes his joke: "No, that won't go in the Plane, but you can take a rope and tie it on behind the plane and let it drag. It can't slow up that plane any."

But as it happened, I drew a Fairchilds and had a wonderful trip into Tampico, and then right along the ocean on up to Brownsville. Then with J. I. Moore, the Boy Scout aviator of Kelly, right on into San Antonio.[9]

Watching the Way the Wind Blows

I must tell you, the first time I flew with Lindbergh I had been down to San Diego to speak at his dinner, when he was on that tour, and I felt mighty proud to speak before him, and I gave a lot of thought to my speech. I did want to have something different from all the other speeches I had heard by the Governors and Mayors, where it was always, "Our Boy! Our Hero, who flew from here to France!" Well, I had an idea the Kid knew where he went and there wasent any use bringing that up, so I told him that as time went by and Planes got better, that his time would, of course, be beat by far; but that there was one record that I thought he held that would go down through the ages, and that was that he was the only man that ever took a ham Sandwitch to Paris; and that all our Speakers always referred to him as an inspiration to our youths.

"Why, if our youths followed you, Colonel, they would all be in the Atlantic Ocean. I have two boys.[10] I want them to admire you, but I don't want 'em trying any of these stunts that you are pulling around here. I want the boys with me a while yet."

Then everybody that ever introduced Lindbergh anywhere always refers to him as the Columbus—the modern Columbus, and Columbus of the air. That just shows you how much all these old long-winded Speakers know.

They just pick out some name in History and bring it down to now; they don't know if it fits or not. When they call him Columbus, they don't know their history. Columbus was lost when he found this Country and don't know yet where he landed. Lindbergh knows where he landed in France, but we can't pronounce it. Columbus just touched the Queen for a mess of Jewels and lit out. It dident matter to him where he landed.

Well, the next day, as he dident have any town to make, he took a big new Ford Plane, three-motored, and took a lot of us back up to Los Angeles. I was sitting out in the Pilot's seat with him and we were about to land, and it was not at a regular field, as they wanted to avoid the crowd. There was no Hangar or wind Indicator; it was just a stubble field.

So I asked him, "How can you tell how to land when you can't see which way the wind is blowing from?"

He said, "Why, dident you see the way those clothes was blowing on that line back there?"

Now dident I see the way some washing was blowing on a clothesline about ten towns back? I dident even notice what clothes were on the line.

And then I told him: "Well, suppose it wasent Monday—what would you do? I supose we would have to fly around up here till somebody washed." But say I wasent kidding him.

He come right back at me—he has a good sense of humor—"I wouldent fly over such a dirty country."

Well, that's about all the scandal for now.

Yours,
WILL.

SAN ANTONIO, TEXAS.

MR. CALVIN COOLIDGE,
   President of these United States and
   Dictator of Republican Convention.

My Dear Mr. Coolidge: Well, here I am on my way back home. Just flew in from Mexico City. And, say, don't overlook this valley down here on the Rio Grande that I flew over today. Why, I never saw as much junk raised on one little plot in my life. That wouldent be a bad place to tell your friends to drop a little investment. Mellon has saved up most of his salary there, and if he will just stick it anywhere down here in Texas it will fix him so he won't have to argue with Couzens and Congress all his life.[11]

Say, what great fields they got here. Keep after this air stuff. Lor', here I am tonight, and left Mexico City yesterday in the late afternoon, spent the night with a lot of fine Americans in Tampico, and then to Brownsville for lunch, and here for dinner. No Bandits, no Wrecks, no heat, and it's the only way to see the country. And what a fine bunch of boys in the air service. One of the Du Pont boys is enlisted here at Kelly. You know, there is a lot of rich kids that have given up the coonskin coat and the homemade gin and are taking to the air.

Let's get all the planes we can, do all the commercial aviation we can to keep the boys in training, and get our Naval fleet the biggest one. Second money with a fleet is sorter like running second at a Presidential election. It's better to spend more money and have the best fleet, just like it's better to spend more money and get the most votes. But I can't tell you Republicans anything about that. If America has all these things, then just sits here and takes care of our own business, you can bet nobody is going to come over here and pounce on us.

This ought to reach you just about the time the Republicans are ready for their masked ball in Kansas City. Morrow and I while down there talked a lot of politics. You know, he is a pretty shrewd little fellow. I dident know those Wall Street Guys knew anything but bonds and Interest, but he sho does. 'Course I have always had the old sneaky feeling that when the boys lined up at the barrier in November, you would be among those present.

A Foundling

I have backed my whole argument on that word "Choose." To me it's the only word in the world that don't mean anything. It's just "Yes," "No," "I can't tell yet," "Mebby," "who knows," "undecided," "decided," "probably," "not likely." It means all those, and hence means nothing.

Now let's be honest with each other. You dident pick that little word accidentally, did you? You did a lot of research work to find that. Now here is what I claim when the convention gets tied up in K. C. between Dawes and Hoover: A Man will get up *apparently impromptu, and with only eight months rehearsal,* and say:

"Fellow Republicans, are we going to haggle and argue and make a spectacle out of ourselves like those monkey Democrats, over two splendid men, when we have only one man that can assure us of victory, and that man is Calvin Coolidge?"

Hurray! Then the banners will start marching and the Gang will all join in, and you will be unanimously nominated. Then the news will reach you. 'Course you know nothing about this—much. The Baby will be laid on your doorstep, and you as a humanitarian will have to nourish it.

Now I may be all wet. Morrow don't know, and he knows you better than anybody—which don't mean anything. He says there is one thing that might make you run—that is, if the Prohibition and other issues got so strong, and there would naturally be a demand on any other Candidate to come out squarely on them, and whichever way they come out, it would lose them a lot of votes. But with you, you wouldent have to declare yourself. All you would have to say is, "I stand where I have stood." Well, as they havent found out in six years, there is no reason to think they would find out before election.

You know, you Birds are going out against this fellow Smith, and you better get your cleats sharpened. You know, funny thing about this Rep nomination—it's just about the same situation that come up in Cleveland four years ago. The very men who are in the race was in it then, but only for the Vice Presidency. So all we got to go by is that. They was humming and hawing around there over a vice Pres, and when Dawes name come up, why, it was a kind of a spark and he went over with a bang. He has got a good deal of color, and, you know, these dopy Delegates, sitting there day after day, they will fall for any kind of excitement.

You know, having Delegates at a convention is almost a handicap, unless you got six hundred with the Republicans and eight hundred with the Democrats. Outside of you four years ago, I don't suppose in the whole history of either party the man that went there with the most Delegates ever got the nomination. So that's why Dawes is sitting so pretty. 'Course you and Mellon wouldent be so strong for him. You would have to do your opposing him through a third party; for we all know you are too wise publicly to show a preference, for it would kill your Candidate's chances and help any other one that you publicly opposed.

And don't forget Charley Curtis.[12] You Republicans owe him more than you do anybody outside of your Campaign contributors. The trouble is he is so faithful that the chances are he will never be rewarded. He has stayed with you through all your disgraces and never got mixed up in any of them. He is an Indian. I wish he would get in. Us Indians would run these White people out of this country.

I guess Hoover has the popular vote, but the popular vote never nominated anybody. I am going to the Convention, and as a favor to me, I wish you would let me know what room this nomination will be held in. I don't want to have to waste my time over in the Convention Hall with any side show; I want in the board of Directors' meeting.

So tell Hilles and Butler and all the Gang that I want to know who is going to be nominated, not who is going to receive the most votes for the first few days.[13] Who cares who leads into the stretch? It's the man that leads in the last ballot that I am interested in—chances are it will be his first vote. You know yourself, Cal, you or I wouldent take those Delegates flocked down there on that floor serious. They are just here for the trip; they are not here to nominate anybody. They think they are, but ——

If you don't decide to run, and move out, why, Al Smith runs a trucking Company—that's his side line. He can move your things out as he moves in, and mebby cut down the price. I personally don't care which one of you get in—all I want is Ambassador to Mexico. I have watched Morrow long enough now to tell how he does it. If they don't appoint me this time, I will wait four years and Morrow will appoint me himself. You Republicans are going to Kansas City, but it's Houston you got your eye on.[14] Let me know in advance where you are going to send me next. I think I will cover the election in Nicaragua. They say it's going to be on the level, so that would be of great interest and novelty to all of us.

Well, good luck to you. If you don't stay in, I will know it's because something better or Smith turned up.

Yours, always a Diplomat,   WILL.

Letters Of A
Self-Made Diplomat
To Senator Borah

Letters of a Self-Made Diplomat to Senator Borah

VANCOUVER, B. C.
Nov. 20, 1931.

Dear Senator Borah:
Well, your One-Man mission is on its way; I am getting out of here in the morning on the Empress of Russia. I just wanted to drop you a line before I pushed off. There is a few things that ought to be straightened out between both of us, so we will have it clear just what I am to do, and why.

As you know, I took this position with you after weighing the whole thing over carefully. As you also know, I could have gone over for Herbert on about the same terms that I went over to Europe in 1926 for Calvin. That was, pay my own expenses and split what I got out of the letters with him. But darn this thing of continually working for our President—that's what we all are doing. It's all right if you are in his Cabinet and there is no way of getting out; those fellows have to stay there and take it on the chin. But with me it's different. Now, here is a few of the plain reasons that I dident want to go for the President: In the first place, there is no novelty to it; you are just another Hoover Commission. Now, that handicaps you right there; you hand a fellow your card, MR. WILLIAM PENN ADAIR ROGERS, CHAIRMAN, HOOVER COMMISSION FOR INVESTIGATING ALL DEPRESSION WEST OF PACIFIC OCEAN. Now, the fellow you hand it to is going to laugh, for he sees bands of such men every day; Highways, Railways, and even Oceans are clogged up with Commissions going somewhere to see why somebody else is doing as bad as they are. They are not all Hoover Commissions, of course—only about 95 per cent—but it was him that started it. He got other folks doing it. Of course, it was a good time to do it, for most of the folks he would appoint was laying off anyhow, and even a job on a Commission looked better than nothing. He first started out by only putting Big Men on 'em—that is, what we thought was Big Men then—and they was, as long as everything was going good. But when the blow-up come, nothing went as high and fell as flat as Big Men. Well, the Big Men dident know any more

Saturday Evening Post, February 27, 1932. Reprinted with permission.

about stopping it than they knew about preventing it before it happened. And, too, the Big Men had run out of Predictions, so middle-sized and Little Men got so they could get on Commissions. They couldent do any more than the Big Ones, but it was a compliment to 'em to be there. Of course, they would not have been there if the case hadent been hopeless anyhow. But lately they draft men to get 'em on Commissions. You can't get one on there of his own free will and accord.

But you can't blame Mr. Hoover. It looked like a good thing to do at the time, and I doubt if we would have been any better off without 'em. For they revived hopes for a while. Of course, they did collect a lot of what they call Data, but most of the Data was bad, so there was no use collecting it. It's like garbage; there is no use collecting it if you ain't going to do anything with it after you get it collected. You see, there really wasent anything you could do. It was just Commission coming into the Hospital with another epidemic case, when they had found no cure for the others; it was just as well to let him die at home.

But the cards was stacked against Mr. Hoover; not only against him but every Nation. The Lord was wise to the World and he just wanted to show 'em that, after all, he was running things, in spite of the New York Stock Exchange. Well, that was a terrible blow to finance to learn that the Lord not only closed the Market on Sundays, but practically closed it on week days. So, you see, Commissions were not to blame for all our ills. They did, however, draw people's attention to 'em. Now, for instance, there is an awful lot of things wrong with us that if we hadent picked up a Paper and seen where a Commission had been appointed to investigate it, why, we wouldent maby have known we had it.

Of course Wickersham's bunch will hold the record for this and all time, for finding out exactly what everybody already knew.[1]

Of course, nothing was ever done about their Report, except they say one man at Mattewan actually read it clear through. Then he did something about it; he made a bonfire that lasted a week. But what I am trying to get at, Senator, in a few words, is that Commissions are as dead as Protective Tariffs in Alabama. Commissions have contributed more to humor than they have to achievement in American life. So that's why I dident want to just go out to the Orient as "Just another Hoover Commission." I like him, mind, and wouldent mind working for him; everybody that has ever been connected with him in a working capacity has the greatest respect and admiration for him. Even Smedley Butler, the Hero of the real old fighting Marines, couldent get any more followers to go with him into battle than Mr. Hoover can among his Coworkers.[2] So, you see, there is nothing personal about my turning down this job with him; it was just that I wanted more distinction than a Hoover Commission could give. And, besides, I don't like to play Medicine Ball early in the morning. I think that early morning, say from seven to eight, was meant for sleeping. That's when I do all my heavy thinking—is when I am sleeping from seven to eight A.M.

Then, there is another thing. When I worked for Calvin that time, I was about the only one he had out. You wasent confused with any other Coolidge Commission. When I went up to Benito Mussolini and said, "I am here in the interest of Calvin Coolidge," it meant something. It dident mean there had been twelve other Commissions there ahead of me that day. You see, Mr. Coolidge wasent a Commission man; he was a man that dident want to know what was going on. He knew that it was going to go on whether he knew it or not, and he dident want to do anything that might keep it from going on. You never caught him appointing any Prohibition Commission. No, sir; he just said, "I was elected to veto Bills; I wasent elected to count the drinks." He believed that Nature elected him, and he was going to let Nature take its course. If the salmon wasent biting in the Columbia River, or the League of Nations wouldent enforce birth control in Abyssinia, you wouldent catch Calvin sending a Commission down there to bring back the Data. No, sir, if Wall Street sold, Short, Long, or Crooked, you never caught Calvin even reading about it. He just said, "What is, is, and I am not going to try to un-is it."

So I guess I am about the only one that ever found out anything for him, and I dident find out enough to worry him. It was just that he wanted a little check-up on Europe. I even went into Russia for him— that was before they had their Five-Year Plan. They was just messing along a good deal like we are now, without any plan. But it was a pleasure to work with Mr. Coolidge; he never bothered you. In fact, when I talked to him he never even bothered enough to answer me. But what I am getting at is that conditions are different from back in '26, when I was with him. Did you know that Mussolini, Charley Chaplin and yourself, Senator, are about the only big men that have held up over that stretch of years?[3] King of Spain has had some good luck; when somebody knocks, he can go to the door now and open it without peeping out the window first to see who it is.[4] But even the Prince of Wales has lost his appeal among the Young Girls.[5] But, of course, gained additionally with the middle-aged married women.

So, you see, Senator, that is why I picked you to go look things over for. I coundent work for Chaplin, for he looks 'em over for himself, and marries most of 'em. Grandi is working for Mussolini, and he was over here.[6] And he was pratically on the same sort of a mission for the Premier as I am for you. About the only difference, I am clean-shaved. Now the question will be asked, "Why did I decide to go on this trip for you?" Well, I am a man that wants to go with the best. What's the use of going all over Europe, or all over Mount Fuji-yama, or Manchuria, or the

Walls of China, or that long Barroom in Shanghai, if, when I get back and turn it over to somebody like Mr. Coolidge or Mr. Hoover, or Mr. Smith, or Mr. Roosevelt, or Mr. Baker, they, in turn, can't do anything about it; they have to turn it over to you anyhow.[7] You know, yourself, that all my Coolidge reports had to go right on UP to you. So, I am getting tired of that; I says, "Here; what's the use of my prowling and writing, and then have to have them go first to a mere Supernumiary?—there is a good word, Senator, that was brought over here to Canada by the English.

So I just says, "No more foreign reports to Presidents for me. I am going to work for the Head Man." You, as Chairman of the United States Foreign Relations Committee, are the Guy that does business with everything outside of the United States and Idaho. When Mr. Lavall comes, it's Mr. Hoover that gives him the Dinner, but it's Mr. Borah that tells him that "I am very sorry, but you can't get away with it."[8] It's the President they have their Picture taken with, but it's you that vetoes their schemes.

You see, where I got all this idea first was when I was in Europe that time I just been speaking of. I had some letters—not to mail, but to use— and they was from quite a few mighty fine men over home, and I appreciated 'em a whole lot. I remember, Charley Dawes give me some to men who had served on the Dawes Plan.[9] Well, they was in such big banks and houses that it scared me out of presenting 'em. But I had one from you.

Well, when I would get in a tight place and somebody would ask me, "Have you any credentials of any sort—Letters, old marriage certificates, mortgages, snapshots with the Spinx, or any little knickknack that will show us you are not just a Democrat and are thrown on the Country?" Well, I would mention everything I had, till I would get to you. Then, when I would tell 'em, "I got a letter here from Senator Borah," well, the Man would jump like he was shot, and he would say, "You mean your Premier?" Why, it makes even an Englishman move fast, and it so dumfounds a Frenchman that he forgets to keep saying "*Como?*" Why, you got me into Russia, and better still, you got me out. Why, I got so I showed the letter in Cafes and they cancelled the Bill; they figured it was money well spent, at that, for maby you would cancell the debt. Well, I wore out the original one just showing it. The I copied off one myself— only I added to the new one and made it look like I was your Col. House.[10] Well, then, that was the last word in service that I would get.

So that showed me that you was the Fair-Haired Boy in all these Countrys that want something. Now, that's not handing you any Boquets; it's the real facts. You see, we don't have a Prime Minister that looks after all those things like these other Nations have. But you, as head of the Foreign Relations Committee, come nearer to it than anyone they know, and so they just naturally think you are our Prime Minister. You see, France has a President, too, but we never know who he is, and neither do most of them; and they get to thinking that our President is more like him—sorter decorative. They don't know that we think so much of ours that we hold him responsible for everything that happens, whether it be in the Sky, on the Earth, or in a Senate Committee Room. You see, it's not our President's fault that they are not known as well in Europe as you are; they are not in all the time like you are. The minute it's not raining enough and we can't raise anything, or it's raining too much and we raise to much, why, we throw our President out and get a new one. So the World is naturally not supposed to keep track of all our foolishness .

But they do know who has to O. K. any foreign skullduggery that's going on with us. It's Mr. Long-haired Borah. They know that an election in America is no more going to effect you than a League of Nations' decison would Japan. They know what happened to the one man that voted against you in 1920. If we had had a President that had been in that long, why, he would naturally be known well too. So that's why I just says to myself, when I got your offer to "Snoop the Orient," "Fathom the Far East" and "Puncture the Phillipines"—"Why," I says, "me for that job." So, when I say I am the Head, Tail, Chairman, and Executive Committee of the Bill Borah Conservation of Foreign Entanglements Commission, why, brother, I will command respect. From what I gather from what you wrote me, we not only don't want to conserve our Relations with 'em but curtail 'em if possible. In other words, we got too many relations with 'em now. It's great to be friendly with a Foreign Nation, but it's terribly expensive. If the worst comes to the worst and we do have to be friends with any of 'em, why, I will pick out little ones that havent got the nerve to ask for much. And when I do come in contact with some of the Big Ones that our relations have already become so financially entwined that they have no use for us anyhow, why, I will try and keep what they call at these Conferences the "Status Quo." It's an old Cherokee word that means: "This thing had gone far enough; let's go back to where we started from, and next time we will watch each other closer." So, with the ones we are already in bad with, I will keep the Status Quo, and with any others I will watch 'em first. So my business is not to increase our Foreign Relations but abolish 'em entirely. Of course, the Orient, where I head for first, is not in our immediate clutches financially as some of our nearer Sisters. It only shows you the nearer you are the more you become entangled. That goes for all but Canada, where I am writing this now. They have truly been a good Companion; I won't call 'em Neighbors, for they havent borrowed enough from us to be called Neighbors; I would prefer to still call 'em

99

Friends. They are a fine tribe of people. They are hardy—they got to be to live next to us and exist; they have made a great showing with a few people over a tremendous area. The whole of New York City, where 80 per cent of our wealthy people are in storage, if you turned 'em loose in Canada on their own resources, it would be fifty years before one would get far enough away from Toronto to discover Lake Erie. No, Canadians are built of sturdier stock; they have suffered more than their share; they furnished more than their share of men and money in the Great War. Their example was a cause of real admiration to all our Country. Then they come home, and wheat and timber prices blew up.

So, Senator, I want you to do what you can for 'em sometime—that is, of course, if it's just a favor and don't cost much. So, you see, I am turning in my first report mighty quick after leaving home. 'Course, I havent looked over so terrible much of Canada. I just crossed the line down here about twenty miles this evening in an aeroplane, and just had time to see a little of Vancouver before dark, but these are my findings, and this is my report as I find this Country. You see, it ain't going to take me long to look a Country over. I am not going to be like a Commission—take evidence on both sides. That way you just become confused and don't know which side is lying, and you go away not knowing any more than when you come. That's why Juries should decide a case the minute they are sworn in, before the Lawyers have had a chance to misslead 'em. So that's why I can size up Canada so quick, and maby give 'em a squarer deal than if I stopped and listened to everybody.

I flew up here, Senator, from Los Angeles. Your old Toastmaster of the Senate, Charley Curtis, was out there when I left, kinder looking over the movie situation. Ever once in a while they can use a good Lawyer—and maby about next November? Well, he was just getting his application in early. Charley is a good Injun. He belongs to the Kaw tribe, but there's not enough of 'em to get much from the Government politically. When he was out there, he dident know whether to stay with Hoover next fall or stay with Kansas and run for the Senate. Well, I been to a lot of gatherings and meetings, and it's as if somebody says to me, "The Hall is pretty crowded. I can give you a seat down in the Auditorium now, or, if you care to wait and take a chance, maby I can fix you up with a seat on the Rostrum." Charley don't want to get off the Rostrum if he can help it, but, on the other hand, he don't want to be left out of the Hall entirely; so he may take a seat in the Auditorium.

But all this, Senator, has nothing to do with me or my trip. I could sit here and write inquiries to you about Politics and all that Hooey all night, but I got to get up early in the morning and get ready to cross one of our biggest and best-known Oceans. I am here at the C. P. Railroad Hotel. You know, these Railroads, when they built into a Country up

100

here, they built up the whole Town—Hotels, Hospitals, Clubs—everything. They dident just put in a place to sell you a ticket. You know, I know all this will be interesting to you, Senator, for you have never been away from home. That's why we made you Chairman of the Foreign Relations Committee. But, Look! The fellow that wrote the best book on Lincoln was an Englishman—well, not the best, but next to Sandberg's, it was—the fellows that wrote the good play about Hollywood, Once in a Lifetime, have never even been as far west as Chicago.[11] So I think it's good you don't get anywhere.

I would just go on doing like you do—drop out to Idaho every few years; 'course, as you get older and the trip gets harder, why, just mail 'em out some Post Cards. But I would kinder keep in touch with the old home. Boise is a mighty pretty little Town; I been there. Ground kinder sandy, built in on a right pretty creek, bluff up on one side . . . . That ain't where you live, is it, Senator? . . . . I met the old Newspaper Gentleman there, Mr. Cobb, who first found you and got you scrubbed up, and hog-tied you and got some shoes on you, but no sox, and run you for the Legislature.[12] He is dead, I hear, now, but he was mighty proud of you. He showed me lots of clippings and letters from you. He said sometimes you would get kinder boneheded and stiff-necked, and get off on the wrong track, and he would have to bring you back to taw with a stiff Editorial. And, he said, lots of times you would take after a rabbit when he took you deer hunting; said that was your only failing. But take it all in all, he was mighty proud of his Pupil. He had a mighty smart daughter that was a mighty keen politican herself.[13] Is she still there? Give her my regards, will you? I think she was unmarried. That's not why I want you to give her my regards. But she was then.

Yes, Senator, don't "Go Washington;" always keep in touch with the Thrasher Hands and the Boys with the Lambing Jackets on. They are the ones that put you in there with those 95 other Hyenas. Of course, that you have risen from just one of 'em is due to your own effort. I imagine it's one of the hardest things in the World to keep from being just another Senator, but you have done it, and you deserve all the visits you get from Lavall, and Grandi, and McDonald, and little Gandi, if he ever gets over here with his goat.[14]

Oh, yes; I like to forgot; what I started to tell you a while ago, about these railroads up here in Canada, there is two of 'em—the Canadian Pacific and the Canadian National—it's now government owned—But they were originally two separate, privately owned, and what one would do the other would do. If one built a big Hotel on the top of a Mountain, the other would pick out an opposition Mountain. One started out to get to the Pacific Ocean, and the other one took out after it. Canada, north and south, is about as wide as the whole U.S., including Central and

South America thrown in, so, did these R. R.'s scatter out so they could cover some opposition territory? No, sir, not these Babys. They just took after each other and went west hand in hand. One place they come to a Mountain, and they had to split for a few miles. But it liked to broke the Directors' heart, and they got back together on the other side, and were chummier than ever from there on. If one went through a town, the other one would go through it, too; even if there wasent enough room in the town for only one track the other would tunnell under. If one had a steamship line, the other one put one in. But he couldent run it till he found out where the other fellow was going to run his, so he could go the same place.

That must have been Englishmen or Americans did that. I don't believe a Canadian did. It was that dogged determination of the English that said "Anywhere you go, I can go," and they generally do, and in this case they sure did. But they are mighty fine lines, got good Hotels, good Boats. Of course, they are not doing so well now, but neither is Ford or Rockefeller.[15] And to this day you can go clear across the vast stretches of Canada by rail; in fact, you can ride tandem, one foot on the C. P. R. R. train the other on the Canadian.

But if you want to go north and south, you better get a horse, tie some snowshoes on behind you, and light out. But, say, wait a minute. Let me horn in here with my pet subject. They are doing a lot of flying away up in that Northern Country. They got several lines; so they told me here tonight, when I landed at as fine a field as you want to see. This should be the ideal Country for flying, with all these long stretches to make, an Amphibian —— Oh, pardon me, Senator, that's a Plane that can land on either land or water; I mean, that can land on either purposely. Any of 'em can do it, but not continuously with the same plane. That's a fine line that I come up on Yesterday from Los Angeles to Seattle too. Mountain Country is mighty pretty to fly over, if you can just stop yourself from continually looking for landing fields—which you never find. If you get a little chance, Senator, with Home Relations, you want to give some of those lines a little Subsidy. They are doing a fine pioneering work. 'Course, don't do it till Andy gets in a little better shape. He ain't in any condition to slip anybody anything now. Did you ever see a fellow as far in the hole?

I kinder hate to be going away off over that far when I could stay at home and go to Washington and see your Show. Let's see, you all are going to meet next week. I figure this ought to be one of the best sessions, for the Audience, that you have ever held. 'Course, it will be a tough session on the Taxpayers, but there will be many a laugh for the Gallery. It looks like, as I am leaving, that the Democrats will have more Members in the Chorus than the Republicans. The Republicans did have the most a couple of months ago, but a lot of them died. Looked like they did it purposely, just to keep from being accused of belonging to that body. But the Democrats—you can't shame them into even dying. They would keep on living just to spite the Republicans.

You know, Senator, here is what I kinder feel: I don't know for sure that the Democrats WANT to be in control of things this session. You see, if they get control, why, they also inherit the blame for the devilement. Now, if they wasent in charge, why, they could, of course, as usual committ the devilement, but the blame would fall on the other Party. And with the election coming on this fall, that makes 'em careful. If it was at last year's session, they would know the Voters couldent remember that long, but they do figure that a voter's mind can retain from winter to fall. So the Boys will all be walking on eggs, and I sure hate to miss it. But I figure that I will get back from over there about the time that all the Relief Bills have been read. Just think, if a hungry man had to stand outside and wait, not till he gets relief but just till all the Plans for his relief was read. If the hungry could eat paper, it would solve the food problem for the whole winter. But I am getting sleepy now, and I got to get up and catch that Boat. May drop you a line before I get away. Now, I hope everything is all clear between us, and I am going to try and find out all I can for you.   Yours.   WILL.

*D*EAR SENATOR: This is written on the Boat, and I will drop it off at Victoria. That's an English Town located on an Island off Canada. Canadians have to get a passport to go over there. Tasmania—that's an Island away off down south of Australia. Well, it was at one time England's Prison Colony; they sent their Prisoners there. But in addition to their Prisoners in England, they have another breed that they always get rid of, and that is about their Third Son—I am referring now to the better Families. Well, the First Son, he stays at home and inherits everything. He has to be pretty handy with a Teacup and be able to get into a Dinner Jacket the minute it starts getting dark, even if it's an eclipse happening in the middle of the day. I have seen an Englishman just automatically get their Monkey Suit on. The Second Son generally goes into the Army or Navy, depending kinder on which branch his Father prefers; but about the Third Son, and from then on down, they are in for a trip. They bundle them off, and they are what they call Remittance Men. They generally try to get 'em as far away from the rest of the family as possible.

Well, Victoria, B. C., is just about as far as you can go west unless you have fins. Not only is Victoria far away but that B. C., as you remember —— But I doubt if you do, being a Senator; I doubt if you have ever read the book; but there is a book that has a meager circulation in parts of the United States that tells quite a bit of what happened around and after B. C. Now, we United Staters —— There is another thing I want to call your attention to, Senator, that I learned from the late and GREAT Dwight Morrow.[16] There was A Man. I may bring up later on, in my advice to you, as to how he solved lots of problems that the State Department thought was Diplomatic, but that Morrow told me in Mexico, that they were nothing but a plain little bit of everyday business, the same as other business men solve every day. But they get 'em solved because they don't call 'em "Diplomatic."

Ah, you would have liked that fellow Morrow, Senator. Too bad you other Senators were too busy talking to meet him and get acquainted with him while he was sitting there listening to you all that time, and having a quiet laugh. In fact, I think that's what made him ill, was just conceiling so much merriment inside—that good taste did not permit him to exhale—that it finally impaired his helth. Well, you would, perhaps, got to meet him if he had lived, for in 1936 he is the one that you would have been going to have breakfast with, to report as to what you had done the last few days in regard to funding debts from the late Russio-Japanese War, the late Italy-France Embryo, and various others of the late wars.

But what I started to tell you was about one of the many things I learned from him. He was never Ambassador from America to Mexico. He always insisted that he was Ambassador from the United States of North America to Mexico—lot of difference there, see? Mexico kinder figures that she is in America, too; and they have some legitimate claim to the fact. Then there is all the Central and South American Countries. When we call ours "America," they also feel that they are in a kind of a sort of distant way America too. So he always paid the other Nations the compliment of saying that he was "from the U. S. of North America." So that is just a tip for you, Senator. We are not the whole of America, we are just a part of the U. S. of North America. So remember that, will you, Senator? And as Foreign Relations Head you are liable to make a lot of friends by following this advice. And Senators could use a friend now and again—not only could but do when they can accidentally find one.

But later on I may tip you off a lot of things that Morrow did that a Diplomat dident do. In fact, he told me one time that he dident believe he would have had the nerve to tackle the job, if it was not that he had the example of Diplomats to watch, so that he could do the opposite and feel sure of success.

But what I started to tell you away awhile ago, before I got off on this

United States business, was that we in the United States never could figure out just why the British would want to root these later-day Sons of theirs off. We always figured—that is, the ones of us that had met the First Son—that they sent away the wrong Son; for some of these later ones are mighty fine fellows and turn into good Citizens, and in lots of cases go back and bail out of hock the favored Son. But there is no understanding people, Senator; it always will seem funny to us United Staters that we are about the only ones that really know how to do everything right. I don't know how a lot of these other Nations have existed as long as they have till we could get some of our people around and show 'em really how to be Pure and Good like us.

So, you see, Senator, in leaving home, I had no more than traveled one day than I can report to you on the manners and customs of two foreign Countries—Vancouver, Canada, and Victoria, England, B. C.—the B. C. means, Before Canada. Well, before we sailed today I stirred around the town quite a bit; went to a bookstore and layed in a supply for the Boat. Told the fellow I wanted something of a historical nature that delt with our United States, for I wasent very well posted on our History, and in case I got into an argument in the smoking room of the Boat—not over who would pay the check, but about some part of our History in comparison to theirs—why, I wanted to be well-healed with some historical data.

So the Canadian Bookseller gave me Cross Marks the Spot, by an Author who not only knew America but had a Camera. The One-Way Ride was another historical best seller; Al Capone, the Man, by the same Author that gave us the lives of Washington, Lincoln and Jefferson; and this book had brought in enough that it made it possible for him to keep on writing of some of our earlier Characters.[17] Hooey and Applesauce, a best seller, he told me, that delt with inner workings and skullduggery of highly paid officials of our National Capitol. Washington a Washout was another of the same scholastic value. Why We Can't Catch 'Em at It was, the clerk told me, a true story of Democratic official life in New York City, written by a Republican who had been on 234 Republican Investigation Committees. It was a very frank exposure, by the Author, who just admitted he was too Dumb; that he knew the City Hall was being carried away, but they couldent prove just what Street it was being carted down. Then he sold me a giant affair of twenty-four Volumes, called, What's the Matter with the United States? Also a little short—practically a Pamphlet—called I Saw It Coming and Ducked, by Calvin Coolidge, the Author Himself. Another called Don't Shoot the Piano Player; He is Doing the Best He Can, by Herbert Hoover, a Mining Engineer. Another he sold me was, Jesse James Would Have Been an Ameteur Had He Lived to Today; How I Made Agriculture Pay, and HOW, by the Farm

Board; We Got to Get Back To Fundamentals, and Model T's, by Henry Ford. Another Best Seller was, The Time, the Place, but Where the _____ is the Man? written by the Democratic National Committee.

He had a lot more there that delt with our type of Civilization. But I figured that after I got through these, I would be in shape to step into any kind of foreign party and pass as a College Proffessor. I would be so well informed on America, her habits and customs, they would perhaps take me for an English Novelist and Lecturer. He was to deliver them all to the Boat. Just as I was going out, he says, "Here is a Treatiste in thirty-six Volumes that I can't sell, and as you will perhaps recall some of them, I will give 'em to you." Predictions That We Have Made That Have Gone Wrong on Us, by 100 Ex-Prominent Americans. Sure enough, the Bookseller was right; I picked up a Volume of it—took both hands to do it—and just casually turned its pages, and there was some of the old, remembered Babies: "This Country is Fundamentally Sound, and you can't keep it Down."...You remember that old Bird, don't you?... "Prosperity is right around the Corner, and We must have Confidence." ...How many years was it that that one did service?..."It's only in the Minds of the People."...You recall that one, don't you?..."If everybody would spend what they've got ——" I remember that one well; it was uttered by a Man that dident have anything...."Why, I can remember in '93 ——" "It's not Hunger the people have; it's Sciocology."...Well, I shut the book up and told him, as they were free, to send 'em down to the Boat, and I would give 'em out to the other Passengers for a Laugh when they was seasick; there might be one in there: "Why, it's not seasickness that's worrying you; it's a state of mind."

Well, we shoved off right on time, and started across those beautiful inlets and bays; they say you can go clear to Alaska on what they call the Inland Passage. I wish to the Lord we could go to Japan by one. On the Atlantic I generally get seasick just as they are pulling up the anchor. But I stood it out pretty good today, so I am still up and going. You told me to find out everything I could on this trip that would be of interest to Americans—Beg pardon, "United Staters." Well, I started right out, soon as I got on the boat, to find out all I could that would interest us U. S.-ers, and I found it. Yes sir, right away; it wasent a Big Bar but it looked like it had a lot behind it. It was what I would call a Bar with a good Background. At first I couldent see it; I could just read the sign over the heads of the other U.S.-ers. I finally pushed enough of 'em out of the way till I could get close enough to give you an accurate report. 'Course I had to get some evidence; this might be like a soda fountain down home, where, if you don't know the Sign or the Caretaker, you are liable to get just soda. And sure enough it was just like home; only you dident have to know this fellow, or even how many raps to give on the counter.

I could tell right away that the other Clients there were U. S.-ers, for they kept referring to "Liberty" and the "Persuit of Happiness." I couldent get in the conversation at first—everything that I said was drowned out by the gargling from glasses.

Finally I thought of a way that might get me some measure of recognition. I said, "Boys and Girls"—for by this time they had discovered where to find their Husbands, and was reprimanding them by making them buy them one—I said, "Boys and Girls, I don't want to butt in, but will you have one on me?"

Well, that's Our native introduction. 'Course in England—that is before depression—you couldent meet an Englishman that way. You had to have a letter of introduction verified by the British Consul, a Letter of Credit and a Virginia Birth certificate. But with my own Countrymen, when I decorated the mahogany with a five-dollar Canadian bill and announced that "it was theirs as far as it would travel," why, I had an entrée into the hearts of my Countrymen that was better than a letter from Bishop Cannon.[18]

So we hadent got out of the Vancouver Harbor till everybody was slapping each other on the back and complimenting the other fellow on having each other's company for the next eleven days—weather permitting. As I got deeper into the crowd at the Beverage Fountain, who do you think I found? Well, if it wasent the noted Radio Entertainer and Champion War Correspondent of all, Floyd Gibbons.[19] You all remember Floyd. He did that fine bit of radio work of announcing all that had happened in the news. He delivered more words to the minute than anyone ever did. Senators have delivered more words in a day or a week than anyone, but Floyd held it for a three-minute stretch. But the Senators took it away from him on pure endurance. Of course his three minutes still holds a record for WHAT he said, compared to WHAT they said in the week.

Then, of course, Floyd covered an awful lot of wars, and a lot of awful wars too. It has practically got so that if Floyd is not at a war that war is not legal, and they have to fight it over. I sure was glad to see him, 'cause he knows his way around. He can speak pretty near everything. Had been in New York the last three years and, naturally, picked up Russian. He has read everything, so when I would start some argument that I dident know anything about, I would slip him the sign and he would come and pick it up for me, and as a team we did pretty good. I would think of some fool thing, and all he had to do was to finish it.

Floyd, of course, is going over to the war; I, of course, am going to attend the Peace Conference.[20] I noticed all the wars of the last few years have had more fighting at the conferences than they have at the original, so I don't try to make the original any more. It's kinder like Hollywood weddings. I get a bundle of Invitations every day to attend the weddings, but I would always rather wait a few weeks and take in the Divorce. Weddings are always the same, but no two Divorces are alike.

So, if the war is over when we get over there, Floyd will have 'em put it on again, and I will just sit around and drink some tea with the Geisha Girls till the Peace Conference.

Well, we are about to get to Victoria, where I have to have this letter to mail. Will have to put a stamp on it too—not like you. I can't help increase the Post Office Deficit like you fellows. We can't get the Farmers any Subsidy, but you Boys managed to get yourselvs quite a few little rake-offs. Well, we are pulling into little London. Here, Senator; I hope you appreciate what I am doing for you on this trip. It's long, and it's hazardous, and it's inconvenient, but you want the facts, and that's what I am going after for you.

So, so long; you won't get another letter from me till I get clear over and it comes back. We can't spend the Government's money with a lot of junk by cable tolls, like the Diplomats can. They keep us broke cabling back what they found out, but don't tell us why they found it out.

Well, here is Victoria, and the English customs are coming aboard. Remember, while I am watching this war, you keep us out of one over home. Watch Stimpson and don't let him issue a Statement.[21]

If Garner is elected Speaker, he will sit there with that big, heavy Gavel and crack those Soft-Shelled Pecans that he raises that I broke three teeth on down at his home a couple of weeks ago.[22]

Now, you Progressives, remember now; don't do anything till you size up the offer from both sides thoroughly. You fellows never was in better shape than you are this year. No Dog in a Manger was ever laying prettier.

Well, so long, Boss. Mail me some Reviews of the opening of Congress; I want to see how the Show got over this year. You got more Comedy than you ever had in it before, but I don't know if the Story and Cast will hold up. Well, anyhow, the Government has spent enough money on it; if it flops, why, of course, it's Mr. Hoover's fault, as usual. Well, again, so long.

Keep 'em guessing as usual, Boss.

Yours,
WILL,

P. S.: A Canadian on here can't understand this English Custom man's English.

Letters of a Self-Made Diplomat to Senator Borah

DEAR SENATOR: Well here I am, over in Nippon. I have to start right in explaining the meaning of things to you, on account of you never having been anywhere: "Nippon" means "Sun." I have had very little trouble with the language. 'Course, I don't know all the words, but I can carry on a pretty fair conversation with the three words I have: "Nippon"—Sun—"Banzai"—meaning a word of exultation, as, say, like if a Republican Senator would die from a Democratic stronghold, the yell among them would be, "Banzai! Banzai! Banzai!" It means a little more than joy. Then I can say, "Harry Carey." Now, "Harry Carey," in English, means a darn good Western actor that can play any part; in fact he played Trader Horn.[1] But the same word in Japanese means "to commit suicide." So I can say, "Hurrah, go commit suicide, in the Sun." Then they got a word, "Ohio," which means "hello," or "good morning." Over home, Ohio means the difference between being elected President and being just another Ex-Candidate.

By the way, Senator, speaking of our Ohio—'Course, it's not exactly OUR Ohio, for the Pregressives never got anywhere in there—But I mean the Ohio. I just heard my very good Friend, Dave Ingalls, Assistant Secretary of the Navy in charge of Aviation, was going to run for Governor.[2] I was kinder sorry to hear that; I hate to see Dave leaving a Constructive work to go into Politics—especially Ohio Politics. There is Politics that are not so bad, but they are not in Ohio or Indiana. You have to hunt away out in the uninhabited sections to find Politics that are reasonably respectable. Now, if Dave is going out there to run, tell him, for goodness sake don't let it be known that he is a Hoover Candidate, or even any President's Candidate. This don't apply only to Mr. Hoover, but it does to all Presidents; there is nothing that will send a candidate to bed as drunk and dejected on election night as for him to be indorsed by a President. Look at Butler that time in Massachussetts. Coolidge wouldent even tip his hat to a Candidate before that election, for fear it would be construed by the People as being favorable to that Candidate. But, of course, he did come out for Butler. Well, Butler was just good enough Politician that he knew he was washed up the minute Coolidge's

Saturday Evening Post, March 5, 1932. Reprinted with permission.

indorsement come out. He says, "Well, you can't buck that." They just don't like a President butting in. So tell Dave to get Mr. Hoover sore at him if he can, if he really wants to be elected. Which I can't possible understand why he should.

But that's not Japan, and before I get onto Japan I better tell you a bit about our trip. Had a fine, congenial bunch on the Boat. Was, of course a Standard Oil man on there, going out to the Far East and Batavia to look over their possessions. His name was Walden, and he is with the Jersey Standard.[3] You know, Senator, every State has its own Standard; some are pretty low, but they all are Standard. You remember how that all come about, don't you? Well, it was when you Senators got the idea that the Standard Oil Corporation was too Big, so you made it split up. So it did. It split up in forty-eight States, with each State Corporation bigger than the whole original one. You fellows did an awful fine job with that; you broke up one little one into forty-eight Big Ones. It's just little things like that, Senator, that make your Body so well remembered. But this Jersey fellow was a nice man. I had met him one time when I went and spoke at one of their dinners, and Young John D. was there.[4] We became pretty good friends—I mean John D. and I—and I afterwards got into his home to eat, ONCE.

Well, listen, Senator, just while I think about it, these Russians are giving them a run out here. They are shipping oil into Manchuria now, and are just about to run the Texas and the Standard Co. ragged. You see, they call it dumping. That is if the other fellow sells cheaper than you. 'Course, if you sell cheaper than him, that's Mass Production. But I knew you want to hear about this Russia thing. Well, this Russian Oil has got the Oil people right where the Russian wheat people have got the Farm Board. Nobody knows what the Russian Five-Year Plan is doing; only that it is underselling everybody else. Well, that's just about all there is to know about it. In fact, it's too much. We wish we dident know so much. Up to now, however, their Coal Oil is not so good as our Companies', and that's still a big business; for there is ten thousand lamps to one Model T yet. So we got the Coal Oil business now, but we don't know how long we will have it.

There was a funny old Boy on our Boat; he had him some Bees—500 hives of 'em—taking 'em over to China. He was a Komical Cuss and got everybody on the Boat sore, because in every argument he knew more about everything than anyone else; and what made us all sorer still, he did know it. He had read everything from Confucious down to Bob Shuler and Dean Inge.[5] In a religious argument he would lose me early. The Minute he left the Methodists and the Holy Rollers, I had to drop out. We had the biggest Cargo of live things that ever crossed on one

Boat—10 million bees, 350 Chinese, 40 Japanese, and about 150 mixed breeds, and One Democrat.

There was a Japanese Proffessor—a very learned man—had been studying high scientific things with Doctor Milliken and Einsten and all that Gang of Low Brows at Pasadena.[6] He was a nice fellow, but we couldent get much out of him. He never would give us a direct answer: "Well, Proffessor, what do you think of the weather today?"

"Do not know. Maby be sunshine; in fact, very probable. But more than doubtful that won't, but will perhaps be both. But is possible to be neither. But am not sure, but feel highly honored that you ask me."

Even Gibbons, who has spent a lifetime missquoting prominent people for the paper, couldent get from the proffessor even whether his eggs that morning was Fried or Boiled. We just had to figure out, well, they must have been scrambled. Funny thing 'bout that, for since we been here in Japan and prowling around, we can't find out much more. They sure are accomadating people. They just break their neck to please you, but they are sure tough to find out anything really direct from. I know now how they can go to all these Conferences and bring home the Bacon while we are gabbing our heads off about "Humanity," and "We want to dissarm down to the last man," and all that Hooey for home consumption. Why, they just sit there and take it all in, havent said a word, but when the Ratios are added up that every Nation is to have, they go home with the Tonnage.

We had some terrible rough weather coming in here, and it looked for awhile like you would have to send out another Boy. We had a Lifeboat washed off the top Deck. Now, those things are not just tacked up there; they are as solid as a Manafactures Association of Pennsylvania's Tariff Bill is when it's given to Dave Reed and he is told to pass it or ELSE.[7]

When that washed away, I said to myself, "The Old Senator has the right idea. Get your Foreign Relation news from a book."

One whole 24 hours we only made 50 miles, and most of that was up and down. But we had a fine Captain and a fine crew and a good Boat, and we made it. Even the Bees got seasick. Did you ever see a seasick Bee, Senator? They are the saddest-looking things you ever saw. No, not the saddest things you ever saw, for you have been in that Senate and have seen real sadness—besides, you have heard Presidential messages.

We got into Yokohoma at night about eight o'clock, couldent see much of it, but did afterwards. You know who met me at the boat? Senator Bingham's Son.[8] I know his Daddy mighty well on account of us both being Nuts on Aviation. His Son's been out here quite awhile and is making good. Went up to be the Guest of an old Friend, Cameron Forbes, the only man older than I am that plays Polo.[9] Well, he is our ambassador out here, and is doing a good job. You know, he used to be in the

Phillipines, and, say, you know who was there at the Embassy as Guest on his way home? Dwight Davis, our Governor-General of the Phil-lipines—he and his lovely Daughter.[10] This fellow Davis did a mighty good job, too, they all say over in the Phillipines. He was one of the biggest favorites of any man we ever sent out. He is the man, you know —— But, of course, you don't, for you are a horseback rider and don't mess your time away with Tennis. But he is the one that the Davis Cup is named for; in fact, he is the Cup. Well, we did some sight-seeing together—he and I and his Daughter. Young Bingham was our Guide.

We went to a Theater—a Real one, where they had real live Actors. There is a thing I think some day will come back in America, is a live Actor. Well, Sir, I hadent seen one in years—not only Japanese but Occidental either. . . . Oh, yes, I got to stop and explain to you again, Senator. This letter is about one-third news and the other third Explana-tion. . . . Well, Occidental don't mean a College, like it does in Los Angeles, but it means a race of people, and we are it. We are what they call Occidentals. Not Accidentals, Senator—Occidentals. I dident know it either till I got out there; I got about half sore when the fellow called me that first. Well, it's anything that don't live in this Territory; like we call everybody that is dissatisfied with everything and everybody a Progressive.

Well, it was as big and nice a Theater as we have anywhere—only difference from ours, this was filled with people. Now, this one they dident make us leave our shoes outside, but some of them they did; and I was so sore when I come out and my shoes were not shined that I wanted to ask for my money back. But this one we just wore the old Dogs right on in. Another time, when we went in to see the Geisha Girls, we had to take our shoes off, and I just thought how lucky it was that you wasent here. This is no place for a sockless man. As luck would have it, mine was in pretty fair shape. This Actor was a Famous Male Star, one of the best Dancers in Japan, his name was Kikaguro Onaye, at the Kubiki-za Theater.[11] He was like Me Lang Feng, the Chinese one that was over home, you remember. . . .[12] Never mind, let it go. It was mostly short sketches—old historical things, mostly of sword Play, of which their Actors have to be adept. Ours are shifty on our feet from dodging—but not a sword. Their talk is kinder high and Sing-Songy, and you can't get much sense out of it. You would have been right at home there, you could have shut your eyes and heard Hiram Johnston or Senator Moses.[13] Only these Sketches dident run long. They were mostly sad; that also made it more reminence of your troop. Japanese love to cry in the Theater, and the Actors love to cry, and the Manager loves to see everybody cry, for that means he won't have to. I just joined 'em and cryed, too; but it was because my feet was cold. Our American Actors

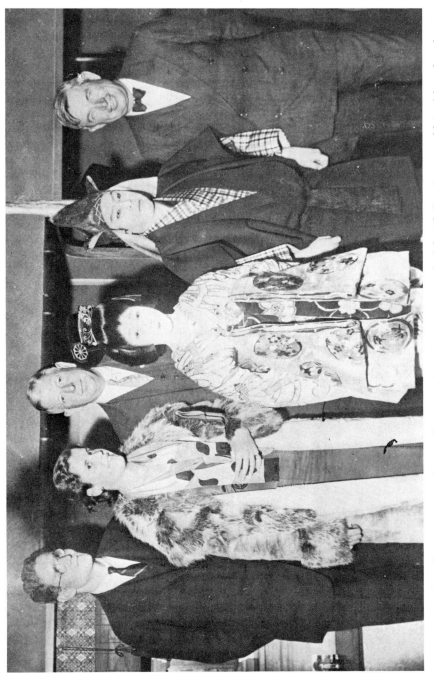

Will Rogers in Tokyo, Japan, with Dwight F. Davis, governor-general of the Philippines, and his eldest daughter, Alice. In traditional dress are two Kabuki performers from the Japanese stage. The identity of the gentleman on the left is unknown.

113

would be awful good over here, for it's not much trouble to get him to cry nowadays. Some of their sketches was what you would call up-to-date; 'course in these old Countries they date everything up-to-date that has happened in the last 900 years. But they did everything mighty graceful. And say, here is a funny One, Senator; they had a Runway out off the stage and down over the audience. Remember the old one at the Wintergarden?...Oh, pardon me, Senator; I mean you must have seen Pictures of it. Well, we thought that was just about the last thing when that hit New York. Well, a Japanese Theater that's the first thing they put in it, and has been that way since the Woo-Hoo Dynasty, which was in 302 B. C. It's like I saw a Movie one time taken in mid-Africa, and the Natives were doing the Charleston exactly as we tried to copy it from 'em.

The Japanese don't use this Runway just to show Girls; they use it for Real Actors to Act on. It's a part of their play, not just a part of their display. Then we were taken back to his dressing room. It was a tremendous big stage with a revolving stage in the middle. Now we had to take off our shoes when we went into his dressing room, for that was his home or house for the time being. But he had some slippers there that you could slip on. He was making up, but smiled and, through the Interpreter, wished us welcome. He had about ten assistants, dressing and helping him; reminded me of when I used to put on my Chaps to get ready for my old Follies Act. I would have liked to see that many handing me two Ropes. We went back and saw the rest of the show, and everybody in the audience had another cry. But, too, if anything funny come up, they would laugh. But crying was the main thing. Sadness prevailed and Meloncholy run rampant.

But this fellow was a fine dancer and Actor, and everything was well done. About 80 per cent of the audiance was in native dress—Men with Kimonas on. Kinder had me stuck there for a little bit; I couldent call my Sexes right quick. They wore the Shoes—Getas—where your Sox are split between the big Toe and the next bunch, and you have the Cord between your Toes that hold 'em on. They get to be skilled with those Toes; they could swim the Atlantic and never lose a Geta. As a Consequence of this, their big Toe kinder stands out from their foot like a Thumb. Lots of 'em are made out of wood, with some wooden Cross Cleats on the bottom. When a bunch of 'em are walking on a stone pavement, it sounds like a bunch of shod Horses loping on concrete. But say, they are not all dressed like that. No, Sir, Senator, the influence of the Movies has made Flappers out of the World. I bet the Head Hunters and the Zulus have those Princess Eugenie hats, and a high-heeled shoe that hurts their foot just as much as it does our folks.[14]

But say, while I am on the subject of Theaters, I must tell you about the

Movies. Japan has got more Movie Houses per head than we have. They are plum Cuckoo over the Movies; and here is something I bet you dident know, Senator, and you are supposed to keep your eye on foreign trade: Japan makes Seven hundred Feature-length Pictures a year herself. In the U. S. we only make between five and six hundred. They make a 150 more than us just to show in that little Country; so you see somebody has got to do a lot of looking.

They don't go in for shorts or news reels much—not enough crying in that. They will take a news reel if its sad enough, but in a short picture they can't hardly get started crying good till it's over. There is one street in Tokio that is just like a Street in Coney Island, with just one after another Movie Houses on it. I bet there is 100 on that one. About 20 per cent of their Movies are foreign—mostly ours. I saw Chevalier's latest Picture there, and they got all the laughs—and the subtle ones, too—right where they would at home.[15]

I went in about a dozen Houses where they play just their own Pictures, and here was one I will never forget. Of course, they got to make 'em pretty cheap, and they are crude as to production beside ours, but this Story run like this: It opened with a chase—one fellow after another, running. That went for about two reels. He couldent have possible chased him that far, or he would have had him clear out of Japan. Well, he caught him; then he started in to kill him, but he wouldent entirely kill him. He would just part kill him, then he would cry—both of 'em would—the Killer and the Killee. Then he would pound him some more with his sword; then he would rest and cry awhile—I mean, both of 'em would; for up to now the Killee is able to cry, but the Killer would cry while he was resting from the beating. Then he would get tired crying, for of the two things he was doing, the crying seemed harder on him. Well, finally he killed him; then he had a good cry.

Up to this time, we don't know, according to my Interpreter, what he run him for, what he killed him for, or what he cried for. But he is doing a mighty good job of all of it. Then another fellow comes running up, and he starts in all over again to kill him. Well, this crying and beating that he had done to the first fellow just seemed to get him opened up good. He really hadent misstreated this first man. He had killed him, but what you might call gently, and his crying over the first one, while I thought it splendid at the time, was really not crying at all, in comparison to what he was doing on this second one. There was really as fine a batch of crying as even a Japanese had ever dryed an eye too. I was kinder blubbering out of self-defense, and commence pulling my feet up, for by this time the tears was around ankle-deep, handkerchiefs had been wrung out dozens of times, and everybody had rushed into service those big Kimona sleeves. Now, when you cry one of those full, you have just about filled a steamer rug or a Saddle Blanket's worth.

I says, "This can't go on all night, or we will all swim out of here—those not too weak to escape." For you can be weak from the loss of tears just like the loss of blood. Then across the Landscape, rushing down what, of course, was Mount Fuji-yama, come another figure, running toward these two that was dead—dead not so much from punishment as from crying—and the Killer, or the hero, or whoever he was, who was still standing over them, crying really more than ever, if possible. Well, when I saw this third one coming and I knew the thing then had gone eight reels, I says, "If that Guy comes and he starts in beating and crying over him, I am not only going to cry, I am going to scream." I was worse than the Japanese; I couldent possibly stand to see this thing go on all night. There must be some Mercy somewhere. Is there no end to these people's tears?

But this last one was a Girl, and that halted the beating, but it seemed to just stimulate the crying of this fellow, this Hero, or Villian. That was the longest I ever saw a picture run and you couldent guess the plot. Now I have told you the whole thing as it has been cryed up to now. Now, what would you say was the answer? Well, when the Girl come, I thought, "Maby I will get a clew here. It's his sweetheart." But no, she didnt rush into his arms; she just stopped and started crying. I couldent tell whether it was with him or against him; anyhow, it was in unison. Well, that seemed to give the audience its second breath of tears; they wasent dripping then. It sounded like rain in the house. Now, if the Author wanted to keep the audience in doubt as to what he was after, he sure had me not only in doubt but I was practically Nuts.

My Companions suggested that maby I would like to go. I says, "No! Not if I never get to Manchuria, or a War, or China, or anywhere. I am going to stay here till that Guy crys himself to death or gives me some slight inkling as to who or what he is, and who the two other Birds were? And if it's so terribly hard on him, why did he kill 'em?" But the thing just won't clear up. The plot was just drowned out in tears by now. Then a third man come running up. Well, it certainly was a relief to see some new faces in the plot anyhow, even if they was going to get killed right away. But I had guessed wrong again. The last fellow looked, then started to run away, and the Hero, or Villian, or—by this time I knew so little that maby he was the Ingénue.

I was glad when he took after this last fellow, for that will slow up his crying. He can't keep that crying and running both up; he has got to give up one or the other. Well, he fooled me again; he did keep 'em both up till he caught him. But he didnt kill him—evidently too weak, or had decided to quit his rough ways. Instead of hitting him, he hugged him;

116

and when he did, that's what started the super-crying, for this was near the finish, and you have to save your very best crying for the fade-out.

Now, do you think you got a line on the plot which cleared up in the last Title of the Picture? it was a silent, or we couldent have stood to see all that weeping, then heard it, to boot. What do you think he killed the first two fellows for? Killed 'em by mistake. He mistook 'em for the fellow—each one of 'em—who had made love to his Girl. The third fellow was the really right one; he was the one that had made love to her, but by this time he felt so bad over killing the wrong men, that he hugged this fellow, and the reason the Girl that we saw in the Picture and him dident rush to each other's arms or do something, was she was not the Girl. She knew his Girl, and knew the man that had been making love to his Girl, and she told him that they were the wrong ones, and that one of them was her sweetheart; so that accounted for her crying. So we never did see his Girl, and it faded out on him and his opponent in Love crying over each other—certainly a new plot and a new fade-out.

This is not, however, like all their Pictures. The man said it was a little, cheap Picture, just made for the smaller Houses and for the more sentimental trade. Well, if a person wanted to cry, I never saw a Bigger Bargain in my life. I asked the fellow what the name of it was. He told me the English translation was, A Joke on Everybody. I says, "There is a great Title, for it's sure been one on me." They got some good Pictures—not all tears for inches like this. But they like to cry. Over the Hills would have been a Comedy compared to this one. But that's all right; a Nation with sentiment will get somewhere. Look at the Irish; they have got everywhere.

Now, from there, Senator, we went down to a Geisha Party. I hope I am not telling anything on Dwight Davis, but the whole thing was so respectable that it was practically astonishing to us. I must tell you about these Geishas. Stop me if you've heard of 'em.

This Geisha business is a real high-class, legitimate proffession. It takes years to learn all the dancing and playing that three-string Instrument, which is the first instrument—that I will stake my life on—that sounds worse than a Saxaphone. They have regular places—Geishayas, they are called—where they live. The Girls are rented out to Parties, Banquets, or any other of those forms of gatherings, or you can go there and have your real Japanese meal served, and they entertain—well, I won't go that far, but they are there during dinner. I don't want to knock the Girls, and I doubt if what I have to say will cut down their business, but for downright entertainment at a Dinner, they are a good deal like a Rotary Speaker. They got on awful pretty Kee-Monas—that's correct. Over here the accent is decidedly on the "Kee"; not "Ki," as we say it. They got a big wide Band wound around 'em that's tied in a big knot at

117

the back; it's called an Obi. The Obi costs more than the whole other Japanese dress, and their dresses cost plenty. In fact, that's one of the principal reasons they are adopting our type of clothes, is on account of economy. Those real Japanese clothes run into dough.

But we got to get back to the Girls! First you take off your shoes outside, and put on cloth slippers; that kinder helps hide the darning. The rooms don't have a thing in the world in 'em—nothing but pannelled walls and matting on the floors. No chairs, no beds, no mirrors, no sofas, no whatnots. No beareau—not even a Cocktail Shaker. It's the barest thing you ever saw. There ain't a furniture Store in Japan. Then they set a little low table about eight inches high, and some sofa Pillows; but this is only brought in when you eat. You can hire as many Geishas for the Party as you want; you pay by the hour for them, and they do their little dances—which for us is Not So Hot. They got a lot of grace, but it's that sickening whitening that they put on their faces; then they are about the only ones left that put their hair up in that tremenous mess that you have seen in the pictures.

But when they ain't dancing they are pouring Sakie. Sakie is a thing that the Japanese have been deluded into thinking is a drink. You know, there is something funny about a Japanese. These Geisha Girls doing this terrible slow dances is just about the heighth of cussedness with him. Did you know the Japanese don't have any cuss words? That's why, when they get sore, they just look like they are going to swell up and bust sometimes. It's because they got to find a way to let it off. To swear wouldent be "honorable." Now, that's the way they are with this Sakie. By all the laws of Beverages, it's got no business being classed as a Drink. I am not an old Conniseuer, but this Sakie is not quite even a stimulant. But they heat it up and it's served hot; that helps it a little. But it's just the last word in Japanese devilment to get that poured into a little cup, and especially if it's done by a Geisha Girl.

The Geisha just watches you like a Hawk, and when you take a sip she loads it up again; in fact, that is their business. Well, they had a lot of Japanese Dishes, but knowing the Party was partly American, they had a few knickknacks of ours, like Sandwitches, and they had some cheese, and I dug up some crackers, so Floyd Gibbons and Mr. Davis swore that all I did at this wonderful Geisha Party was either go to sleep or eat cheese and crackers. It was like this old Rat-bate cheese we used to get at home that you bought a dime's worth of cheese and crackers. I thought I was back in a country grocery store in the Indian Territory. The Sakie was too weak to be alcaholic, and too bad tasting to be a drink. But I did lay in the cheese and crackers, and every little bit take a nap.

Now, I know I am doing these Girls an injustice, for they say that when you can talk to 'em, they are especially bright, and are trained to be witty and amusing. They claim they are well informed on all affairs of the day, so it's all my ignorance in not being able to be able to chat and compare Coolidge and Hoover with some of their Emperors, and exchange laughs on their Congress and ours. But say, listen. Don't you get the idea that all the girls in Japan look like these Geishas. No, Sir, they got some beauts.

Their Congress is called Diet. Now, ain't that a hot name for Congress? That's what our Taxpayers are on, just on account of our Diet. Did I tell you about the Chopsticks? Well, we had to eat with them. Now, a man that has had as little practice with a fork as I have, can't jump right from a knife to Chopsticks. That's to decided a leap. I think that's what drove me to cheese and crackers. I handled that À la natural. But, you know, those Chopsticks are really not so difficult; with just a little practice you can get so you can do quite a bit of gastronomical damage with 'em. They are great if you are on a diet, or have a tendancy to eat too fast. I got so finally I could catch flies with mine.

Say, did I tell you about Our Embassy in Japan? It was just finished; he had only been in there a week. Oh, it's the finest one we have anywhere, and I expect as fine as anyone has, even England, who take their Foreign Relations serious. It's a business with them; it's a hobby with us. But for us this Establishment is a bear. How Mellon ever O. K.ed it is more than I know. Now, don't take this up in the Senate, Senator; you do those things sometimes. It's all done and over with now, so let's just let it go.

Did you ever ride on one of those Rickshas, Senator? A man pulls you. 'Course, you havent. Now, anybody knows that you are not going to let any man pull you. Both Calvin and Herbert offered to pull you. They dident exactly get in the shays, but they would if they thought it would do any good.

That's an awful big means of Transportation over here, is those little carts. It seems awful gratifying to some folks to have another man pull you—and by the way, they was invented by a Missionary.

This is a beautiful little Country. It's winter, but there is lots of green about. And these folks do love Flowers and things that grow. Now, all the Geisha Girls—in fact, all the Girls—their names translated into English mean: "Little Miss Potato Bug," "Little Miss Navy Bean," "Miss Holly-hawk," "Little Thistle Flower," "Lotus," and "Christanthamum," and "Cherry Blossom," and "Peach Limb," and "Little Miss Limbertwig"—all those are just like Smith and Jones over home. "Little Miss Cornbread" and "Little Miss Cucklebur" were among some of our entertainers. Japanese love Nature; they love rocks and trees. They all got some sort of little rock garden; they even polish 'em up to make 'em slick. Their paintings and drawings always contain a flower or tree; beautiful embroidery work on their Screens.

They sure do like to go in for Progress, too, like ours or England's—

119

that is, if you can call the stuff we are doing now Progress. But they will build anything they ever did see. Even if it don't run, they will build it. They are really overdoing Progress; they are adapting themselves to things so fast that they really havent got time to get used to 'em. Japan is learning to crawl, walk, run, and dance, all at the same time. Now, you got to kinder take those things in rotation, like a Baby. It's got to grow into 'em. You can't rush him from a crawl to a Two-step, just because you are in a hurry.

They have everything fixed up over there just as up-to-date as you can find it anywhere. Tokio looks like a part of any American City in the business part. And you know the greatest thing about 'em, Senator? They all play baseball. Yes, Sir, and really play it. I just missed our Big League Players that were there—part of the Athaletics and Cardinals. They played over there against College teams to as many as fifty thousand people at a game. The parks on Sunday morning are just simply packed with teams, and all in Uniforms. I never saw as many ball players.

Oh, yes, Dwight Davis and Daughter and myself went out to the Studio to see 'em make Movies. They make all silent Pictures; they did make a couple of Talkies, and you know what the ingenious Birds did? They manafactured their own apparatus to do it with. They have big Movie Favorites of their own just like we do. We met some of the Stars. Don't get the idea their Pictures are all like that one I described. When you consider they make them at an average cost of $5000 a Picture, it's remarkable the high class they put in some of them. Any Picture over home would not run less that $150,000.

Well, I got to tell you something about the War. Of course, the whole Country is excited over Manchuria, and knowing we were going over there, why, they were naturally anxious to talk to us about it. A bunch of very high Officers—all Generals—had Floyd and I for lunch one day—a real Japanese feed—and me and the old Chopsticks just went round and round. I cleaned up pretty near everything, and afterwards Gibbons said to me, "You dident eat that raw Fish, did you?" Oh, Boy, when he told me that, and I had eaten it raw, Wow! They told us a lot about Manchuria, and gave us the whole War—of course, from their angle. Some of these men were connected with the Intelligence Department of the Army. For once in my life, I let Floyd do all the talking. He was explaining what he wanted to go over there for, and what he would like to see.

Well, they couldent figure me out at all; I dident tell 'em what I had in mind to do over in Manchuria, for I had nothing in mind. Only, if there was a War, to do some very long-range Reporting. We spent, oh, I expect two or three hours with 'em; several of them spoke English. Well, then we went down to another General's office, and we had some more tea;

he was nice and friendly, and Gibbons and him talked away for a long time through an Interpreter; then he finally looked at me, and asked, "What's he want?" You see, Floyd was O. K.; he was legitimate, but they couldent dope me—in other words, "What business did I have at the War, and how did I ever get away from home anyhow?"

Well, I told the Interpreter to tell the General that I was as much mystified as him; That I wasent particular about seeing a War, but if they had one handy that I dident mind attending purely as a Spectator, that I just wanted to get a Tourist's slant on hostilities. Well, the old General, he kinder smiled, and he went on back to attending to Gibbons.

Now, the next morning I pick up the paper and I see a big story about Mr. Floyd Gibbons having a long interview with the Minister of War, General Minami.[16] So I says to Floyd, "Say, what's all this Hooey about you interviewing the Minister of War? I was with you all day yesterday and I dident see any Minister of any War?"

"You're Cuckoo as usual. That was the Minister of War that we went to see last, and sit in his Office for a half hour and drank tea."

"Was it? Well, I dident know it. I just thought it was another General."

Here I had seen the biggest War man in Japan and dident know it. It was a terrible dumb thing to do, but all their names are so queer to me. Well, it would be just about like somebody meeting you, and then go away thinking they had seen just some Senator. I wish you would take it up through the Japanese Ambassador and apoligize for me. I mean for me personally. I know you wouldent apoligize for anything for yourself. But with me its different; I come from a doubtful State.

They all showed us every courtesy, the same as everyone else did in Japan. It's quite a Country, Senator. 'Course, now, Senator, I am not going to pass any opinion on this late muss between them and China till I get over to Manchuria and see the cause of the dispute; then on over into China and get their side. That will give me both sides and the middle—I first spelled that muddle; so I was really right accidentally, wasent I? So now I am just giving you what the Newsmen in Washington call a Background. That's when the Washington Officials beat all around and don't say anything; they call it a Background.

They are going to kinder tip us off when there is anything doing, so we are liable to be on our way any minute. Manchuria won't be anything like this; besides, it's warm here. I dident have anything but some little cotton shorts, and there is a noted Cameraman here named Aerial Barges; he shot everything that ever was shot in everybody's War, or in peace. He is the World's greatest Character and notedest Cameraman. He don't shoot "Spot where Body was found"; he knows about it ahead of time and shoots "Body as it was falling."

Well, he has been in some cold Countries and he give me some long woolen drawers. Gosh, I havent heard that word in years! But that's all they were. Then he give me a kind of padded Jacket. Wouldent turn a bullett, but he said it would turn a lot of snow.

Well, we will leave any minute now. Say, what do you know about this Town? They got the Taxi Dancers here too. Hall just packed this afternoon, some mighty snappy-looking girls—most of them dressed in modern clothes; "Grab a Japanese, ten cents a Dance."

Well, I am a poor hoofer, Senator. I used to rattle a mean pair of hocks in the Follies in the old days with little Ann Pennington, but I am getting all spavined up; been fired three times.[17] Say, you know these Guys got a Subway here, too, and lots of electric trains—I mean trains, not street cars. Well, what do you know? Mr. Forbes, our Ambassador, give us another Geisha Party, had all the folks from the American Hospital. It's a wonderful institution out here, about as fine as anywhere at home. We met an awful lot of nice folks from it; had a Japanese Meal. This was a real one; you sit down and you cooked it right there before you—each couple had their own little stove. It was the cutest thing you ever saw. 'Course, this was a big party—lots of Americans, and Japanese that spoke English, fine Doctors, and all that. It was just as high a class Clinic as I ever ate at. We had a lot of fun at this, and I dident go to sleep. I made up for that other one. This had better food, but the Geishas were about the same; there dances are mostly of an Interpretative nature; One dance might be called Raining on the Cabbage, and they interpret Rain and what happens to the Cabbage, or one might be Mount Fuji-yama in Eruption. But at this first party no one had told me the ideas of any of them, so that left me groggy. When you know what they are getting at, why, you can kinder pull for 'em and hope they make it, but when you just see 'em waving and holding one foot up, kinder like Fanny Brice used to do in her Dying Swan Dance, why, then you may not know that that means Moonlight Kissing the Butterflies.[18] But now that I had all these Officials and Doctors and Japanese to tell me—all differently— what the Girls was getting at, why, I could enjoy and still feel that I knew as much about it as they did.

But say, before I am called out of here I want to tell you we don't get any news out here about your Congress, or even you. Now Congress must have met by this time. Of course, I hope they haven't, but I am just afraid they have. I think I will fly over to Manchuria. I carry no camera, so I guess I won't get arrested for going over fortified Territory. I guess they are reading the Relief Bills by now. How you going to get your extra taxes—out of the rich, or just out of the poor, as usual? Some say there is a kind of a split between the War Department and the State Department over the handling of the War here. Where have we heard that before? Say, if you want to read a frank statement on that line, read General Graves'

Book on Our Siberian Adventure, or some name like that.[19] I read it coming over. He sure gives the straight of it; he don't write like a retired Army Officer at all.

Get that Book, Senator; it's right up your alley—on Foreign Relations. He opens up by saying he don't know what American troops were doing in Siberia, and he says it on every page, and closes and still says: "It's eleven years later now, but I still don't know what we were doing in Siberia." It sounded like you must have colaborated with him on it. Well, it's getting late, so I must stop. The League is still argueing over Manchuria, China is trusting the League, and Japan is trusting this General Minami I was telling you about. We don't belong to the League, but a little thing like that never stops us. We can get into more things without a Membership Card than anybody. We are the One-Eyed Connelly of the Nations.[20]

Well, so long, Senator. Yours faithfully,   WILL.

Letters of a Self-Made Diplomat to Senator Borah

MUKDEN, MANCHURIA. Late Chinese Territory.

D EAR SENATOR: Well, I been stepping pretty fast since I last dropped you a line. These Japanese! Now, here is something I better tell you right off the reel: Don't ever call a Japanese a "Jap." Now, I dident know that till I got over here; I just thought that it was about like Englishmen calling us "Yanks"; even if you come from Alabama, the English don't know but what you are a Yank just like Mr. Coolidge. But this Jap business is a serious matter with them. So when their Ambassador comes in to see you about something he wants fixed up between us and them, why don't start bellowing out, "Why, Hello, Mr. Ambassador. My Compliments. I see where you Japs are doing pretty well." 'Course, we can't understand it, for it seems to have no disrespect, but they just naturally love ceremony. The longer you can palaver and make anything seem important the more important it becomes to them. Then, too, the word "Jap" is short, and they are very sensitive about their size anyhow, and "Jap" makes 'em sound shorter still.

Now, you take Horses. Now, naturally, my mind is on Horses more than it is on Diplomats, but with the Japanese right here in Manchuria, the greatest Pony in the World, bar none, is the Manchurian, or Mongolian, Pony—which is practically the same. They are the toughest, hardiest little Beasts in the World; carry more, go farther, stand the cold and the hardships more than anything. But I have yet to see a Japanese on one. They get some big old Horses from some place—the bigger and clumsier the better—and then there they are, perched upon this big old plow Horse, and their legs come just down about even with his mane. But by getting up that High they retain their dignity. It takes a long time for 'em to climb up there to retain it, but they make it some way with a Crane, or a Step Ladder. Japanese may become the greatest Country in the World but there is one thing I will bet on, and that is they will never astonish the world with Horsemanship. You see, if they rode these wonderful little Ponys that are acclimated and used to this Cold winter and the rough feed here, it looks like it would be good Military precaution. If I ever hear of the Japs losing one of their wars in Manchuria—

Saturday Evening Post, March 12, 1932. Reprinted with permission.

which you can also bet they are going to have—I will know just what caused it. Records will read: "They lost the War, but they still maintained their dignity on a high Horse."

But we have things that are just about as Crazy at home. It all depends on what you are looking at. But don't call one a "Jap" and don't let Stimson do it either. You kinder got to watch Stimson. Mr. Hoover won't do it, for, naturally, he has been out here and knows. And I expect there has been times in the last few years when he wished he was back out here. You Boys must make it pretty tough on him there sometimes. And they say it's the same with a Chinaman, too; don't go calling him "Chinaman." He is always a Chinese, but never a Chinaman. 'Course, you don't have to warn the Boys about Chinese, for he has no Army or Navy and don't go to the Conferences. So you don't have to worry about whether he is Proud or not. 'Course, there is 400 Millions of 'em, but what has humanity got to do with a Conference? That's just for the Countrys with Navys.

It is funny, Senator, what a respect and National Honor a few Guns will get you, ain't it? China and India, with over half the Population of the entire World, have not only never been asked to confer but they have not even been notified what was to be done with 'em after the other Nations had decided. Yet you give India England's Navy and China ours, and they would not only be invited to the Conference but they would BE the Conference. Now we gather to dissarm, when a gun has put every Nation in the World where it is today. It all depended on which end of it you were—on the sending or receiving end.

Every Guy in England could have been a Shakespere, but if there hadent been a Lord Nelson every few years, England would have had a Breechclout and a Nany Goat, and Gandi would have had on a Tuxedo and a Monocle. And as for us, Cortez would have had every Senator fighting Bulls instead of throwing 'em, and the Capitol of Mexico would have been about Claremore, Okla. And then they tell you not to Arm?

You must get quite a kick out of it, sitting in a reserved seat like you are, Senator. When you write your Memoirs —— That's another Cherokee word; means when you put down the good things you ought to have done, and leave out the bad ones you did do—well, that's Memoirs. Well, when you write yours you ought to call it, Hooey as I Have Seen it From the Ground Floor . . . . But, Gosh, how did I get off on all this? It's Manchuria we got to get going on. Well, as I say, the Japanese have everything, and they have a fine Aeroplane line from Tokio right over to Manchuria. Goes to Darien, but they are going to extend it clear up through Mukden to Harbin, and one more little Amateur fuss like this and they will have it right on into Vladivostok.

We took off from Tokio kinder sudden—Floyd Gibbons and I—for we

125

got a tip, and these Japanese run their Wars just like they do their trains—right on time. If they are billed to take a Town at ten o'clock on a certain day, if you want to see it taken you better be there at ten, for ten past ten they will be taking another one further on. I want to tell you, Senator, War is a business with these folks. When a War shows up, they don't have to stop and put in a Draft and sing songs, and make three-Minute speeches, and appoint Dollar-a-Year men. All that has been attended too long before the War ever broke out. All their Soldiers are trained between Wars—not after one starts. You see, we have been lucky that way; all of our Wars have waited on us till we could get ready. But these Japanese figure that they may have one where the enemy won't wait. So, when it is booked, all the preliminaries have already been arranged; each soldier not only knows where he is to go, but knows practically Who he is too shoot.

You think that's kidding? Well, you are just Another Senator if you do. That's just the way this War went right here in this very Town I am sitting in now, writing this. War broke out at 10:30 on the night of September the eighteenth, and by nine o'clock the next morning the whole City of Mukden was in the Japanese hands just as solid as the Pennsylvania Senators and Congressmen are in the hands of Joe Grundy.[1] It started that night over two Chinese Soldiers blowing up a bit of the South Manchurian Railway, that belongs to and is heavily guarded by Japan.[2] They, of course, killed these two soldiers, and then took the whole City in just as efficient and methodical way as you Birds put through a salary raise for yourself. China had the biggest Arsenal in the World, supposed to be held alone by 20,000 troops. Couple of Truck Loads of Japs—pardon me, Japanese—went up and took it over. Dident take over the Aviation till the next morning, as they were rushed with more pressing matters. But when they did, there was every Plane there. No one thought of issueing them orders to fly away. Not a Pilot had flown away, yet the trouble had started the night before, and this was 8:30 in the morning.

The whole thing sounds like a Movie, to hear it told by men that were there. Now, of course, the Young Marshall, Chang Hsueh-liang, who was the War Lord of all Manchuria and North China, this was his home Grounds; the very backbone of what they thought was China's greatest and best-equipped Army.[3] Well, I have since seen the Young Marshall and talked for hours with him about it, and he says that they dident want to put up any resistance, that they had faith in Diplomacy, and also felt that the League of Nations would come and help 'em. Well, I don't know how he expected the League to get there that night, all the way from Geneva, but that's his story, and he said he was going to stick to it anyhow, till he could think of a better one. Now, Senator, here comes all the conflicting stories. All the Newspaper Boys from all over had gone

126

over every angle of the case. There is lots of sides to it. The Chinese angle is that the two dead Chinese Soldiers were Plants and were just the Alibi. The argument was, "Why would they have blown up the road right in front of an encampment where they were?" Japanese left the Bodies there for a long time to prove the evidence. Which, some thought, if it had been on the level, they wouldent have thought of doing that, or even cared to try even to prove it to anybody. Some said a Military Officer saw the Bodies and said, "Why, the Insigna on the men show that they were infantrymen. Why, if we blowed up a railroad, it would be our Engineers." Next day another Military Observer from another Country looked at 'em, and the Insigna on 'em was Engineers.

It's just like the big War. We used to think that it was started by some old Austrian Bozo being bumped off in one of those little Truck Garden Countries down there somewhere. Since then, if you read Col. House's Books and have read Lord Gray's book—who was looking after England's foreign affairs then—and both of 'em admit that they had been working on the war for months.[4] In fact, Lord Gray's really showed that everybody in all the countries—Germany, France, England and all—they all knew it but the people that was going to fight it. The actual start of it come at a moment's notice, but it was known that it was practically assured. 'Course, the Duke was the Alibi, and it all wound up by killing 5 million.

Well this one started over killing two soldiers; and look one time what Germany did to China; they had two German Missionaries killed. Chinese Government dident kill 'em but somebody did in China. So Germany, in payment for 'em, got the whole Kiachow Peninsula. That holds the World's record to this day for top price ever paid for Missionarys. Now, these two Chinese Soldiers come pretty high. They cost 'em Manchuria. In the one case, Germany charged 'em a whole Peninsula for killing two of them. But in this case, China has to pay ten times as much for getting two of their own men killed. So China is going to lose some Territory whether they kill or get killed.

But now let's get the other side. The Japanese claim, in this particular case, that the reason they were all so quick to go and do a certain thing at the right time was not because it was planned for that night at all; it was just a part of their Routine duty that they had been drilled and trained in; that they knew that trouble with China was inevitable, and so, naturally, they had their plans. So that's what I was telling you a while ago, Senator, when I started on all this—was that these Japanese take this fighting business serious. They are almost what you would call natural Soldiers. Their life belongs to their Emperor, not to them or their folks at all; it's their Country's, and if they can give it in service of their Country they attain immortal salvation. Now, you can't beat patriotism like that.

127

And it's not fanatical Patriotism; it's just what they feel they owe to their Country. Gibbons had a General show him letters that Mothers and Fathers of Boys that he had in his command wrote, saying that the Boy's life was his to give for his Emperor, or Country. They are symbolical. They are hardy, they drill all the time.

Of course, that cold away up north in this Campaign froze lots of their hands and feet, and during the siege of Titzihar, Aviators had their faces froze. The cold did 'em much more injury than the enemy. Our War Co-respondents that have followed 'em will tell you that they will sure fight, and skillfully. 'Course, it's admitted that there was not much opposition, the way the Chinese were going, and they were GOING. But it's very probable that they were told not to resist, as they knew it was hopeless and would have just meant extra loss of life. The Chinese could fight if they could get a Leader, But he is always so far back the men can't hear him give Commands. Then another thing: Where, with the Japs, it's all Coöperation, United Command and the heighth of efficiency, with China, just as they go to shoot, they will find that somebody who was supposed to have charge of the Ammunition has given them .38 Calibers when their Guns is .44's. They start to send back for it, and they don't know where to send.

I don't suppose there is an Army in the World that can have as many things wrong with it to keep it from fighting as the Chinese. I doubt if the Dublin Fussileers could fight handicapped with both China's Generals and her inneficiency combined. There ain't nobody going to stand out there and get killed for nothing, like a Chinese would have to do. Here he is fighting in Manchuria, and maby he come from away down at Canton. He don't know whether he is still in Manchuria or Scotland. He is in the Army because he was either forced in, or went in to get something to eat. He don't know anymore what the War is all about than 12 million White Men did 15 years ago. A Japanese wants to die for his Country, but the Chinese, he ain't going to let patriotism run away with his life. He wants to live; he loves life, he enjoys it. Life ain't serious with him like it is with the Japanese. The Japanese feel they were put on earth for a purpose, but the Chinese, he feels he was put here by mistake. He wants to get a little piece of land, live on it, die on it, and be let alone. He is, naturally, a compromiser. He wants to trade you; he don't want to fight you. In a lawsuit, they don't want to take the chance of winning it or losing it entirely; they want to have it settled by compromise. If there was some way in a War where you could show him that he would at least get second money—but he knows there is no second money. So why go in there and get your head blown off?

Now, that's all right. It's a commendable thing to be a peaceful Nation. China and India are the two biggest in the World and the most peaceful in the World. How do they stay the biggest? It's not by fighting somebody every day. Your warlike Nations rise to great heights while they are on a winning streak, but let 'em lose a few games, and they not only pass out of the League but sometimes out of existence. You know it's pretty hard for Nations to give advice to China. Giving advice to China is kinder like a Son telling a Father what to do. So it hasent been entirely proven yet but what China has got about the right dope on this war business. I know if I saw a man charging down on me with a Bayonet, I would sure kinder like to talk it over with him first and see if there wasent some way of buying him a drink, or offering him an Apple, or something. Anyhow, fix some way so we could both walk away from the place—not just one of us.

An American was out here trying to sell a Chinese War Lord a Submarine; told him what it would do, that you "could sink any boat out here; just dive down and let 'em have it."

The Chinese said, "You mean it sinks the boats it takes after?"

"Sure," said the Yank.

"Oh, I don't want to sink 'em; I want to capture 'em. How do you suppose I am going to make a living if I sink or kill everybody I meet?"

He had the right idea on war—get something out of it besides a Coffin. They was having a Civil War over here in about '27 or '28, and the Northern Armies had a couple of Hundred thousand men at Hankow. The South was coming up. An American that was observing it for his Big American Co., so they could tell which side to jump too—that's an Old American Custom: "String with the Winner"—Well, he wired his company that the North was bound to win; they had thousands of more troops. But while he was sending the telegram the South come into Town and got the North on the run, and when he turned back to look, his big army was hot-footing it for trains to get out of Town for Peking, or Nome, or Montreal, or anywhere north. Now, get this: It was a single track; they had all their trains there, waiting to do this very thing, in case the South did come in. So their Military Plans was working 100 per cent. Each General loaded his train. The first train started to pull out, but the other Generals stopped it; they wouldent let him go on alone. You wonder why? Well, get this reason: They were afraid, as he got out ahead of 'em, he would stop and blow up a bridge behind him so they couldent get out and would have to stay there and fight. There's Coöperation for you. No one would trust the other, even in retreat. So, you know what they did? They hooked every train all together and pulled 'em out as one long train, miles and miles long, so nobody could double-cross the other one.

Now, what chance would even the Blue Devils of France have if they had Leadership like that. So it's not due to cowardice—in fact, in this same engagement they did blow up the tracks ahead of the last General and his Gang to get out, and he stayed there alone and put up a great fight. This American said it was really a heroic thing. Cowardice or Bravery is never racial. You find both in every Country. No country has a monopoly on Bravery; great deeds of heroism is liable to break out in the most unexpected places. The first man to get the Victoria Cross in the wonderful Princess Pat Regiment of Canada was a little Piano Player in a Moving-Picture House; it wasent some big Rough, Tough Bird. Leadership is what keeps Soldiers fighting, and from what I hear of the Chinese War Lords and Generals, there couldent possibly be anymore justification for not fighting than to fight for them. It's all just to get him a soft position somewhere.

They got one old Boy over here they call the Christian General; He is a sort of a Methodist or Babtist or something.[5] He has his men singing Hymns. He sends 'em into battle singing Hymns. But old "Him" himself is leading the Choir from about twenty miles back. He has imbibed enough Christianity to offer his Soldiers' life up, but he feels that there is still work to be done here by Him yet. He babtised his men—some Thirty-five Thousand of 'em whom he had just proselited from Budda and Confuscious the day before for purely Christian reasons. Well, that's a pretty big Gang to initiate into a combination Church ritual and bath all in one day; especially if the Heathern enemy is marching on you. So he borrowed a Fire Hose and turned it on 'em. This was in Tiensin. He took 'em off to War and they all did pretty good. He come pretty near being President one time, and if the Hose hadent run out, I expect he would. He is a big fellow. I got a picture of him; looks exactly like Babe Ruth.[6] I see where he come into Nanking, the Capitol, the other day. But he wouldent put his trust entirely in his spiritual safety; he brought 50 Body Guards. Get that, Senator. Think of General Pershing dropping in to Washington with 50 armed Guards.[7] But that ain't got anything to do with what we was talking about. I bet a Chinese troop, properly led, trained, fed and equipped with Bulletts that fit their Guns—I bet they would cause some opponent a lot of grief.

These Chinese always got an answer. Some were on the Boat coming over, and I asked one if he was going to War. "No. No Likee War; likee Earthquake better." I don't know the answer to it. I guess he meant that for downright destruction and doing a good job, why have war. Just put on an Earthquake. Then, here is another thing that might have been in his Nut: the Earthquakes happen IN Japan, not in China. So that might have been why he wanted an Earthquake. I asked another one if he was going to fight Japan. He said, "No. Japan win war all time. China no win. Why fight?"

They just figure they are going to live and kick along no matter what happens. The patriotism angle don't enter into it when your whole life is just a battle for the bare necessities of life anyhow. You see, the Chinese will still have a lot to say in it. You see, there is only a Million Japanese to 30 Million Chinese, and 800 thousand of these Japanese are Koreans; so that only leaves 200 thousand Japanese. Well, 30 million is more apt to gradually suck them in than the 200 thousand is to inhale the 30 million.

But let's get back sorter to the start and see what all the shooting was about, and how we got over here to see where it was. We left Tokio and we flew to Osaka—that's their biggest town, and it is a whale, too. Met a lot of Newspaper Boys there that night and they showed us around. That Japan has sure got some live papers; just as up-to-date as any we have. Only we don't get any American news much; neither do we publish much Japanese news. She was raining and a Fog, but this old Japanese Pilot come through it for an hour. We passed by Fujiama, the Mountain that they keep for Post Card purposes. Went to the Japanese Movies that night and saw some good Pictures. Next day, right along the Inland Passage—that's from Kobe down toward Nagasaki—beautiful inlets and Islands. It's supposed to be one of the most beautiful trips in the World by Boat. Well, it's better by plane, for you can see it. Then into Fukuoka, where we stopped for gas. Then we headed across the Sea of Japan for Korea, and this is in a Land Plane too. That dident look so hot, but we made it great.

We landed at some little place for Gas, and there I saw my first Koreans. Then, on that night to Seoul, or, as the Japanese call it, Keijo. . . .Why is it that, Senator, when a Nation takes over another Country they always want to bring some of their names with 'em. But these Koreans are mighty patriotic toward the old things and old Country before they were under the Japanese. But I will get to that later. We went to a very nice Hotel. These Japanese have splendid Hotels. This one I am sitting in in Mukden is one right here—plenty good for anybody, even a bunch of growling Newspapermen. There is about twenty-five of 'em here, waiting for the one-line battle of Chinchow. They been here off and on for three months just waiting for that. An old Russian Newspaper Boy here named Fleepack, he got a House and sent for his family; he figured that there would just be continuous war in Manchuria.

Now about this Korea. Now, here is where I got some reporting to do to you. On account of you wanting to know about foreign relations, you naturally want to know how one Country goes out and Gobbles up another. I know you are agin that, so I will report in detail. Here is the place where Japan first lost her head. She thought the more Country you owned the bigger you was. She dident know that Idaho, one of our small States, was one of our best. Well, this Korea was right by Japan, and woe

131

be to a weak Nation if they live by a strong one. They either got to play with 'em or join 'em. You see, in this Manchurian mess, if Japan had never taken Korea, you wouldent hear so much complaining from the rest of the world now. But they point to Korea, and say, "Manchuria will be another Korea." It's the first Horse you steal that always is thrown up to you. Korea originally leaned toward China. Well, Japan dident like that. Then they and China both agreed to get out of Korea; then Korea invited China back; then Japan said China had no right to come back without her. China says, "Well, you wasent invited back."

So one word brought on another, and the other word brought on War; so Japan and China had a War—that was in 1894—just when Bryan was advocating what has taken the rest of the world thirty-seven years to find out.[8] This's how far ahead the Democrats are, Senator.

Well, Japan whipped China, which shouldent have had anything to do with Korea, but it did, for whipping China Korea went under the partial domination of Japan. You are following me, ain't you, Senator? I am just showing you how these big Babies work. Now, here comes the Russians; they get a lot of big lumber Contracts from Korea; they lease Port Arthur from China, and they start fortifying it, and were putting on quite a "Gazottsky" all through Manchuria. Now, mind you, Manchuria is still China's, and Korea had leased to Russia. So Japan says to Russia: "You are getting too friendly with Korea, and just for doing so, we want you to get out of Manchuria."

Now, get this: Manchuria is Chinese. Well, one word brought on another and a war; so Korea is the innocent cause of another War—this time between Russia and Japan—that's in 1905. That's when Roosevelt says, "Ain't they cute little fellows?" Russia says, "Yeah." Well, that cooked Korea's goose for Liberty. Japan took an extra hold on 'em, also got Russia's Concessions from China. Now, what did China have to do with this war between Russia and Japan? Nothing; only it furnished the prize at the finish. There was a War. China lost without being in it; so, you see, you can't tell whether it's cheaper to enter or stay out. Now, Korea hasent been in any of these, yet it loses its independence.

But, mind you, Japan had got Manchuria once before; she charged China that much for whipping her, but Russia and France and England advised Japan she wouldent get away with it.[9] Russia was waiting so she could get it, so, you see, Japan feels that it was beat out of her spoils. You see, after all, this War with China was not entirely for just Korea's Independence. Now Russia gets it, and then Japan whips her and she gets it again. But the Foreign Powers once more make them make Darien an open Port, and Japan feels that she is robbed again. Now, here is Manchuria that hasent personally been in any of these Wars. It's only been the Battle Ground. And Korea, who just happened to be living next door, is the goat. So Japan feels like she finally ought to have Manchuria. She has fought for it three times now; all the Battles she ever had was in and over Manchuria—Victories 3, Defeats 0. Her dead are buried there; every Station has a sign on it telling what battle was fought there or near by. Monuments all over the place. Japan really kinder forces her patriotism; they keep Children marching to the trains to see Soldiers come in in Mukden, and looking at the various Monuments. Now, Kids are not just naturally that historical—not in ten-below-Zero weather. But that's how they keep patriotism going, and it's brought pretty good results up to now, as far as the net return on War is concerned.

So you see, Senator, it reads kinder like the Phillipines, don't it? Always the Big Brother is helping the Weak Sister. But I don't care how poor and inefficient little Weak Sister is, they like to run their own business. Sure, Japan and America and England can run Countries perhaps better than China, or Korea, or India, or the Phillipines, but that don't mean they ought too. I know men that would make my Wife a better Husband than I am, but, darn it, I am not going to give her to 'em. There is a million things that other people and Nations can do better than us, but that don't mean they should handle it.

When you take a country over you only help a certain class—that's the Foreigner doing business in there, and the Wealthier people of the Country you take over. You protect their investments, you make it easier for them to make money, but to the 90 per cent of the people away back in the Jungles and mountains, you don't help them. They never even know you have taken it over. Then you get in wrong with all the other Nations, and you get credit for exploiting and getting away with really more than you do. No Nation should be fathered or annexed unless it's at the almost unanimous Vote of them asking for it. Then you can rightly claim you are doing them a benefit. Then get out when they want you too; then you are a real Humanitarian. You go through these countries where they are under the protectrate of some other Nation, and see who is the domineering one, who cusses the native if he gets in their way, who has the right-away with every privalege—why, the foreigner of that place. That's all fine, and maybe it's what should be, but it don't look so good.

We fought for our Liberty when we was enjoying at the time a lot more of it than these Nations are. What if England had asked us if we was ready for a free Government? Why, we wasent ready for anything, and because we finally did struggle through and starved and fought among ourselves and finally got away with it, now we think no one else could possibly be as smart or as deserving as us. Let 'em go their own way, run their Country any way they want. The trouble in all these things, Nations won't tell the truth; they always give one reason and then have another one. Nobody don't have to take some other Country in order to protect their own, especially if it's across a sea. Now, Japan has had three wars, all off from her own Country, claiming she had to do it for protection. That would be like us saying we had to take Canada to protect us against England coming in through Canada. The whole thing in all these claims is a lot of Hooey. Why don't they just up and say, "We need the ground. Got to expand. We are naturally ambitious and so we are going in and get it."

But mind you, Senator, I don't think they really want to take it over right now. It's too big; it's too hard to hold; it would take more to protect its borders than they would make out of it. The Chinese, they all say up here, was getting a little Cocky, and I guess he had been flee-biting the Japanese; and they really thought, with all this Army, they could fight. So, they say, the Japanese just figured here is a good time to show these folks who is papa, and they knew that the Nanking Government was going to blow up about then. "So we will just clean the whole mess out, and then drop back afterwards to our original positions. But it will be a lesson they won't forget soon." Then they wanted to get rid of this Young Marshall.... This Young Marshall is a Son of Chang-So-lin.[10] There was a real old He Hoss. He was the Pancho Villa of this neck of the Forest. He was blown up right here on a train a few years ago. The Chinese say the Japanese did it, and the Japanese say they dident. This place is pretty near as bad as home to find out the truth of anything.

So, you see, all these things over here in Japan and China and Korea, they all run in what they call Dynastys. You know what it is—a Dynasty? No. Well, then, I can tell you better if you don't. It's where one Family, or one Gang, run a Country till they get thrown out on their ear. That's a Dynasty. We are now, at home, going through what they call the Republican Dynasty. That Dynasty flourished and floundered from A. D.—After Democrats—1920 to 1932, when it looks like it will fold up. Over here those things are heriditary. Take, for instance, the Chung Dynasty, from 1302 to 1348, ruled by Bum Chung. Then it passed to Mo-Bum Chung, his Son by a Concubine; and then little Mo-Bum Chung, and so on. You want to read some of the historical records over here sometimes; they sure are racy.

But back to our homemade Dynastys. There was the Republican Dynasty with Emperor Calvin. You see, there is really nothing that one Nation has that the other hasent got in some form or another. Japan had the Sho-Gun. Well, the Sho-Gun was a man that really ruled the Emperor. As Civilization come along in Japan, the Sho-Gun was gradually eliminated. Now, for instance, at home there was the Calvin Dynasty, with Sho-Gun Mellon. Then come the Commission Dynasty, with the same Sho-Gun held over. You see, One Sho-Gun might outlast two or three Emperors. Then you have, under the Big Sho-Gun, Little Sho-Guns—smaller accomplices scattered around, like Little Sho-Gun Grundy and Little Sho-Gun Dave Reed. All of this, in Japan, was, as I say, eliminated by Culture and Education, and there is no more of the Sho-Gun Racket, but as both of these accomplishments we have so far avoided, why, we still have the Sho-Gunate type of Dynasty. It flourished to a vast extent during the McKinley Dynasty, with Sho-Gun Hanna.[11] Then there was Sho-Gun House. Then, as the Ruler, or Emperor, would be changed, the Sho-Gun would be changed. The old Rulers and Sho-guns passed out at death, but ours passes out when found out.

Everything they got here we got at home—China had her Confucious; California has her McPherson. Out here you are born into what they call the Privilege Class, Just the same as back home. Over here, men adopted the dress of Women and wear Kimonas; Over home men adopted the Dress of little Boys and wear Knee Breeches. I just been having a laugh over History. I read the Korean History, and they have never done a wrong thing in their existence: they have continually been oppressed. Then, here is an outline of Japan's History. Every move they have made for Korea was only for their good; every war Japan ever had was just forced on 'em by the enemy. Now, here is China's: They have lived all their lives just according to the teachings of Confucious; they have always acted square, honorable; never broke eny treatys, and so on. Now, each one of those is taught to their own people, but they don't see the other side. I doubt if there is a thing in the world as wrong or unreliable as History. History ain't what it is; it's what some Writer wanted it to be, and I just happened to think I bet ours is as cockeyed as the rest. I bet we have started just as much devilement as was ever started against us— maybe more. So as far as facts are concerned, the better educated you are the less you know.

And say, Senator, they call Korea, "Chosen."[12] I thought New York was "Chosen." But the Koreans won't call it that; they still stick to Korea. In 1907, Korea sent a Deligation to the Hague Peace Conference. All they got out of it was the trip. The Ex-Royal Family of Chosen was allowed to be called Prince, and they framed up so he married a Japanese, and he is given at first 1,500,000 Yen—that's $750,000 bucks—then it was raised to 1,800,000—$900,000. He was finding the going kinder tough, so he got the raise. I saw the House where he lived; dident get in. Imagine a poor Country having to give a guy like that $900,000, just for nothing, and our Presidents, for worrying their lives out trying to please, get $75,000.

Well, that was the biggest laugh I got in Chosen. In 1905, when they was taken over, they dident have one cent of National Debt; now they owe 325,966,000. Sounds natural, don't it? There is nothing like Progress to get you in debt. Look, when we only had a Horse and Buggy, how little we owed. Now, our debt, they don't add the Millions any more, they just count the Billions. But take it all in all, Japan has helped the Country in many ways—same as, I guess, we have helped the Phillipines—but when it's all added up—the cost of the Wars, and the management, and the lives lost, and the criticisms to stand—I bet they would have been better off if they had never went in; and that's about the way it would be with any Country that has fought for and annexed another. Say, Senator, these folks all wear white Clothes—even the farmers in the field—all in white Cotton and the world's funniest hats. They are good workers. There is lots of Gold here. I met some Americans out here—Gold Diggers, mostly Male.

Well, I got to stop. I could ramble on all night. Here I have done all this Gabbing and havent even hardly got you into Manchuria—where I am now—but in my next letter I want to take up Manchuria. I am going to Harbin. That's the place where all the White Russians are—any Russian is a White Russian if he is not a Red Russian. There is where the pretty Girls are. This Manchuria is quite a Country. It's well worth taking; of course, if it wasent there would be NO War. If I was a little Nation I would find the poorest land and Country in the world, and then settle on it. I might not make a living, but I would at least be let alone anyhow.

Gosh, I wish I could hear from and see what you Guys are doing there in Washington. I was not sure that Congress ever met; I never had heard. But you must have, for I read the other day where "conditions were getting worse, instead of better"; so I knew then you had met. But that's the first mention of you all that I have read. The U. S. may be big at home, but it's certainly insignificient out here.

I will drop over in China from here; they are always cooking up something over there. What did they ever do about Capone? He is better known out here than Jimmy Walker.

Well, your old Servant is still on the job.

All the Rumors that's fit to Print—that's what I am sending you, Senator.

Yours.
WILL.

136

Letters of a Self-Made Diplomat to Senator Borah

HARBIN, MANCHURIA.

D EAR SENATOR: Well, the old fact Ferret has worked his way clear up here to Harbin. Even the Senate must have heard of Harbin. Harbin is one of the few unique Towns that never amounted to much, but still was World-famous—it and Newport, Rhode Island. Geography made Harbin, while a Tuxedo and Cocktails made Newport. This Harbin come pretty near being in Siberia; it's a junction point on the Trans-Siberian Railroad—that is, the Chinese Eastern, which is a part of the Siberian line. Here is where another line turns south to go to Mukden and Port Arthur. What made this Town famous was the Russians that got out of Russia. It's like Tia-Juana, Mexico. What's made it World-known is the Americans that have escaped over the line and got into the Bars there. Harbin in the "good old days"—you see, these Countrys had "good old days" too—when the Democratic Dynasty was flourishing at home, the White Russian Dynasty was at its top hole here. They say it was the Paris of the Far East. 'Course, that might have been a Chamber of Commerce Slogan. You see, they got those things over here, too; you can't have progress without its accompanying ills.

Well, the Night Life in Harbin is what made the Town livable. You couldent exist there in the daytime—you practically had to leave Town till night come on—but when the shadows of the evening broke over the Siberian Stepps, why, the "Scandalousness did begin." Where in our early Western Civilization "every other house was a saloon," why in Harbin every house was a Cabaret. They just Sang, Danced and Drank themselves through two Wars and a half dozen Peace Conferences—that they have in between Wars, to prevent wars. The Russians are a Gay lot, when they got anything to be gay on, and even when they haven't they don't just fold up and holler hard times like the New Yorker does. They take it on the chin, dig up some more Vodka and stand the Fiddeler off for another gazottsky. 'Course, the Bolsheviks have made everybody in Russia serious, but it's taken a Gun to keep 'em from laughing. For at heart they love fun and amusement.

You see, here is a thing you want to get straight, Senator: All these

---

Saturday Evening Post, March 19, 1932. Reprinted with permission.

Railroads that this late War is over, that the Japanese are taking Manchuria to Protect, were all built—not by them, or the Chinese either—they were built by the Russians. Had there been no Russians building Railroads there, you would never heard of Manchuria; so the Russians are the real ones that unconsciously made Manchuria worth fighting over. So give the Devil his dues; these Russians have contributed something to the world besides whiskers. The Russians spent six hundred million Rubles, on Railroads here alone—that's three hundred million in Mellon's Money. Now, that was a lot of Jack in 1900 to 1904—that's more than we owed at that time. 'Course, now that would just run us over the weekend. So all these investments that Japan talks about in here was mostly Russian investments. But, on the other hand, Japan put up a tough fight to get it; they waited till Russia got it all finished before they started the War, but they did battle, and they lost about one hundred and twenty-five thousand men, and they feel they paid pretty dear for it. For, you see, Senator, all these other Nations, they don't just go off and have Wars, and then just come back home and claim nothing at the end, like we do—or did. Maby we will be wiser next time.

'Course, in the Historys, War always starts "for patriotism's sake," but you read on and get down to the Peace Conference and you find that the historian has to write pretty fast and veil things over very cleverly, or the reader is apt to discover what changed hands at the finish besides a mere satisfying of honor. You look at all Wars and you will find that there is more new deeds for land signed at these Peace Conferences than there is good will. Did you ever look on a map and see the Colonies that Germany lost at Versailles? All the Nations that are crying Debt Cancellations, you never hear 'em mention a word about returning Colonies to Germany so she would have a chance to kinder use 'em to help dig up this Reparations. So, you see, in Wars the Slogan is Honor, but the object is Land. They are always fighting for Independence, but at the finish they always seem to be able to use quite a snatch of the defeated opponent's land to be Independent on.

But I guess the Russians was getting ready to go in and gobble it up themselves as soon as they got everything all set; so maby the Japanese just beat 'em to it. Pretty near all these Wars have got two sides, and some of 'em are like dice—they got six sides. But we can at least get this straight: The Russians are the ones that built up Manchuria—that was the White Russians. Harbin was their main place of operations. Well, everything was going along lively till Russia sees Red about 1918. The Reds signed a separate Peace with Germany at Brest-Litovsk. The Allies not only dident know they were signing it but they dident know—and don't yet—where the place was they was signing. It's like Japan signed Peace with China in 1895 at Shimonoseki. It would take another War to

138

find that place. Then they jump clear over home to find another town to sign in that no one ever heard of—Portsmouth.[1] Roosevelt, always being original, dug that up, and buried it after the signing. You see, they have to hunt out-of-the-way places, for they haven't got the nerve to come out and demand such loot in a real civilized Town. The Humane Society would get 'em for cruelty to animals for making 'em sign such terms.

Now, in 1918, when the Bolsheviks had made peace with Germany, the old Czarist Russian commenced hunting a hole—in other words, he took to the Tulies. With a Red Russian on his tail, he didn't have long to tarry. So he figured on getting out through Siberia; that's a cold, bleak land, inhabited by close-lipped, close-trading Natives, occupying their northeast country, exactly comparable in all these respects to our New England. Now, if they did get out of Russia, all they was in was Harbin. Now, this local War I am talking about is around 1918. Now, we hear of it, and, of course, we have to get in. "Why did we have to get in?" Because we hadent been in anything out here in years. So we sent General Graves and about five thousand men. You see, by this time we had helped so many people out in Wars that it was just a mania with us. We would send men anywhere that could get ten signers to a petition that said they wanted us. We was in the Humanity business, and we was going to do it right. "Just bring on your cause, and we will help you see it through."

Well, our Troops stayed here two years, and all they did was freeze— "froze for Dear Old Siberia." In 1920 we brought 'em home; the Senate and War Department had had two years to think up a reason for them being here, and couldent; so it was decided to bring 'em home and let 'em thaw out. Then, if someone could think of why they had been here, why, they could send 'em back; but up to now no one has ever done it, so they are still at home or in Nicaragua. At that time there was also present in this neck of the woods fifty thousand Czecho-Slovakians that had deserted over in the European War and were trying to get back to Europe by way of Vladivostok. When the Czechos desert, they do a real job of it—fifty thousand at a clip ain't bad deserting. But what always looked kinder odd was them coming six thousand miles across Russia, then going around the world to get back to where they had deserted from in the first place. They seemed to know more about deserting than they did about Geography.

Now, Senator, there is a page in History that you kinder want to watch: With the Bolsheviks in control, that left the other Russians without a Home, a Country, or a place to go, just because they didn't stay at home and become Reds. Now, we are not arguing who is right. Maby the Reds are; maby the ones that left are. It was just a difference of opinion. In any Country there is always a difference of Party or opinions; so you can't exactly blame the White Russians for leaving there at the time, thinking things would adjust themselves soon, and they would go back. But that's been just fourteen years now, and it may be forever. Now, that's quite a stretch to remain without a Country, when you consider that you dident commit any crime. A big part of them were Army Officers who had fought with Russia in their Army that they had been trained in, thinking they were doing their patriotic duty just as much as our troops, or France's, or Germany's, or England's. But because this revolution was a whole new plan, of which they knew nothing about and dident know if it would work or not, why, they have to leave their Country and never return. Their folks are there yet—can't get out, and they can't get in.

Now, I know nothing about the merits of either side. All I know is that there is thousands of people that are absolutely on the very mercy of the World, with no Home, no Country, no Consuls to apply to; not one speck of protection from anywhere. Now, this Harbin that I am sitting in here now is the gateway, their only partial touch with the Country they were born and raised in. They escaped through here, they come back here to try and get in touch with their loved ones still in Russia.

'Course, the Bolsheviks say, "Why dident they stay with us in the first place? We were fighting to free them from the Czar. So what mercy should they get now?" Well, that may be all right. It's not the cause of all this I am telling you about, it's the condition as it exists today.

All down through China, Shanghai, Tientsin, and everywhere, there is thousands of these White Russians; the men, lots of 'em, doing practically Coolie work, but it's the Women that have had it tough. These Girls, simply to eat, have had to live under the most degrading circumstances—at the mercy of the lowest class of every race of people under the sun.

There is nothing happened during our generation that has done more to lower the standing of the White Race than what has taken place right here in this Town and all Manchuria and China. Years ago, the White Man had a standing, especially Social, that put him apart. But since these thousands of white Women have been, for the sake of their very existence, thrown at the feet of people who, before this time, couldent have even spoken to them, why, it looks like somebody is responsible. It's no fault of theirs, it may not be any fault of Red Russia's, as they will say: "Well, they are not in sympathy with our Government, so why have 'em here, causing trouble?" But it's the fault of somebody. Your League of Nations is always into everything. Well, here is a purely humanitarian problem that they could solve in some way, give these folks somewhere to go and some manner of protection some place. White civilization, in days to come, is going to have a lot to answer for, for this. For nothing has lowered your boasted superiority of the White Race like what has happened to these Women. That's where you lost your caste in the Far East. All your examples of boasted superiority will never live that down, for, naturally, they can't see why—if we are such Superior people, and our morals are one of our most cherished traditions—"why it is that you don't do more to protect your White Women?"

It's not Gay in Harbin; there is a semblance of attempted gayety—lots of little cheap Cabarets—but it's just sad. It's not lively, it's not amusing, it's just depressing. They are like any other gathering of Girls or Women—some are beautiful, but their whole manner and looks are just of lost hope, just licked, just whipped. The suicides will run higher here than anywhere in the world. They say they generally hit the dope, and then to the River. The Russians—the Bolshevik ones—in conjunction with the Chinese, control the Chinese Eastern Railway, and Harbin is its big center. It runs through Chinese Manchuria for more than nine hundred miles east and west, with Harbin in the middle. Then there is the south line that joins the Japanese line a couple of hundred miles south at Changchun. Now, that means that there is several thousand Red Russians here that run these Railway lines; they are all working; they have their Consuls, their Protection, and everything. They are all getting along fine. They had a big entertainment last night in their big Recreation Hall, which we went in to see. They were all well dressed and would compare with such a gathering in any Railway Town at home. You see, there is all these Reds and all these Whites, then two or three hundred thousand Chinese, a good many Japanese and every other Nationality in the World. There is no place like this. The National City Bank, of New York, have a flourishing Branch here, as they have all over the Far East; Standard Oil, Texas Co, American-British Tobacco Co, Ford, General Motors—these are just a few of the leading firms that you run onto all over out here.

You can't visit Harbin without one memory that sticks. It's our American Consul General, George Hanson.[2] I call him the Emperor of North Manchuria—best known, best liked, most competent, sleeps less, prowls more, works harder, done more favors for more Nationalities, and I expect is one of the best Representatives we have in any Foreign Country, be it Ambassador, Consul, or foreign emmissary of any description. He is a big, old kind of a funny-looking, bald-headed fellow; he is not anything like what you pictured him from the phrases you had heard.

You would figure that about three o'clock in the morning he would have to get that old bald bean into the hay, but he is just getting organized by then, and this has been going on for twelve years right here. This old Bird—I don't know how old he is—he would have Mayor Walker hollering for help in less than three nights. This is the Guy ought to be mayor of New York, for he can do all that and, in addition, tend to business. He is in that Consulate from nine A.M. right till the devilment starts at sundown. He is the man should have been appointed on this Commission coming out here to see how much indemnity China will have to pay for losing Manchuria.[3] He knows this Country, and all sides like him—like him and trust him.

Old General Ma—remember the Chinese General, Ma, that fought at Tsitsihar—well, he was just across the river from here this week, conferring with the local authorities that are running this Town.[4] I kinder wanted to go see old Ma, but he had gone back into his Mountain retreat. Hanson could have taken me, but listen, Neighbor; it was thirty below when I stepped off that train here at 6:30 A.M. In that kind of weather old Ma would have to come see me. I wouldent go out in this cold to see Napoleon.

Now, Senator, I am serious about these Russians. If you can do anything toward getting 'em a country, why, do so, will you? I think there is going to be an awful lot of Countries go in the hands of the receivers by fall, so save one for the White Russians; they may make just as big a mess running it as they did their own before, but give 'em another chance. The reason I am writing you so much about this particular town, Senator, is, in the near future you are going to hear so much about it that it will become like Chicago to you. For this will be the main Town in the Russo-Japanese War. You see, out here, Senator, they arrange their Wars away ahead; they commence getting lined up, sometimes three or four years before the Whistle blows. So don't say I dident tell you about it.

Well, I am going to get out of here; was to stay another night, but a Man from Hollywood has got no chance following this old Hanson. I would go to sleep on him in every Cafe last night, but he would wake me up and drag me out in that cold to another one. Not another night like that for me, even to get the facts for you, Senator. Here is the place where a bunch of Washington senators would like to Investigate. And How! Say, did I tell you I could tell the difference between a White Russian and a Red Russian—that is, if it's a Girl? If she is pretty she is a White Russian. That's right, Senator; these Reds are mighty hard-looking. There must be something about that "everybody split up what you got with me" idea that makes 'em all look alike. When you got everybody looking alike, that should be the heighth of Communism.

Well, anyhow, you are enough of a Humanitarian to help try and get both Whites and Reds straightened out. Write you from Mukden.

Yours
WILL.

MUKDEN, MANCHURIA.

DEAR SENATOR: Well, here I am back in Mukden, after Harbin. Snow is about six inches deep, but it don't keep these poor Coolies from pulling their Rickshas in a long trot right through it. About twenty Newspapermen are here still at the Hotel, waiting for Chinchow—they call that Chinjo—to break. Gibbons has joined 'em, and I will lose him here. He is investigating for Mr. Hearst and me for you.[5] I must tell you a good one on me. I was to go this morning by train to Peking, but that's the line all the Robberies is on, and some good friends advised me not to go: "They will kidnap you and hold you." Well, in this type of weather I dident relish standing out there in the snow while Beverly Hills and Claremore, Okla., passed the Hat. With the price of everything else off at home, ransom money on Comedians wouldent be any exception. I might not be able to make these Bandits understand that while our Country was not at war like theirs here, it certainly is not at peace; that if U.S. Steel was 36, a U.S. Citizen couldent possibly be quoted at over 15 cents.

I wouldent mind being with these old Bandits in the summertimes, and ride these cute little Mongolian Ponies and try to show 'em how to rope, but this is no weather to be giving an exhibition to the Chief. Anyhow, I got cold feet and am going down to Dairen, and then over by Boat. Things are as quiet here in Mukden, you would think you was in the Supreme Court room there at the Capitol. This is a big Country, Senator—as big as Texas and Oklahoma combined. In fact, it looks just like Oklahoma did before we went in hock for life to build the roads for Kansans to cross into Texas on. It's a pretty prairie, and it's main crop is Soya Beans—65 per cent of the World's Crop of them is raised here; they jumped in production from thirty-five million bushels in 1915, to five and one half million tons—not bushels—in 1929. Three million Tons of these go to Oil mills of Europe. Why, Senator, did you know? But, of course, coming from an Agricultural State, you wouldent. But it's a fact that the Manchurian Soya Bean has revolutionized the whole dairying business and cattle-raising business of Holland, Denmark and Sweden. They make everthing out of 'em here, then live off the curd. It used to bring about one hundred million Dollars. A.M.—Andy's money—into this Country NET.

Now, Senator, we got to let you in on some Scandal. The War Lords of Manchuria, to support an Army of three and four hundred thousand men, they levied heavy taxes against these Farmers. It was by far the richest and best-paying part of China. In fact, there is a question as to whether it is, or ever was, a REAL part of China.

None of the Taxes ever went to China proper. They always remained here. Incidentally, over half of our trade with China was in Manchuria. It

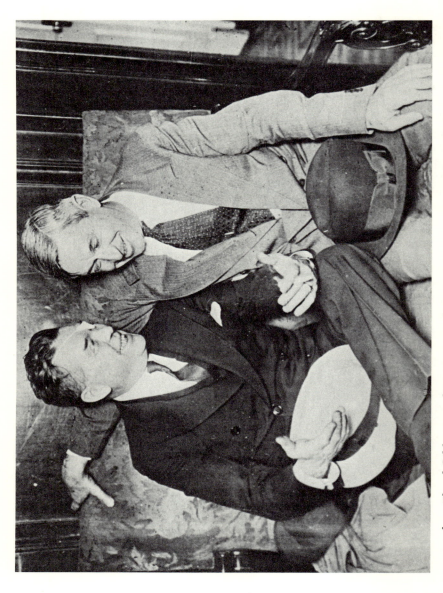

War correspondent Floyd Gibbons and Rogers in Yokohama, Japan, in December of 1931. (courtesy of the Floyd Phillips Gibbons Collection, Special Collections Department, Raymond H. Fogler Library, University of Maine, Orono, Maine)

was the up-to-date live Market of all the Far East. Now follow me close on this, Senator, for you Birds in there are trying to scheme up ways to get some more Taxes out of the voter and NOT lose his vote. Well, get this what this old War Lord up here did. He was ambitious and he moved his Capital from here to Peking and embraced all Northern China; so, naturally, he had to have some more dough. Now, get this: He issued an order that the Beans couldent be sold to a buyer, or Middle-man, or direct to the shipper; that they must be sold to a Representative of his Government, which he would name in each Community, and these men would pay for them with a special Government specie, or money. Well, he dident have this money, but he sent and got some printing presses, and he just made it. As the Farmer would thrash his beans the War Lord would thrash out their money. No Farmer ever received newer money in the world. Was there anything back of this money? Nothing but a printing press.

For a little while, when the demand in Europe for Beans was going good—that is, when Europe was Bean-Minded—why, these paper notes did have some value in trade and at the banks. But Chang took the beans and sold them to the Shippers for Gold. Funny you boys in there never thought of that. Clever people, these Chinese. The whole of this gold went to pay for his big Armys. Well, a hard-working people like these dident need any Army. Ever once in awhile he would hear of the Brokers manipulating around with this Rag-paper money and selling it away below its stamped value. He just had 'em arrested and brought in, bumped off, and the notes went back to par. The amount of shootings denoted the price of the notes. But, of course, the thing had to bust; and they estimate today that there was in all these years upwards of one Billion dollars, A.M., scattered about. Today, well, you can take your old Confederate money over there and you can get a trade for it, even. Now, Senator, there is an Idea for Capper to pay off the wheat Farmers.[6]

Will drop you a line from Dairen. So long, Boss.

Yours

WILL.

DAIREN, MANCHURIA.

D EAR SENATOR: Say, this is one of the most up-to-date Ports you ever saw; more modern buildings here than any Port I ever saw. This is the terminus of the South Manchuria Railway, and, say, they build all their own cars and engines. 'Course, all this end of the Penin-sula is under lease to the Japanese for ninety-nine years—with a renewal

145

clause. The Russians were the first builders of this too. This is what Japan got after the Russian War—like as if you whipped me, Fox Film Co. would have to pay you my salary. This afternoon Young Mr. Kinney, one of the Officials, drove me down to Port Arthur, about thirty miles over a fine, paved road.[7] After seeing Port Arthur and all those Monuments—one with ten thousand of their troops buried beneath it—their War Museum, 203-Meter Hill—remember that during that Russian War? That was one of the famous sieges of history; it run for months. The Russians were cut off from supplies by sea and land—the Trans-Siberian R. R. By the way, Senator, they are double-tracking that and getting it in real shape. . . . Eh, what?—but both sides fought heroically here. A Japanese training ship was in here today at Port Arthur, and all the Cadets were doing the Historical spots as we were. These folks keep this Patriotism thing going at top speed. This is hallowed ground to them. Port Arthur and Manchuria was the making of them as a Nation. Some say war don't pay, but it's guesswork as to where Japan would have been without this Chinese and Russian War. So, if you think the League of Nations or anybody else is coming in here and demand that the Japs get out, well, they better come with a gun instead of a Resolution.

Did I tell you this, Senator: the Army in Japan is only answerable to the Emperor, not to any other part of the Government. The State Department has nothing to do with them. In fact, in this trouble there has been some friction, but nothing much. When these Babies go out to do something, you can bet it's UNITED. That's Japan's middle name is Unity—when it comes to dealing with any outsider. That's why poor old China has her problems; if they have a Representative in Paris or somewhere promising something, that night he will get a notice that the Government he was representing is washed up; he is simply not dealing for anybody. That happened this week to Mr. Sze, their Representative in Paris.[8] I see where the League is sending out a Delegation, Well, there is still talk of appointing a Committee to find out "who started the big war?" So there will always be Committees, same as there will always be Wars. Well, sailing in the A.M. Will write from Peking.

Yours,
WILL.

PEKING.

DEAR SENATOR: Well, here I am at last in China, and what a time I had getting here. Left Dairen in a little Japanese Tub; it was a Covered Wagon with a rudder. We got out—it's supposed to be a couple of nights and days to a little Port near Tienstin—well, we run into a storm; we plowed through it half a day; then the Captain—a fellow that played Checkers, or a game with two or three hundred buttons, all the time with two other Japanese Passengers—he decided to turn around and go back and spend the night in the Harbor at Port Arthur, but wouldent let us go ashore, and we run out of beer and food. We never noticed the food. A Ford Dealer from Shanghai, a French Aviator, a little Jewish Fur Dealer from New York and an Ex Oklahoma Comedian—but he wasent working at it on this trip—oh, and an English Newspaperman—Mr. Gorman, from Peking—who had covered the whole war and was going home to make up his mind.[9] The Ford Dealer was sore because he not only hadent sold anything in Manchuria but half of his Sub-Dealers were off in the war, and all his Fords were in it. The little Fur Dealer had been to Harbin—by the way, I forgot to tell you, that's the Fur Market center.

But get this, Senator: They don't get furs out of Russia. Russia sells direct and cuts out the middle, or, from what this fellow said, the twelve middlemen that they have in the fur business. Well, the little Fur Dealer was downhearted too. The war had killed off all the Dogs, and that left no Fur Business, and it had been rather a discouraging trip for him, and nothing can be as blue as a New York buyer; and when the beer run out he was practically unconsolable.

He perked up on the Dock, however; there was a lot of Mongrel Dogs there of every description, colors, shades and sizes, and his eyes just beamed. I thought he was going to take 'em to the slaughterhouse direct from there. The big French Aviator had had his plane captured by the Japanese when they took over the Airport at Mukden. He knew the war was on, that night of Sept. eighteenth, but he dident know it was "on him." We played some Poker—a game which any of my friends that know me know they never even saw me attempt. Well, I livened the trip up a bit for the boys by paying their passage and incidental expenses. I contributed very little humor, but something much more substantial, to the trip. Now, I know no one will ever see me play it. Did you ever see a little boat turn a Somersault and light on its feet? Well, this one did, and does.

Well, we finally got ashore, and what a relief to get off that Baby. The Furrier is still eyeing the Manchurian Flee Hounds: The Ford Dealer is cussing hundreds of carts pulling up with little Manchurian Ponies, unloading Soya Beans for the boat. He figures if they had civilization, Fords would replace 'em. I asked him if he took Ponies in trade-in on his cars. I told him over home they take in old Cook Stoves, Bureaus, Burros, Radios, Saxophones—anything—to make a sale nowadays; so I told him it was him that wasent keeping up with civilization.

After hours of freezing and waiting, here comes the train. Oh, get this:

147

We have only been on it about a mile, and it stopped at a little station, and what do you think piled on, about fifty strong in a drove? American Gobs.

"Well, if it ain't old Will! What are you doing here, Will? Yes, it is; that's old Will. There ain't another face like that in all China."

"Hello, Will."

"Say, wait a minute, you Guys. Quit piling over me here. Where did you come from? What Boat you from, out here in the prairie?"

"From the Tulsa."

"Tulsa! Why, you must be anchored right close to the Battleship Claremore. What is this Tulsa tug anyhow?"

"It's a Gunboat, and we been stuck on the bar here for six months."

"Does the Navy know where you are?"

"It don't look like it. We havent heard from 'em in years."

"Well, maby I have done some good out here anyhow; I have found a Gunboat that I never heard of, and I doubt if the Navy has. Who was you sent here to shoot at, and why?"

"Well, we had orders to go to Peking, but Peking is inland; the Navy thought we was an Amphibian."

"You got any Aeroplanes aboard?"

"No."

"Well, then, I got no use for you, then. I have a good notion not to tell the Navy where you are."

"What you doing out here, Will—a Missionary?"

"Yes, I am out here for Sister Aimee."

"Why dident you bring her with you, and we would all have been converted."

"Missionaries do pretty well out here, don't they?"

"Better'n they do at home."

"Who's going to run for President, Will?"

"Why, Mr. Hoover."

"What? Again? Ain't he got any mercy on us?"

"Who will the Democrats run?"

"I guess they will run Hoover again. They are the ones that run him the last time."

"Ah, boloney, quit your kidding. Who will they run?"

"Well, Boys, I don't know; they hadent drawn straws up to the time I left."

"Did they ever find the corner that Prosperity was hid behind?"

"What they going to do about Prohibition—just keep on drinking, or are they going to cut down on it?"

"What's Al doing, Will?"

"Why, he's got the highest building in the World, and he is just standing at the bottom selling Tickets to it. Got the best thing in New York."

"What do they want to go up there fur—to jump off?"

"You got any Marines on your Boat?"

"We did have some, but we drownd 'em."

"Here, where you get that stuff?"

"Sure us Marines are on board. We have to be, to keep the Chinese from carrying off the Sailors with their Chop Sticks."

"Is there anything doing here in Tientsin, where we going tonight?"

"Sure, just had a war there last week; shot up the Japanese Concession."

"Have we got any troops there?"

"Sure, got the Fifteenth Hoof—infantry. Grant sent 'em out right after the Cival War to protect the Missionaries."

"Have they been here all this time?"

"Sure, what's living have; the ones that's in the regiment now was born here."

"Say, why don't you Bloaks cut it out? Will don't want to hear our daily menu. How's Clara Bow, Will?"[10]

"That-a-boy! Will, tell us about Clara, and that Greta Garbo.[11] Tell her she can have my end of the Tulsa."

"Ah, Will don't know about them. Fifi Dorsey is his Racket.[12] How's Fifi, Will? Nes Pau, Say-vu-play, 40 Hombes and 8 Cherval. I ain't forgot the language yet. Bo-coup, Fano."

"Well, so long sailor Boys; here's the Station. Will see you around town somewhere tonight. I am going to hunt up some of the Fifteenth Hoof."

And sure enough I did. The Col. rounded 'em all up in the Mess Hall that night, and I dug up a little old piece of Cord line, or Chinaman's Que, or something, and we had a show. Told the Boys I was going to arrange 'em passports and have 'em visit America some time. They are a fine regiment, getting along fine; been there thirty years and never fired a shot—so the Col. told me. They may not have any Guns—I don't know. Met lots of nice folks. They all asked about you, Senator.

They want to get you out here some time. But you better stay where you are, though, and let me do the looking for you. 'Course, here is what you're up against here: They been out in these Countries so long that they can't see our angle at home, and we can't sit at home and see theirs. So that's another one you will have to dope out yourself. Everybody out here is mighty nice folks, however, and I would hate to see anything happen to 'em.

Say, here is something you would like over here. It's the Mongolian Ponies. They got the prettiest race Courses. They race these little fellows—about thirteen hands, and thirteen one. They are the greatest things you ever saw. They had a Cross Country race, some ten miles—just think of that—ten miles—and every one of them carrying one hundred and fifty, one hundred and sixty and some up to almost two hundred pounds. The jumps are mostly ditches. I went out to see it. They are the best animal for their inches, I guess, in the World. They ship 'em down from up in Mongolia; they only send down so many each year—two thousand, I think it is.

You see, Senator, when you are in a Heathern Country like Mongolia, you can regulate supply. They don't ship all they raise one year, then everybody go on a dole the next year. Just two thousand a year. If you send any out besides that, well, you better go with 'em. Then, they thought Gov. Hughey Long, in Louisiana, was crazy![13] Lot to be learned from these Heathern over here, Senator; and say, they play Polo on these little Rascals too.

I come up to Peking here—by train it's about three hours. Here is the Old Capital; it's where the Capital was till just a few years ago, when they moved it to Nanking. You see, over here it's the Party that's in that designates where the Capital will be. For instance, if you was in, it would be in Boise; if Al Smith was in, it would be out on the sidewalks of New York; Bill Murray would move it to Tishomingo, Okla.—that's if the U.S. was run like China.[14] It was a good joke on the Foreign Embassys; they had all their soldiers—well, not all of 'em, but part—in Peking—Peiping—same Town—and then the Chinese moved their Capital right out from under 'em. So all these foreigners have been sitting up there in their fine quarters, and NO government to deal with; it's thirty-six hours by train to Nanking, and it looks like it might move to Canton—that's like from Washington to Seattle. Now I think that's funny. These Diplomats over here don't seem to derive any humor in it, but to me it's komical. These Chinese got humor, don't kid yourself.

I been looking at Walls and old Palaces today till I am groggy. The Forbidden City—that's the way to attract attention to anything; call it "Forbidden," and you couldent keep an American out of there with a meat Ax. Well, this wasent Forbidden any more than Palm Beach, but by calling it that, they grabbed off the Yokels, me included. Then they got a Gag they call the Temple of Heaven; about like a thousand others, only that name "Heaven" is a great Sales Argument. But this is a great old Town, if you like old Towns. Personally, I like new Towns. Tulsa, twenty years ago, was my idea of a real City. 'Course, it's aged now, kinder like Peking. But when she was new and had no Tradition, she was a hummer.

Say, Senator, if I dident run onto another patch of Marines here! Marines are not Soldiers; they are Tourists. I find 'em all over. I have gotten out of maybe an Aeroplane in the oddest places in the World, not thinking there was any civilization in a thousand miles, and there would be six or eight Companies of Marines. They are likable cusses; been everywhere, seen everything—but America. Some of these spoke pretty fair English. Had dinner with 'em, and, of course, had to work for my meal after by telling a lot of the old ones. They was a fine audience and we had a lot of fun—me more than them. Here is the Town where all the Writers and Artists, and the ones who "love China for China's sake" live. It smells and sounds just like Carmel, Cal., and Saugatuck, Conn. They got no use here for Shanghai. Shangai Art is about on the level with St. Louis's. But this is a great old place here. Wish I could stay longer, but I have to keep moving with the Government, so I am off tomorrow for Nanking, Shanghai and Hong-Kong. I sure would like to get a letter from you, Senator, but I guess the Democrats got you dodging so.

Well, so long,

WILL.

Letters of a Self-Made Diplomat to Senator Borah

DEAR SENATOR: Now, Senator, you sent me over here to look over these Chinese and turn you in a Diagnosis. I believe I can do it, for it takes a Comedian to look at China. Historians, Writers, Tourists, Professional Observers, Missionaries, returned Business Men, and League of Nation Commissions have looked 'em over and can't make head or tail out of 'em. The way to do it is to look at 'em from a Comedy angle. It's just like a Zoo: Every day you look at 'em, they are doing different Tricks. What you got to do is get in quick, look at 'em and get away. If you stop to solve 'em, you are lost; you can't solve 'em. China is a Country that you mustn't stop and think over; if you do you are sunk. You see, that's what they are doing themselves, is stopping to think things over. They are standing still, looking backwards. And if that is what we do, we will be more lost than he is, for he can see something back there; his whole Life has been spent looking over his shoulder. But we can't see nothing but our shadow when we look back. That's the biggest difference between the two races, Oriental and Occidental. We are a foresight people, and they are a hindsight people.

Now, pick your choice of Civilizations—the one that looks into the Past where they know what's happened, or the one that looks toward the Future, where they don't know anymore about what's going to happen than a Weather Bureau Man. It's a bad Country for a White Man to meditate in; make up your mind quick, put your bet down, and tell the Dealer to go ahead. Every Writer tells you that it is a Country of contrasts. It's not a Country of contrasts at all; no Nation in the world has done the same things as long as they have, and yet the White Race hasn't been smart enough to find out what it is they are doing. So get in, look 'em over, and get out before they begin to get in your hair. There is millions of 'em. Nobody has ever counted 'em; and that's one good thing about this Country; there is no statistics in it. We have eleven million Unemployed at home, counting the four million that do nothing but keep Statistics on things that we would be better off if we dident know. Well, nobody can give you any Statistics on China. That's one thing makes me believe they are really civilized; they abandoned that Statistic foolishness during the

---

Saturday Evening Post, April 2, 1932. Reprinted with permission.

Coo-Coo Dynasty, 2100 B.C. China is a country that can only count so many anyhow. They count by a Board, looks like a Cribbage Board or Faro Layout; it's a lot of buttons on a string, and they move 'em up and down. They subtract, multiply, get Weather Reports, Stock-Market Closings, the Sex of a contemplated baby. Anything under the sun you ask a Chinaman, he runs to this Oriental Weegee Board and moves these buttons up and down awhile and comes up with an answer. You've seen 'em in a Chinese Laundry. He can't tell you whether you had a Shirt or a Nightgown laundered till he runs to this Monkey Board.

Frank Hawkes, the Flyer, is the same way, only he uses a Slide Rule— you know, where one Rule slides up and down between two others.[1] He has a lovely Wife, fast Plane, Cars, everything, but none of 'em would mean a thing to him if you took away his Slide Rule; he eats by it, washes his teeth by it, orders his soft-boiled Eggs by it; flying, he never looks ahead at the Horizon, it's just at the Rule. You ask him, "Frank, what town is that that we are to play at eight o'clock in the Morning?" He goes into a huddle with the Rule and comes up with: "Batesville, Arkansas." "Do you think Coolidge will run?" and away goes the Rule on another tour. He tried to pay his Income Taxes by it, but the Income Man was a Straight-Rule Man. Frank is a direct throwback to this Board and Button Dynasty somewhere. The Chinese are not only married to one of these Boards, but they sleep with it.

But anyhow, roughly, they say there is four hundred million of 'em over here. That shows right there they have mastered Mass Production; they had it before Henry Ford had ever thought of making Detroit anything but a One-Night Stand. They are the only ones that have mastered Mass Production and mastered Distribution too. They have arranged Wars, Famines, Droughts, Floods, and Disease so that it takes care of the Surplus. Four hundred million have lived on the same Farms for four thousand years, so that shows that they got Farm Relief pretty well doped out. They can't overproduce anything. If they do, they eat it. If they don't produce it, they don't eat it; so you can't beat that for a Balance of Production versus Consumption. We got twenty-seven Hoover Commissions trying to figure out this same Problem; if they raise too many people in Prosperous and well-fed years, they starve 'em when bad years come. So the problem that has got the rest of the world Nutty don't mean a thing to Confucius' boys. They got it settled before it happens.

You know, they are the most patient race of people in the World; they have waited four thousand years for something good to happen to 'em, and as it hasent, they are all set for another four thousand. They are the most fortunate Nation in the world, for they know that nothing that happens to 'em can possibly be worse than something that's already

153

happened. Our "Fall of 1929," when Prosperity dived and hit her head on the bottom and hasent come up yet, why, a little Catastrophe like that would be just like a Thanksgiving Dinner to them.

The Chinese Problem! We are always hearing about the Chinese Problem. To the Chinese it's no Problem; it's just another Fact. We dident find that they had a Problem till we found they had some money to buy something we had. Then we found they had some things to sell cheaper than the rest of the world, so that, naturally, made them a Problem. Then you start studying 'em. What is their Characteristics?

Ain't it funny the Chinese don't get wise to themselves and really learn how to live right? But they just don't think that a Car and a Radio is essential to their happiness. So it will just about be their luck to go on living like that another five thousand years while we will have everything down so perfect that we can live a whole Lifetime in a couple of years. But we won't spend any more time on how to live, for we got that figured out in our Country; so there's no use wasting time on a trifle like that. What we want to do is get all other Nations fixed up now like us.

But now that we and European Nations have gone in and taken their Ports and Customs, got lots of Missions, and sending lots of their sons to Harvard and Oxford, why, we have practically settled all China's troubles. They will have easy sailing now, after all we have done for 'em. Just get half as many more educated by us, then half as many educated sons returning, and their troubles will be over entirely, practically for all time. There will be no more China. You never saw a thing turn out as well in your life. It's all been wonderful. Students return from Abroad, go into Politics to "save their Country," end up by saving enough to get themselves a fine Home in one of the Treaty Ports under foreign protection and then start a Campaign to throw the Infidel out, and hope to the Lord they don't go; for if they go, he will have to go with 'em.

Now, here is another thing, Senator, you want to get straight: The Chinese you see over home and all over the world, they are not just all kinds of Chinese. They are just one kind; they just come from one part of China. That's a place down south called Canton. Did you think that all those that keep us clean over home come from all over? Well, that just shows what sitting in that Foreign Relations Room in the Capitol all your life will do for you. Say, there is more breeds of Chinese than there are of Republicans. Now, you know how much you are like Senator Fess?[2] Naturally, you hope you are not, and you got your wish. Yet to people that don't know any better, you are both called Republicans. Does Senator Moses and Hiram Johnson strike you as being the same Race of people? Still, in a Congressional Dictionary they are under the same head. Is Brookhart like any other Republican you ever saw?[3] Well, you see there, that's just the same with Chinese; they ain't all Chinese any more than you fellows are Republicans. Anyone that ever gets his nose outside China is a Cantonese. That would be just like as if all the Americans abroad would be from New York. 'Course, that would be great for us, but tough on the rest of the world. So, you see, the Chinese we meet don't give us a real line on the whole Race. A Cantonese has a Language that is purely his own; a Manchurian wouldent know if he was talking Chinese or Cherokee. But it's them that are the adventerous ones; they do all the prowling. They are just as restless as a lot of old Maids, some Chinese Commercial Travelers must have dropped into Canton away back; in fact, that was old Marco Polo's town. So that old Gad-about left a Mess of Offsprings there, I reckon. Just give a Cantonese a Washboard and some Soap, and he will see more of the world than a U.S. Marine. And even the ones that stay at home is not satisfied; they are always raising some Devilment. Here just last week it was the Canton Crowd that threw a Cat into the Electric Fan of Government up at Nanking. They are the ones that busted the whole thing up worse than a bunch of Renegade Democrats. You know, come to think of it, Senator, the Cantonese are what we, humorously, at home, call Progressives. He has either got to be moving, or stopping something that is moving.

Not that that Nanking Government dident need something thrown at it. I have seen some Comedy Governments in my time—some of 'em right around your Range, Senator—but these over here are hot Sketches. You got to be a General here before you can be anything else. When I get home and go down and tell my pet Country —— You know, I got two pet Countries—Mexico and Ireland. I am sure high on them, Senator. Well, Mexico will be tickled to death to know that there is a way of having more Generals to the square inch of desk space than they have got.

You see, you get into politics here with a gun; over home there is no Qualifications. If you had a bad night the night before, and wake up feeling that there is nothing left in life for you, that you are no good to yourself, the World or your friends, why, one day later finds your name on an Election Ballot running for something. But over here you get in power through an Army. You ask, "How do you get Votes with an Army?" Votes! What do you mean—Votes? There is no voting in China; there has been nothing voted by the people in China since Jenghiz Khan called for a Vote of confidence in twelve hundred and something, A.D.— Almost Democratic. He not only called for the Vote, but, Brother, he got it. Senator, that was China's last Popular Election.

If a Cabinet Member in a Chinese Government accidentally stumbled onto a Voting Box, he would think it was a Bomb left there by some enterprising Cantonese, and run till he hit the Great Wall. Voting as we know it just ain't done in up-to-date Chinese circles, and as for a Chinese Coolie Voting, why, he wouldent know any more what to do with his

Vote than a Hoover Democrat will next November. Even their Patron Saint, Sun Yat-sen, got in, not after counting the Ballots but the Bodies.[4] He freed 'em from something—I don't know what it was, and they don't either yet. Then another Modern-Educated one come along—Chiang Kai-shek.[5] He give 'em some more oratorical Liberty; so, as I say, they are just practically resting on Easy Street now.

I read some of the Platforms that these new Presidents get in on—Prosperity, Lower Taxes, Equal Rights for the Workingman, and Throw the Foreigner Out. Outside that last Clause, sounds just like our 100 per cent American Campaign Pledge, don't it? Well, this Pledge was fulfilled, too, just like ours. So you see what our Modern Education has taught 'em. In the old days in China, the Rulers promised 'em nothing and made good. But with American and European methods, now they get Promises; so you can see yourself how much better off they are. No comparison to the old days. Starting as a Bandit here is another quick way of reaching the top—take over a Province, then make the Government give you enough to feed your Army; you feed 'em on one-third of that, take the other two-thirds yourself, and the very first thing you know you are a Political Leader.

I believe, Senator, over there they are a little short of Patriots. Well, we are short of 'em at home. But the Chinese are the best Talkers, they can put up the most convincing Arguments.

Here is another funny thing I bet you dident know: A Chinese can speak 100 per cent better English or any other Language than a Japanese. That was a strange thing to me. Japanese got a lot of educated ones, but there is just something about 'em that they can't speak English. I don't mean correctly, but I mean right out, without hesitating. The Japanese are so careful thinking of saying the word they are on correctly, that they can't remember the one that follows it. It must be something in the Throat, or Vowels, or something. But a Chinese that's educated, he can just rattle it off—no hesitating. Then, with his marvelous Memory, why, at a Conference or in an argument they can leave the Japanese standing still. If all Chinese Oratory that has been wasted in behalf of China's Independence had been converted into Powder and Ball, and shot it at 'em, why, there would be no Europeans on their shores, or Japanese either. They can show you, with the most convincing and true arguments, where China should be independent, master of her own whole country, but their resistance in the past has consisted mostly of Oratory. They don't figure that Japan got where she is today with a Gun, and China got where she is today through her Diplomats trying to persuade some other Nations to protect and help her out; not figuring that every time they helped her they took a slice of her for doing it.

If China would go worship old Jenghiz Khan and his Grandson, and

156

live up to some of their Traditions, instead of Confucius and his Sayings, why, she would be occupying her own free Ports. Confucius had some awful pretty Sayings, but none of 'em have ever kept a Foreigner from coming in and gobbling up what he wanted. China just picked out the wrong man to Worship, that's all. Old Jenghiz was the boy. He wouldent have met 'em at the shore with a Platitude; he would have made his Cavalry swim right out in the Ocean and get 'em.

Now, I am not taking anything away from Confucius. He must have been a wonderfully smart man. From reading some of his Sayings, I would judge him to have been a cross between our Abraham Lincoln, Elbert Hubbard and H.L. Mencken.[6] But the things he said was meant for the Chinese; they wasent meant for a half-baked Chinese that had a conglomeration Night Club and Tammany Hall political-method Background. I bet if Confucius had known his people would adopt a lot of modern-world foolishness, he would have written a different Book, telling 'em to stay at home. He had life figured out for 'em better than any man in the world for any Nation, and to prove it, it worked for two thousand years; but he naturally thought they was going to stay Chinese.

Then there's Egotism. We always think of the Japanese as the Egotist, but the Chinese got him licked on it. The Japanese is naturally Cocky now over his War and Commercial Records. They believe they can do great things but they still want to learn. They are not right sure yet. He believes his future is built on keeping up, and he tries everything and learns everything he can. He wants to know that his Egotism is well-founded. But the Chinese is a far different Egotist; his is based on Tradition. He has Books to show that he has lived, done Reading and Writing, and been Educated for thousands of years. He knows—and it's true—that everything the Japanese knew, up to just a few years ago, they got from him. And that has naturally given him this superior Atmosphere.

I don't mean he is distant and won't speak to you, like a strange Englishman. No, the Chinese are the most friendly folks you ever saw; they got a smile and laugh. You can't help but like 'em; they are good Fellows. But back in that Nut of theirs, they feel that all this modern Junk you are lording it over them with is just a trick, and that it will pass in time and they will be in command. And the Rascals might be right, at that. A Chinaman looks at a European just like we do at a Monkey up a tree with a Coconut. We know he can't open it, and eventually he will drop it and we will get it. Well, that's the Chinese with the Whites. They know we are playing with a lot of stuff we don't know anything about, and eventually we will drop it and come down to earth. He has spent his lifetime just learning to sit and do nothing. Well, if he is sitting there doing nothing, and likes it, why, he has been taught that he is well off.

157

We like to sit, but it's got to be with somebody, so we can be blowing off to 'em what we are going to do when we get up.

Their whole study in Schools is just memorizing Confucius and the old Classics. He wouldent give you a chopstick full of Rice to know the Date and Birth of Every event in the world if it dident happen in China. Geography or History don't mean any more to them than it did to me when I spent four straight years in McGuffey's Fourth Reader.[7] If a thing dident happen in the old Indian Territory, I dident want to know it, and dident, and still don't. You know, Senator, the Chinese are kinder like the old Virginians or Charleston, South Carolinians: They base an awfull lot on what they used to amount to. England is a good deal like that—they are another Tradition Worshiper—but, like Virginia, they are kinder snapping out of it and beginning to try and dig up somebody they can be proud of this day and time, without having to take the Guests to the Cemetery to worship. What spoiled China was somebody saving their History. The minute you teach a man he is backed up by Tradition, why, you spoil him for real work the rest of his life.

They tell me that the tremendous size of the Country, and the lack of Communication, and the different Languages, even different Races, is why there is no real Public Spirit. Then, I think, along with some real Patriots over here, they need just a little mite more Honesty in high places. Now, that strikes us like a Bomb, don't it? Our whole thought had been of the Chinese's unalloyed Honesty, but I guess your visiting Business Men and the Chinese's own oversea experiences has made him just as modern as anybody. I hate to relate this, but there is a speck of Graft over here. It starts small, but gradually works its way up. They don't call it Graft, though. No, it's called the Squeeze. I will say one thing for these Chinese—when they learn anything from us, they learn it thoroughly. So they have taken Graft. They not only improved on its name but they improved on its method. They introduced Mass Production with their Squeeze. You know, they got places over here where they collect Taxes thirty years in advance. Then they sell the tax-collecting Privilege to someone. Then he can go out and get all over that amount he can. Kinder like us. We got to wait till Congress meets to find out how much they have squandered in the past year; so then they tell us what we have to dig up.

But take it all in all, we got more honesty in Government than any of 'em. You know, Senator, I believe that's what's kept us going so long is that our Public Men in High Office are Honest. You never saw one getting out of Washington with a load that he made while there. It would be wonderful if we could say as much for our Public Men's ability as we can for their Honesty. They all really want to do something worthwhile for us, but they just can't think of anything to do. 'Course, Senator, here is

158

another thing that handicaps the Chinese: Take one separate, and he is smart, alert, able, clever, and can get things done. But let him be joined by another Chinese and their efficiency usually drops 50 per cent.

But there is one thing you sure got to admire in the Chinese. They are great Family People; they are home folks and stay-at-homes. Whole Families for generation after generation are born, live and die under the same roof, especially all the Male line. Everybody brings their wives home and lives off Pa. Not much, you don't. You bring your wife home and you both go to work, and everything all of the whole Caboodle of you earn all goes into the one Family pot. They carry on what their Fathers carried on. They don't believe they should spend a lifetime trying to raise above their Father's position, and therefore they have more peace of mind and commit less Devilment trying to reach some position that they are not fitted for. With us, it's "Nothing is too high; get the Moon. We are just the guy can run it if we can reach it." Whether we belong anywhere or not, that don't matter. Get there, that's all. So I believe the Chinese have got it figured out better; they may never arrive at a point where they can look down on their old Parents with a charitable condescension, but they get pretty near as much pleasure on looking up to theirs. If their Father has carried a wicker basket on his shoulder on each end of a pole all his life, they don't feel called on to go out and get a Wheelbarrow; they think that old Dad that did that was quite a fellow, and if they can live to be as good a man, they have fulfilled a life's Ambition.

Parents are a Tradition with them, and not just a means of arriving on earth. They think that what you have never had and never been used to you will never miss. We think what we havent got we ought to have, and will miss it if we don't get it. Their whole theory of life is contentment, ours is "Come on, Boy. Let's get somewhere, even if we don't know where it is." 'Course, there is just a little difference of opinion and a matter of a couple of thousand years of living. 'Course, we know better than they do, but they just won't see things like we know things are. It's awful hard to convince a Nation it's wrong—especially a big one—but we will do it, because it's up to us to show 'em they are wrong. 'Course, China is like a lot of us; they tried to do things too fast; they went from a Chopstick to a knife and Fork before they was ready, and they been mutilating themselves with it ever since. Japan also jumped from a Ricksha into a flivver before she was ready, and we ourselves went on an eight cylinder basis, and are now paying for it on a Street Car.

China should be ruled over by some real old Chinese—ones that had never any more seen a College Degree than they have a piar of Pajamas. These young ones and old ones that are European and Mission Educated, they mean well, but their Education has just put 'em out of touch with the real Chinese. We don't have an American Cecil Rhodes Scholar to come home and run us.[8] Get real old wise Chinese for three hundred and ninety-nine million of the four hundred million are just Chinese, so that's the bunch to pick your Rulers from.

Just to read the Chinese Treaties and dealings with the so-called Whites, there is a laugh or a tear in every line, whichever way you want to take it. It must have been a big Country to start out with, for every Nation that has reached out to shake hands with China has pulled her hand back with a Peninsula, an Island, or a Seaport. But it's so big and powerful in human beings that she just rolls along, and three hundred and ninety-five million don't know if the old Dowager Empress is still running it, or Coolidge.[9]

A Crisis is just another meal to China. She can lay right down and go to sleep by the side of a Crisis. And don't waste too much pity on Poor Old China; she will be here when some strange Race of People will be excavating some of our Skyscrapers and wondering what Tombs they were. There is none of us that don't feel that China will be here five thousand years from now, and none of us are sure that other Nations will be here through the life of two more flivvers.

So long, Senator. Drop you line on next Boat, maybe, about Philippines.

Yours,

WILL.

A Letter to the Philippines

DEAR SENATOR: Just want to drop you a line before I get away to Shanghai. Say, I kinder stepped out last night; wish you could have been with me. Was you ever the Guest of an Emperor in his own Home? I mean a real live Emperor, with him in the House, not one of those things where there is a Guide showing you around telling you where the Emperor did live. I had been in a lot of them out here in China and Japan, but it was three or four hundred years after the Emperor had done any real Empering.

But this fellow was right there, as we say in the Classics, "in person." You see, an Emperor is bigger than a President; he is what a President would be if he dident have any Congress and Senate to see that he does nothing. This fellow can Behead people. Now, a President can't do that, as much as he would like too. Say, if Herbert could do a little Beheading —Eh, what?

Come to think of it, Senator, that old shaggy Bean of yours wouldent be any to permanently located, would it? But an Emperor in China, he is just about the last word in Empering.

Nearest you ever come, Senator, to being in one's House was, maybe, in the early days, when you come to the Senate, you was called in Emperor Boies Penrose's House to get your Instructions, but when he passed out our Emperor business kinder went in the Rough.[1]

This was at the House of the Emperor of Manchuria and all North China. Of course, Japan has just foreclosed on Manchuria, and it was kinder in the nature of eating with a Lame Duck Congressmen. He is the Young Marshall, Chang Hsueh-liang, son of the old he-horse War Lord, Chang Tso-lin. This young fellow is very Up-To-Date and has put more progressive things into Manchuria than all the others proceeding him put together, or anywhere else in China. 'Course he hasent got the fighting spirit of his Old Man, but he is a very Up-to-Date, Pleasant Chap. I don't know his age; seems in the early thirties. But you can look that up there in the Congressional Record somewhere; there must be some Information somewhere in those things. 'Course, the Japanese never did like him and have been after his Scalp all the time.

His old Dad kinder played ball with 'em, but this young fellow, he

---

Saturday Evening Post, April 30, 1932. Reprinted with permission.

161

kinder thought China owned Manchuria. Well, that was contrary to the Data Japan had on it.

You see, Senator, this whole Manchuria is just a case of mistaken Identity. China thought, because they were Chinese, they owned it; Japan knew, because she had One Billion Dollars in there, she owned it. You see, when an outside Nation commences to pile Money into your Country, right then you better start getting some Deeds ready to sign. They don't come in there for nothing—Us, or England, or any of 'em. Investments is just two jumps ahead of Control. So, if you want your Country opened up and modernized, why, that's fine; but nobody is going to do it for nothing. They next come in to protect their Investments, then send in to protect the ones originally sent in to protect their Investments, and before you know it, the Country is under their Protection, and you, the Original Owner, are the only ones that have no Protection.

But if it's not of the Rights or Wrongs of Manchuria I am penning you these lines; it's about my visit with a 100 per cent Emperor, wonderful Host, speaks fairly good English and understands more. He has around him a bunch of young fellows. Most of 'em were educated at Home or in England; Tommy Lee, a little Frisco Chinese I remember in particular, is very keen; he had a great sense of humor and was full of Fun and Amusement.[2] The Emperor has an English adviser, and they told me of another one—Donald, a Scotchman, that was down in Nanking at the time.[3]

The House was not so elaborate. If we had been putting on an Emperor's Set in Hollywood, we would have walked right by this one without Photographing it. 'Course, there was an awful lot of Buildings and Temples there that we wasent in, but after having looked at the old Dowager Empresses and the Forbidden City all the afternoon, why, naturally, this did look a little Coolidge to me. We talked about Manchuria. I having just come from there, he was anxious to know how the old Home looked. Mukden was his old Home Range; you could see his Heart and Soul were there. Talking about Manchuria was just like talking to an old-time Ex-Senator about Washington; he likes to have you tell him that it's not like it was in the Good Old Days when he was there.

When I told him Mukden was a pretty Sorry-Looking Place, he dident have any harsh words for the Japanese; he gave 'em a lot of Credit for their Patriotism, Organization and Military Machine. He was very generous; he seemed to think that Japan would have a hard time running the Country. Well, he ought to know. He is very dapper, slight, well-dressed, small Hands and Feet—kinder the Jimmy Walker Type.

He brought in some Robes—Mandarin Robes, they called 'em—beautiful things. He asked me to pick one out—all beautiful, fur-lined

Kimona-Effect things. Had me try one on. I said, "Ha! This is not for me, is it? This is a woman's Gown." They assured me it was 90 per cent Male. I said, "Now, won't I look cute prancing in Beverly Hills with this thing flowing and me hollering, 'Whoops, Boys, Mother Rogers is back from China'?" I asked little Tommy Lee which was the best one, and he nodded at one. He had his eye on the same one I did. It was lined with Mink—not Dog Mink but Mink. The Young Marshall said, "That's too small for you." I said, "Yes, for me, but not for Mrs. Rogers." So I Glommed the best one, and Tommy grinned like a Possum, and I grinned more.

But never mind all this Hooey. Let's get down to the Eats. Senator, coming from Idaho and just going nowhere but Washington, there ain't any way you could possibly have ever seen this much Food. Lot of Folks have had Chinese Dinners, but if you havent crossed Chopsticks with a real Emperor you havent seen any Chinese Meal. Any of these others have just been Appetizers. There was only about seven or eight men in the Party—the Young Marshall's immediate friends. This Orgy of Bamboo Shoots starts about 9:30 P.M. At 1:30 in the A.M., when we shoved away from the Table, there is at least ten Chinese bringing in arms loaded with more unnamable Provender. I don't believe even the Host knew what half of it was. I have saved a Menu Card that was in front of me. I am going to have it translated some day and see what all we had. You dident order; they just brought it and put about a dozen different Dishes at a time in the middle of the round Table, and then we all just reached over with our Chopsticks and put it in our own Plate. They don't sit on the Floor like the Japanese. In lots of ways these fellows are better educated; they got Couches and Cushions—of course, that constitutes Modern Civilization.

I wouldent ask what all these Dishes were, for I wanted to enjoy 'em, but I do know that we had Bird's-Nest Soup. It's the Delicacy; it's the Caviar of China. Well, all the time I was eating it I was just hoping that the old Blue Jay that had occupied the Nest was part sanitary anyhow. Then they had Shark's-Fins Soup. Now, you wouldent think any part of an old Shark would be a Delicacy, would you? Well, he is, and he is not bad at all in the Soup. The Soup Course alone run about an hour and a half. Now, that's an awful lot of Soup, and some of it was awful Soup, but whether you eat it or dident eat it, you got another Brand in a minute anyhow.

Then along in the middle of the Dinner they had Lunch. He explained to me that a real Chinese Dinner was the whole three Meals in one—that is, Breakfast, Lunch and Dinner. Now, in the middle of the Meal there was sweets. He said, "We are in the Lunch now." And they did have some of the most novel sweet things—candied Fruits on sticks, and Lord

163

knows what all. Then other things kept coming, till finally, around about 11:30 or 12:00 o'clock, why Dinner started to be served—that is, I mean we settled down to steady eating. Up to now we had just been practically fooling. This barrel of Soup and kegs of Rice and dozens of different kinds of Meats we had eaten was just supposed to whet our Appetite. And the Waiters settled down to steady packing. Then come Peking Duck—and this was in Peking, and this was Duck. Now, there is a way to fix Duck that almost makes it eatable. Being no Hunter, I am not a Duck Man myself, but this was delicious; it was glazed over with something.

When we all give out about 1:30, he told me that this was generally followed by a Supper, but that, this being my first Offense, he wouldent ask that I partake of that. Then he admitted that the "Chinese eat too much, take too little Exercise, and take things too Easy."

Well, maybe some of 'em do, but I had seen some Chinese that dident eat too much. It wasent chronic with the Race to do it, and I had seen some doing quite a bit of Exercising—oh, maybe just light Exercise, like carrying a Piano on their back, or six or eight bushels of Coal, or pulling a load that a small automobile couldent move. But the "take things too Easy"—I dident get exactly what he meant by that. But they say they will if you don't watch 'em. I know, every reader will say, "Oh, the crime of such a Meal as that in a Country where millions are starving." And you are right; it was a Crime; and it's the first thing you think of in China. But it's funny we don't think of it at Home. We don't have any Meals like that, but we have some big ones that the Folks sitting down to 'em couldent eat in a Week. We have some mighty big Spreads, oodles left over, and we got hungry Folks, too; but we don't think of 'em till we read about how some rich man in China or somewhere is wasting the food. So I guess the Young Marshall wasent much more to blame than hundreds of us at Home.

So, you see, Senator, there just ain't anything that you can find in one Country that you don't find is being done just about as bad in our own; where we might have the edge on 'em in one thing, you find they excel us in others. So it's about an Even Break. Well, I must stop; got to grab that Train. He was to send me down in his Plane—a big three-motored one, with an American Pilot named Hutton that I had ridden with at Home—but it's bad Weather and it can't get up from Nanking, the Capital.[4] Snowstorm here today 'bout six inches deep. All these Chinese War Lords got Planes, and their Motors is spinning all the time; they are ready to move, and now.

So long. Take care of yourself.

Yours,   WILL.

SHANGHAI.

D EAR SENATOR: Got in here from Peking; was two days and nights on the Train. We come by Nanking, the present Capital. Their Government had just blowed up, so it was a pretty Sorry-Looking Place. This Railroad we come down on is the one you used to read about the Students laying on the track to stop the Train going; then they would make it haul 'em to the Capital to denounce the Leaders that wasent going far enough in keeping the Japanese out. Well, it was snowing most of the way down, and there was no Sophmores or Freshmen spread out before us. They must have been holding a Pep Rally in their Fraternity House. You know, come to think of it, I have seen old Engineers over home running Trains that I would hate to take a chance laying down on a Track in front of 'em; in fact, seeing College Boys would be more apt to just whet his appetite for more Speed. These Chinese Trains run so Unoften that why the Students dident starve to death before the thing got there will always be a Mystery to travelers.

Doctor Hutchinson, of Peking, was in the next compartment to me; he is an Old-Timer out here, and mighty well and favorably known.[5] He had been Adviser to several Chinese Governments. He made the trip mighty pleasant and instructive. As we get down toward Nanking and Shanghai, we run into the Rice Fields; up north in China they eat Millet, a kind of Grain sorter like Wheat. I remember we used to raise it in the old Indian Territory. By the way, Senator, there was a great Country when I was a boy, growing up, and before we went under the Mandate of the United States. A Territory always had it on a State, but the Politicians must get Statehood and get 'em some Jobs. . . .

As we got into the Rice Fields we saw the Water Buffalo. That's a fine old domestic animal that they do all their work with in Rice Fields, or any place where there is lots of Water. They keep 'em almost in their Houses, they are tied right at the Door. And the cutest thing—in the evenings when the Buffaloes' work is done they send 'em out along the Irrigation Ditches to eat grass. They can't turn 'em loose or they will get in the fields, so they put a little Boy or Girl upon their big, old, broad Backs, and they have a kind of pair of Reins fastened in the old Buffalo's nose, so they can guide him and keep him out of the Rice.

You will see dozens of these Children doing this—some of them are laying up there Asleep—and the old Water Buffalo just grazes along. Then, as it begins to get late and the sun is going down, they ride 'em to their various Houses. You don't see many Ponies in Southern or Central China like you do in Manchuria; the old Water Buffalo is about their only means of plowing.

The whole Country, as you near Shanghai, is flat; it's the Delta of the Yang-tse River. It's all dug up with Canals—some of the oldest in the

World. Did you know that there is still part of this upper Valley under water? And the Poverty and Hardships is terrific. No Charity could be more Humane. But, of course, all these things happen at a time when the need at Home is very great, our own are going through a tough time. But if anyone can afford to help both Causes, this one is very deserving. Charity is the only way to help all these different kinds of people. Anyhow, if you are going to do anything at all for 'em, feed 'em, even if they don't become Christians. Got to tell you about this Shanghai, but I will do that later; I am too busy looking.

Hope everything is going along fine with you there. Still can't get much News from Home. Don't know if Congress met or decided to give the people a rest and chance to recuperate from their last Effort.

Yours,

WILL.

SHANGHAI.

D *EAR SENATOR:* Well, there was a good one on me, Senator. All my life, or ever since I been prowling around, I had heard of the Shanghai Bar. It's supposed to be the very longest Bar in the World. I am not just around the World looking for Long Bars, but as it was one of the Seven Wonders of the World, it naturally wouldent be a hard thing to look at. There is an awful lot of our wonderful scenic sights that incur some Hardships to reach, and no particular gratification of the Inner Man while looking at them. Niagara Falls is wonderful, but I never craved a drink from it; the Carlsbad Caverns at Carlsbad, New Mexico, is a World's Wonder, but even it don't excite your thirst; you are too busy being dazed. My visit to this Shanghai Bar—the Far East's sole contribution to the World's Wonders—happened at what I thought was the most opportune time—it was on Xmas Day. I had been in my room at the Cathay Hotel—and, by the way, this is just about the last word in hotels; it was built by Sir Victor Sassoon, who lives there and has tremendous holdings in Shanghai and India and the whole Far East.[6] He is a very charming man, and well versed in all Far East matters....Well, Mr. Abend, The New York Times Far East main Representative, whom I had met in Manchuria, was home from there for Xmas....[7] And here is a funny one: The Japanese had told him that when they started to take Chinchow, they would let him know. So, sure enough, later he got the Wire to come on; that they had found a Reason for taking it.

Well, Abend and his Assistant called me up Xmas Afternoon.[8] I had just got in the evening before. They wanted to know where I wanted to go or what I wanted to do. Well, I had been in my room writing all day, and I was ready for anything. It was Xmas, the first one I had ever spent

166

away from my Family since committing the Overt Act, and maybe you think I wasent Lonesome. I just thought, "What a Yap! Over here trooping around trying to get something to write about, when everything Funny in the World that is happening is happening right there at Home." But when Abend come over—and say, there is a fellow that knows the East too; he is an Authority on it. And has the confidence of all sides— when he asked me what I wanted to do, I naturally said, "Well, I want to see this sight of the Far East, the Shanghai Bar."

So the three of us piled into a Cab, and off we went to gratify an Ambition that I had had ever since I had first heard of it. I just thought, "What a day to do it. Here it is six o'clock on Xmas Day." I knew the place would be crowded with people from all over the World that were away from Home like me. I am not a Bar Connoisseur, but, naturally, in my Rambles I had seen that, for Length, you could stand in a row about as many friends as you would wish to pay for. Tia Juana, Mexico, has one that, if it was a hundred yards longer, would reach San Diego, California. Some of New York's Speak-easies are only limited by the length of the Block. But this was to be the World's Longest. Time and again I had pictured in my mind the crowd that would frequent such a place. Being in the noted Shanghai, I naturally thought that this place must have been the origin of the Shanghai-ing of Sailors. I could just visualize the Swinging Doors, the Sailors from every Port in the World, the Marines of the U. S., English Tommys, Italian Marines, White Russians, Red Russians, Blue Russians.

Oh, I was just looking forward to this conglomeration of humanity from the four corners of the World. I just pictured the setting, wondered at the amount of Languages that I would hear. I just thought, "What a Story I will get out of this—the World's-Famous Shanghai Bar." Feeling in a Xmas mood, I had secretly planned to ask the House to have a Xmas Cheer on me. Now, you that know me know that I must have been in some kind of odd Mood to ever offer to spread myself like that. I had even cashed a Check at the Desk before leaving the Hotel, for fear the Bar would even be longer than I had anticipated. I sure was reckless.

Well, we got out of the Car in front of what looked to me like a Bank Building or a City Hall. We went up a long row of steps, into a very imposing Entrance Hall. A uniformed Attendant come and took our hats and coats. Great marble pillows looked like snubbing posts in a Corrall. We then went to a great Book, or Register. He asked me various Questions about my Ancestry, my Fraternities, if any. He finally wrote down "Democrat." From the Answers, I kinder got to doubting if I would get in. Now, all the time I can't figure the whole thing out. I dident ask Abend anything; I just says, "Well, maybe this is not the place; maybe this is some place that he belongs to that we just come by on our way to the

Shanghai Bar." Then we are escorted to the Wash Room. Well, I couldnt see any particular reason why it would be necessary that one should be compelled to cleanse oneself before imbibing at this Bar. A Chinese Attendant in the Wash Room had a Racket of guessing "exactly" your Weight. Abend was high in his recommendation of this Celestial Guesser of Beef on the Hoof. Well, he missed me just twenty pounds; had he been a Jap he would have committed Hari Carey, he would have felt so chagrined. This bird couldent figure it out; finally laid it, I think, to my lead feet and fat head.

I still don't know what all this has to do with my Shanghai Bar. I am getting anxious to see the Crowds, to hear that mixed Jargon. Flashing through my mind was the other World's Wonders that I had seen—the Yellowstone, Grand Canyon, Virginia's Natural Bridge, Al Smith's Derby. And here it is, six o'clock on Xmas Day. Can't you just feel yourself anxious to see it, because you have it all visualized?

Well, we finally enter; it was a tremendous Room, and there is the Bar. It had not been exaggerated; Bobby Jones could have just made it in two.[9] It looked like about a half-mile Straight-away. Here was the World's Famous Shanghai Bar. About a niblick shot apart scattered along it, was a Bartender, and standing right exactly in the center on the Purchaser's side was one lone Figure, an Englishman. Well, here stood this lone Englishman, on Christmas Day the very sole Occupant of the famous Shanghai Bar. He had Spats, a Cane, was perhaps sixty, had Sideburns, and, of course, a glass of Whisky-and-Soda. Here went my Illusion of drunken Sailors from every Port, masses of Humanity scrambling for great, foaming Beers; for here stood this lone Figure; he just looked like he was saying, "Prohibition, you shall not pass." Oh, I wish I had been an Artist and painted that picture, it looked just like a One-Man Parade going up the center of Pennsylvania Avenue.

When I saw that there was only one Inmate present, I felt more than ever that I would buy the House a drink. I left Abend and his friend, and ambled over to him and said, in what I thought wasent bad English, "Pardon me, sir, but this being Xmas and my being far from Home, and a spirit of good will within me, would you be kind enough to join myself and my two friends in an Eggnog to the Yuletide?"

He turned on me like I had bit him, and said: "I beg pardon. I don't think we have ever been introduced, sir. Good day." Well, it wasent a "good day" for me. The World-Renowned Shanghai Bar had been a complete Flop; the only fellow that felt worse than I did was, I imagine, the Chinaman that missed me twenty pounds. I had missed my illusions further than that. I don't even remember now if I even had my Eggnog. If I did, I dident enjoy it. I dident know the thing was a Club, I thought it was a Swinging-Door Joint that took in all comers. They told me that around Lunch Time it was pretty crowded. But they never got me near the place again. I can see that lone Englishman standing there now— "Liberty's Last Stand." So, you see, Senator, you can get fooled with your Foreign Relations.

Good night.   WILL.

D EAR SENATOR: Say, Senator, here is a letter I am writing to you, but it's really for the Philippine Islands, so you send it over and see that they get it. Send it to that fellow Quezon, but it's pretty much to all of 'em.[10] You know, Senator, the greatest disappointment I ever had was missing out on my trip to their Country. I was on the Boat headed for Manila when I learned that the Boat that I was to leave from there to go on down to Singapore was late and I would not be able to make my Plane out of the Straits Settlements. The Philippines was the place I was all primed to go too. Pat Hurley had given me a lot of dope on his trip out there, and I sure did want to see 'em and do a little Flying.[11] It was to be my main Piece of Resistance, as they say in Chevalier's Language. So you send 'em this:

Dear Philippines: I sure did want to come over and see you Folks. Now I have to wait till I come out again. I wanted to come over and work with you on your Liberty. You remember, you had a U. S. Senator out there—Mr. Hawes, of Missouri—he come out and give you your Liberty.[12] Then you found out he was the wrong man and dident have the Authority to give it to you. Well, that would have been different with me; if I had given you your Liberty, you could have Depended on it. This fellow was evidently an Imposter—not only an Imposter but a U. S. Senator, which is worse.

Now, you Filipinos know a Senator can't set anybody Free, even the whole ninety-six of 'em can't set anything Free. Then, my old friend, Pat Hurley, was out to see you. He liked you so well, he wants to adopt you permanently. Pat is crazy about you all. 'Course, Pat come out away last Summer, at a time when he wanted to leave Home anyhow, for fear somebody would accuse him of being one of Mr. Hoover's Advisers. You couldent get much out of Pat; he would kinder set you free in the Morning Speeches, and then bring you back in under Old Glory at night. Pat wants to hang on to you fellows because it gives him more to point to on a Map, when he is showing what he rules over. Then, there is no Secretary of War that wants the credit, or blame, of giving you Folks up. They don't want history to say, "Philippine Islands taken under Secre-

169

tary—can't even remember his name now—and given up under Patrick
J. Hurley." That's no way for a Hurley to act—to give up some Country.

But Pat likes you Folks, and if he don't treat you right, let me know.
Pat is in the Cabinet and has to be kinder careful. You know what the
Cabinet is, don't you, Filipinos? It's a band of about nine men that go to
the White House every Tuesday to see if the President has lived through
the past week. If he had Passed Out, they, being in the Cabinet, would be
the last to hear it. News travels slow in the Cabinet. They take up
Subjects—that is, they take 'em up to the White House, then take 'em
back Home with 'em again, then bring 'em back again with 'em the next
Tuesday. Some of 'em have Subjects that they have just wore out bringing 'em back and forth to Cabinet Meetings. 'Course, some of the more
hardy Subjects have stood it pretty well—for instance, the Subject of
Prohibition—why, it can walk up to the White House alone, it's been
there and back so much.

Then, at those Meetings is where they take care of Crisises. You know,
when we sometimes read about a Crisis and afterward wonder whatever
become of it. Well, that's what become of it; they took it up. "What do
they do with it?" Dident I just tell you they took it up; before they get
through discussing it, why, the Crisis is over. It takes a good Crisis to last
a Cabinet Discussion.

But here, I got to get back to you Filipinos. I hear you got a Congress
and Senate and Cabinet, and all, just like we have. Pretty near every
Country that is Suffering from Depression has these.

Now, about you Filipinos and your Freedom? Do you really want your
Freedom, or do you just want to Holler? Personally, I believe a Country
can get more real joy out of just Hollering for their Freedom than they
can if they get it. You have always got Sympathetic Listeners if you are
hollering for Liberty, but when you get it and then start Hollering that
you would like to be able to turn it loose, why, you can't get as big an
Audience. You Folks over there want to realize you lose an awful lot of
Alibi's when you get your Liberty, and no one to lay the Blame on but
yourself. I know I have sat in the Galleries of our Congressional Halls
and heard our learned Lawmakers Hollering for different things that
they hoped they would never get, for if they did, it would cramp their
Style.

But if you Folks out there in the Islands really want your Liberty, there
is really no better way to Get Even with you than to give it to you. There
is nothing that will cure a Nation as quick of wanting Liberty as to give it
to 'em. But if you can run your Country and do a good Job of it, why, I am
sure in favor of giving you your Liberty. Then we can copy your Style
and maybe do a better Job of running ours.

I understand you Folks sent a Commission over Home to go before

Congress and state your Case. Now, Congress is not a very fit bunch to send a Commission before to judge if you are to govern yourself. What you should have done with your Commission is to have them visit a lot of so-called Republics and just see how some of them are run; then debated among yourselves: "Boys, is this what we want?" If you look at a few of 'em, like I have, it will pretty near cure you from Hollering for Liberty.

Now, for instance, here I am in China, a Republic. Here's Democracy with a Pigtail. Yet China is so big that nine-tenths of her people never find out that all these wonderful Benefits that they are enjoying are Liberty.

Now, here is one that we want you Folks over in the Philippines to realize. We had a war to get you, but we sure are not going to have one to keep you. Not that we think any the less of you, but our Point of View has changed. In those days we thought it would be wonderful to have Islands away off somewhere. We had read about England doing it, so leave it to us to Ape the English. Sometimes we wonder what our so-called Society would do if they dident have the English to Copy. But the English had had so many Islands all over the World that they had had Experience, and we dident. England was raised on one, while we had never seen one in our lives.

Now, here is another thing: There is always a lot of talk about if "We get out of the Philippines, why, some other Nation will step in at once." Well, there is a little conceit mixed with that Statement. I doubt if anybody would take you Folks over. First they would ask to look at our Balance Sheet and see if we had made any Money out of you. I don't know how we stand with you Folks financially, but I imagine we are in the Red. If we don't make any Money out of you, I believe I can go back to Washington and assist you in getting your Liberty. Now, you got a big Sugar Crop. If you will let that fail—it may do it of its own accord—but let that fail for about two or three Years in a row. I think that will get you a sympathetic Ear from Congress quicker than a Philippine Delegation or even a Revolution. And if you can guarantee four years of Sugar Failure, why, I can absolutely guarantee you that we will not only give you your Freedom, but we will become absolutely disgusted with you.

'Course, anyone that knows anything about the Philippine Situation knows that we got two angles to it: We got a bunch over home that is "Agin" your Sugar; they raise Sugar themselves. So give you two or three years of Heavy Sugar and you might get your Liberty quicker than if you dident raise any. We got over home what we call the Sugar Beet Non-Expansionists; they don't believe in Colonial Possessions. 'Course, they wouldent mind a few Islands up north where it's too cold to raise Sugar Cane, but they are "Agin" Tropical Expansion. So the Philippines are in the World's most peculiar Predicament. "To raise Cain, or not to raise Cain?" That is the Question. "Whether it's better to raise Cain and please Uncle Sam, or not to raise Cain and please Reed Smoot?"[13]

I know that your Delegation that goes over Home will receive every consideration outside of Liberty. It will be a great Trip. Our Folks will show 'em a great time, give 'em everything but what they come after. The Delegation will get a lot of Laughs, but no Freedom, out of the Junket. Mr. Hoover will put 'em on a Commission to Investigate the Philippines.

I wanted to get to see those Head Hunters you all have in your Country; we have 'em over Home, but we call 'em Income Tax Collectors.

And I did want to meet Aguinaldo.[14] I have always been an admirer of that old Hombre. We used to call him a Bandit. Any man is a Bandit if he is fighting opposite you and licking you most of the time; but if you are fighting against him, why, that's Patriotism. The difference between a Bandit and a Patriot is a good Press Agent. If Aguinaldo was a Bandit, I wanted to meet him and tell him about our Bandits; make him jealous that he lived thirty-odd years to soon.

Every Administration since Lincoln has promised you Folks your Liberty, "when you were Ready for it," and you naturally took that Promise serious, well, that will teach you a Lesson the next time. Another thing against you Folks getting your Liberty is the other Nations are against it. If America got out of the Philippines, why, every Native in the Far East would raise a Holler to have England get out of China, out of India, out of the Malay Straits; France out of Indo-China; Japan out of Manchuria and Korea; the Dutch out of Java. In other words, it would be an example in "Freedom for Determination of all Nations" that would shock the World. It's the opportunity of a Lifetime to be in this position where we could, perhaps, start this, but don't think for a minute we will do it. It's too big and good to be true. It would make a Sucker out of the other Nations, and, of course, we couldent Dare Do That.

We will drag along with you Folks on the Pretext that we are protecting you, and some day we will get in a War over you, and if we ever do, we will lose you before Lunch. Japan can be in there and have a Crop planted before we could get a Fleet across that Ocean. Any Nation that thinks they can go six thousand miles away from Home and fight somebody is Crazy. Lot of folks over Home think there is a Filling Station in the middle of the Ocean like there is on every vacant lot over Home. We got no more business in the Far East than we have in the Far South or the Far North. That Country is run by two Yellow Races, the Chinese and the Japanese. We dont understand either one of 'em. They know more about each other than we know about them.

The Japs are not going to take China, whether we send 'em Notes or not. Nobody is going to take China. China, even if they never shot a Gun for the rest of their Lives, is the most powerful Country in the world. You could move the whole of Japan's seventy millions into the very heart of China, and in seventy years there wouldent be seventy Japanese left. China is the only Country in the World that needs no Protection; its principal Enemies are the so-called Educated ones that come home and try to change it. Now, as far as our Trade is concerned, you can't, by being in a Country, force 'em to buy your Goods. Japan has found that out, to her Misery, right here in China. All this Open-Door stuff is a lot of Hooey. Any Door is only open to those that have the best product at the cheapest money. A manufacturer can sit in his Office in America, and if his car is cheaper and better suited to China than any other car, Chinese Dealers will come clear there to buy 'em, for they are the best Merchants in the world. Now, all Nations are finding out that there never will be the amount of Exports and Imports that there used to be. It's the same the World over; every Nation is trying to live more and more within itself; each Nation is going in the Hole and pulling the Hole in after it. But, seriously, I hope you Folks get your Liberty. It would be mighty gratifying to every American to say, "We don't hold under any kind of subjection any Country. What about the rest of you Birds?"

But we will Stall you off and say you are not ready for it. If your Freedom was left to a Vote of the whole American people you would get it two to one. But anything important is never left to the Vote of the people. We only get to Vote on some man; we never get to Vote on what he is to do. You see, that's what I was telling you about Liberty a while ago. There is things about it that is not just exactly 100 per cent Kosher. A Delegation of Senators and Congressmen will be the ones to decide just how far advanced you are in Intelligence and how many years away from Freedom, it won't be the people that will do that. So until the American People get some Freedom, why, you Folks can't get any. So, no telling when either one of us will be Free.

Buenos dias, Phillipinos. Señors y Señoras y Politicos y Pendayos Tambien. Algunos Phillipinos gusto Freedom. (Como se yama Freedom in Castillian?) Yo habla Castillian Puro. Poco ustades no savvy me Castillian; Castillian is para Intelehensia, con franco muy alto. Ahora yo vamoos para Estados Unidos muy pronto; no tiene muchos mas Plata. Yo habla con Señor Hoover, el Patron, el gran Henerial. Yo dece Señor Hoover, "Señor Hoover, el Phillipinos cara para poco mas Libertad?" Dece Patron Hoover, "Cara para poco mas Libertad? Phillipinos tiene muchos mas Libertad y el Americanos ahora. Phillipinos tiene Vino Blanco, y Colorado, Aguardiente, Cervesa mucho frio. El Phillipinos Hombres muy loco; no savvy quando muy bien." Yo diece, "Señor Hoover, una Hombre nombre Hawes give—como se yama "give"— Hawes give Phillipinos Libertad." Señor Hoover diece, "Senator nombre

Ha-Ha's?" "No, no, Señor Presidente, no nombre Ha-Ha's, nombre una Ha's solo." Señor Presidente diece, "Yo no savvy Hombre nombre Ha's. Yo savvy Señor Patrico Hurleyico. Patrico Hurleyico trabahar para me. No trabahar mucho; no Hombre trabahar mucho para el Presidente. Cara para Plata, no cara para Trabahar. Yo no want presente Señor y Señoras Head Hunters con Libertad. No, no Phillipinos tiene mucho Asucar; me Presidente gusto mucho Asucar en me Cafe. Yo Bebe Cafe con Asucar. Todos Americanos gusto Asucar para poco Plata. Phillipinos Libertad? No, no Señor Giermo Rodrigues—Will Rogers—no Libertad ahora para Philippinos." Pero me Amigos Phillipinos, in el mes Novembre, Señor Patron Hoover finis. Una otro Hombre dormier in el gran Casa Blanco, en al Capital de Estados Unidos. El nueva Presidente uno—como se dece "Democrat" in Espanol.

Adios Amigos Phillipinos.

Yours,

GIERMO RODRIGUES—
WILL ROGERS.

NOTES

A LETTER FROM A SELF-MADE DIPLOMAT TO HIS CONSTITUENTS
(January 8, 1927)

[1]Calvin Coolidge, president of the United States from 1923 to 1929; vice president of the United States from 1921 to 1923. Known popularly as "Silent Cal," Coolidge was a Republican, a native of Vermont, and a former governor of Massachusetts.

[2]Rogers' observations on Europe, which he recorded during an extended visit to that continent in the summer of 1926, may be found in his *Letters of a Self-Made Diplomat to His President*. Almost immediately after his return, he embarked upon one of his famous, so-called "lecture" tours of the United States. His itinerary can be followed generally in *Will Rogers' Daily Telegrams: The Coolidge Years, 1926-1929*.

[3]Betty Blake Rogers, wife of Will Rogers. The couple was married at the Blake family home in Rogers, Arkansas, on November 25, 1908.

[4]Everett Sanders, Republican United States senator from Indiana from 1917 to 1925; secretary to Calvin Coolidge from 1925 to 1929.

[5]Grace Anna Goodhue Coolidge, wife of Calvin Coolidge. An educator and a graduate of Smith College, Mrs. Coolidge enjoyed wide popularity as first lady.

[6]*Mayflower*, name of the presidential yacht that the Coolidges regularly used for cruises down the Potomac.

[7]Irwin Hood "Ike" Hoover, chief usher at the White House during six presidential administrations; a member of the White House staff from 1891 until his death in 1933.

Herbert Clark Hoover, United States secretary of commerce from 1921 to 1928; Republican president of the United States from 1929 to 1933. As Food Administrator during World War I, Hoover was responsible for controlling the production and consumption of food.

[8]William Harrison "Will" Hays, president of the Motion Picture Producers and Distributors of America from 1922 to 1945. A prominent Republican from Indiana, Hays served as postmaster general from 1921 to 1922.

[9]Warren Gamaliel Harding, Republican president of the United States from 1921 until his death in 1923. Harding's Airedale, Laddie Boy, was one of the most famous dogs ever to inhabit the White House.

[10]Marie, queen consort of Rumania. Queen Marie, accompanied by a large retinue, conducted a highly-publicized tour of the United States in the fall of 1926.

[11]George Brinton McClellan Harvey, American editor, publisher, and diplomat; ambassador to Great Britain from 1921 to 1923.

[12]Charles Evans Hughes, United States secretary of state from 1921 to 1925; earlier, Republican governor of New York and associate justice of the United States Supreme Court; later, chief justice of the Supreme Court from 1930 to 1941. Rogers and Hughes returned together from abroad in the fall of 1926 aboard the S. S. *Leviathan*.

[13]Antoinette Carter Hughes, wife of Charles Evans Hughes.

[14]During his return trip from Europe aboard the *Leviathan*, Rogers staged a benefit show for victims of a devastating hurricane that struck Florida in September of 1926. Hughes and other fellow passengers also lent their talents to the charity show.

[15]Alfred Emanuel "Al" Smith, Democratic governor of New York from 1919 to 1921 and 1923 to 1929. Smith, an Irish Catholic and anti-prohibitionist, ran unsuccessfully for president in 1928 on the Democratic ticket.

[16]Emily Price Post, American author and syndicated newspaper columnist who became famous as an arbiter of good manners; author of the bestseller *Etiquette* (1922).

[17]The City of Philadelphia held a massive Sesqui-Centennial Celebration in 1926 in commemoration of the 150th anniversary of the Declaration of Independence.

[18]Charles Sherman "Casey" Jones, aeronautical pioneer and veteran of the French flying service in World War I; test pilot and executive with the Curtiss Aviation Corporation.

James Joseph "Gene" Tunney, American pugilist who won the world heavyweight boxing championship in September of 1926 in a match against William Harrison "Jack" Dempsey. Tunney held the title until his voluntary retirement in 1928.

[19]Carmi Alderman Thompson, Ohio politician, businessman, and attorney who was sent by Coolidge in 1926 as a special commissioner to survey internal and economic conditions in the American-owned Philippine Islands.

[20]The Preliminary Disarmament Conference, which convened in Geneva, Switzerland, in the summer of 1926, was sponsored by the League of Nations. The meeting ended with the United States, Great Britain, and other conferring nations failing to compromise on significant differences.

[21]The World Court, or the Permanent Court of International Justice, was established to supplement the machinery of the League of Nations. The United States never joined the world judicial body.

[22]Vladimir Ilyich Lenin, Russian revolutionary leader, founder of Bolshevism, and the major force behind the Soviet Revolution of 1917; virtual dictator of Russia from 1917 until his death in 1924.

Leon Trotsky, Russian Communist leader who participated in the abortive Bolshevik uprising in 1905 and in the successful revolution in 1917. Trotsky was expelled from the Communist party in 1927 and banished from Russia two years later. He was murdered in Mexico in 1940.

[23]James Putnam Goodrich, American attorney, businessman, politician, and special presidential commissioner to Russia; Republican governor of Indiana from 1917 to 1921.

[24]Nancy Witcher Langhorne Astor, one of the beautiful Langhorne sisters of Virginia; wife of Lord Waldorf Astor of Great Britain; the first woman to sit in the House of Commons, serving from 1919 to 1945.

[25]Rogers was slightly more than one-quarter Cherokee Indian.

[26]Coolidge claimed some Indian blood through his maternal ancestors.

[27]Brigham Young, American religious leader who headed the Mormon Church from 1847 until his death in 1877. A polygamist, he was survived by seventeen wives and countless children and grandchildren.

[28]Theodore Roosevelt, president of the United States from 1901 to 1909; highly popular progressive Republican.

[29]Aimee Semple McPherson, phenomenally successful California evangelist who preached a Pentecostal, fundamentalist, faith-healing doctrine; founder of the International Church of the Foursquare Gospel, based in Los Angeles.

[30]Alice Lee Roosevelt Longworth, daughter of President Theodore Roosevelt, wife of Speaker of the House Nicholas Longworth, and famous Washington hostess.

Evalyn Walsh McLean, mining heiress and Washington society hostess; wife of publisher Edward Beale "Ned" McLean. The young McLean's estate, Friendship, provided the setting for some of the more glamorous social events in the nation's capital.

[31]James John Davis, United States secretary of labor from 1921 to 1930.

[32]William Morgan Butler, Republican United States senator from Massachusetts from 1924 to 1926; confidant of and political adviser to Coolidge.

[33]Theodore Elijah Burton, Republican United States representative from Ohio from 1889 to 1891, 1895 to 1909, and 1921 to 1928; United States senator from 1909 to 1915 and 1928 until his death in 1929.

MORE LETTERS FROM A SELF-MADE DIPLOMAT TO HIS PRESIDENT (May 12, 1928)

[1]Benito Mussolini, founder and leader of the Italian Fascist movement and dictator of Italy from 1922 to 1943.

[2]Andrew William Mellon, United States secretary of the treasury from 1921 to 1932; Pittsburgh financier with interests in coal production, aluminum manufacturing, and banking.

[3]The Washington Conference of 1921-1922 resulted in several treaties between major world powers to limit naval armaments and to recognize territorial rights.

[4]Hugh Simons Gibson, career American diplomat; ambassador to Belgium from 1927 to 1933 and 1937 to 1938; chief delegate of the United States to the Preliminary Disarmament Conference at Geneva.

Hilary Pollard Jones, rear admiral in the United States Navy; commander in chief of the Atlantic fleet from 1922 to 1923; naval delegate of the United States to the Preliminary Disarmament Conference.

[5]The United States launched a much-publicized but unsuccessful punitive expedition against revolutionary bandits in Mexico in 1916-1917.

[6]Dwight Whitney Morrow, American lawyer, banker, diplomat, and Republican political figure; United States ambassador to Mexico from 1927 to 1930; United States senator from New Jersey from 1930 until his death in 1931.

[7]John Pierpont Morgan, Jr., chairman of the board of J. P. Morgan & Company, one of the most influential banking firms in the world.

[8]Florenz "Flo" Ziegfeld, Jr., American theatrical producer, best-known for the *Ziegfeld Follies*. First produced in 1907, these elaborately-staged musical revues

featured a bevy of beautiful chorus girls and many of the leading stage performers of the day. Rogers appeared with the *Follies* from 1916 to 1925.

[9]Albert Martin, mayor of Laredo, Texas, from 1926 to 1954.

William Lee "Will" Wright, captain of Company D of the Texas Rangers from 1917 to 1925 and 1927 to 1933.

[10]Thomas Johnstone Lipton, British tea merchant and sportsman. Lipton competed for the America's Cup yachting trophy five times between 1899 and 1930. Although he never won, he became a great favorite of the American sports public.

[11]Daniel James "Dan" Moody, Jr., Democratic attorney general of Texas from 1925 to 1927; governor from 1927 to 1931.

[12]James Thomas "Tom" Heflin, Democratic United States senator from Alabama from 1920 to 1931; prohibitionist, nativist, and anti-papist.

[13]John Garibaldi Sargent, United States attorney general from 1925 to 1929; a native of Vermont.

[14]Maximilian, French-imposed emperor of Mexico from 1864 to 1867. Mexican nationalists defeated Maximilian's troops at Queretaro, where the Austrian-born monarch was captured and executed in May of 1867.

[15]Thomas Arnold Robinson, American businessman in Mexico City who married Ernestina, a daughter of Plutarco Calles, in 1927.

Plutarco Elías Calles, president of Mexico from 1924 to 1928 and "strong arm" leader of the country during much of the 1920s and 1930s.

MORE LETTERS FROM A SELF-MADE DIPLOMAT TO HIS PRESIDENT (May 19, 1928)

[1]Arturo de Saracho, mayor of Mexico City.

[2]James John "Jimmy" Walker, dapper and flamboyant Democratic mayor of New York City from 1925 to 1932.

[3]J. G. White & Company, a major American engineering and construction firm, built several irrigation and reclamation dams in Mexico during the 1920s and 1930s. Albert Sears Crane and E. G. Williams, executives in the company's home office in New York City, and George W. Caldwell, the local manager, and F. E. Welmouth, the chief engineer in Mexico, represented the firm during Calles' tour of northern Mexico.

[4]Elizabeth Cutter Morrow, American writer, educator, and charity worker; wife of.Dwight W. Morrow.

[5]James Smithers, American importer and exporter; close friend and business associate of Plutarco Calles.

[6]Rebecca, the name of Mrs. Coolidge's pet raccoon.

[7]Patricio F. Healy, Mexican journalist; founder of the Mexico City daily newspaper *Excelsior* and publicity adviser for General Motors of Mexico. Healy, a supporter of Calles, accompanied the presidential entourage as a special correspondent for the *Excelsior*.

[8]Álvaro Obregón, Mexican soldier and political leader; president of Mexico from 1920 to 1924. Obregón was elected again to the presidency in 1928 but was killed before taking office.

[9]Francisco "Pancho" Villa, Mexican bandit and revolutionary leader. In 1916, hoping to draw the United States into war against Mexico, Villa raided Colum-

bus, New Mexico, killing sixteen persons and burning much of the border town. He was assassinated in 1923.

[10]Javier Sanchez Mejorada, representative of the National Irrigation Commission of Mexico.

[11]Charles Gates Dawes, Republican vice president of the United States from 1925 to 1929; Chicago industrialist and attorney, noted for his salty language.

MORE LETTERS FROM A SELF-MADE DIPLOMAT TO HIS PRESIDENT (May 26, 1928)

[1]Edward Ballard, millionaire Indiana horseman and hotel man; builder and owner of the West Baden Springs Hotel, near French Lick, Indiana. In 1934, with a decrease in business due to the Great Depression, Ballard gave his $7,000,000 hotel to the Jesuits for use as a college.

Thomas "Tom" Taggart, Irish-born American politician and hotel proprietor; Democratic "boss" of Indiana; United States senator in 1916. In 1901 Taggart purchased a hotel at French Lick, Indiana, site of the world-famous sulphur spring "Pluto," and developed the property into one of the most famous health resorts in the country.

[2]Several political scandals erupted in Indiana in 1928. The incumbent Republican governor was tried and acquitted of bribery charges that also involved a former governor who already had been convicted of the same crime. In an unrelated case, Republican members of the Indianapolis City Council also faced charges of bribery.

[3]John Davison Rockefeller, Sr., American oilman and industrial tycoon who founded Standard Oil Company in 1870. Although well-recognized as a generous philanthropist, Rockefeller also earned a reputation as a parsimonious tipper, frequently bestowing only a shiny dime as gratuity.

[4]William Edgar Borah, Republican United States senator from Idaho from 1907 to 1940. In the 1920s Borah became the most powerful force in foreign affairs in the country, particularly after December of 1924 when he became chairman of the Senate Committee on Foreign Relations.

[5]The McNary-Haugen farm relief bill was designed to ease a post-World War I depression in agriculture by providing federal assistance for the control of surpluses and the stabilization of prices. Coolidge twice vetoed the legislation.

[6]Augusto César Sandino, Nicaraguan revolutionary who supported a liberal insurrection in Nicaragua in 1926 and waged guerrilla warfare from 1927 to 1932 against United States Marines who intervened in the conflict.

[7]William Hale "Bill" Thompson, Republican mayor of Chicago from 1915 to 1923 and 1927 to 1931. In the mayoral election of 1927, Thompson attacked his incumbent opponent for permitting the use in Chicago public schools of history textbooks that Thompson considered pro-British.

[8]Krupp, prominent German family of armament manufacturers and mine owners.

[9]George V, king of Great Britain and Northern Ireland from 1910 until his death in 1936.

[10]Christiaan Rudolph De Wet, Boer soldier and politician who commanded the Boer forces against the British during the later stages of the Boer War. From

1902 to 1903 Rogers worked as a cowboy in South Africa and toured that country with a wild west show.

[11]Joaquín Amaro, Mexican secretary of war from 1925 to 1929; veteran military leader of the Mexican Revolution; modernizer of the country's armed forces.

[12]José Gonzalo Escobar, Mexican general who led rebel forces in Mexico from 1928 to 1929.

Gilberto R. Limón, Mexican military leader and revolutionist who led a brief, ill-fated rebellion against the government in 1929.

Juan Andreu Almazán, Mexican medical student who abandoned his studies in 1910 to join the Revolution; federal general who opposed the Escobar rebellion.

Roberto Cruz, Mexican general and the chief of police of Mexico City; staunch supporter of the Calles government.

MORE LETTERS FROM A SELF-MADE DIPLOMAT TO HIS PRESIDENT (June 2, 1928)

[1]William John Bulow, Democratic governor of South Dakota from 1927 to 1931; first Democratic chief executive in the history of the state.

[2]James Eli Watson, Republican United States senator from Indiana from 1916 to 1933; a determined conservative who advocated high protective tariffs, a strong defense, and isolationism.

[3]Izaak Walton, seventeenth-century English writer and naturalist; author of *The Compleat Angler* (1653), the fisherman's bible.

[4]George Rublee, American attorney; associated with Morrow on the Allied Maritime Transport Council from 1918 to 1919, as legal adviser to the American embassy in Mexico from 1928 to 1930, and as adviser to the London Naval Conference in 1930.

[5]Paul Whiteman, American bandleader who became famous in the 1920s for pioneering "sweet style" as opposed to the traditional "classical" jazz.

[6]Clement Vann "Clem" Rogers, Indian Territory rancher, banker, and political figure; father of Will Rogers.

[7]Constantine, unidentified.

[8]Charles C. "Cash and Carry" Pyle, American businessman and sports promoter who, in 1928, staged the "bunion derby," in which athletes ran across the United States in the first such transcontinental marathon.

[9]Charles Augustus Lindbergh, American aviator who made the first solo, nonstop transatlantic flight, from New York City to Paris, May 20-21, 1927. An international hero and a booster of aviation, Lindbergh made a well-received good will flight to Mexico City from Washington, D. C., in December of 1927.

[10]Following his return to the United States from France, Lindbergh made a nationwide tour to foster popular interest in aviation. The trip was sponsored by the philanthropic foundation of the American industrialist and capitalist, Daniel Guggenheim.

[11]Alexander J. "Sandy" Macnab, American army officer; military attache at the United States embassy in Mexico from 1927 to 1930; close friend of Charles Lindbergh.

MORE LETTERS FROM A SELF-MADE DIPLOMAT TO HIS PRESIDENT (June 9, 1928)

[1]James Alexander "Jim" Reed, United States senator from Missouri from 1911 to 1929; maverick Democrat from Kansas City.

[2]Henry Cabot Lodge, United States senator from Massachusetts from 1893 until his death in 1924; urbane Boston attorney, editor, historian, and author; conservative, party-line Republican.

[3]Genaro Estrada, Mexican foreign secretary in the Calles administration; diplomat and author; originator of the *Doctrina Mexicana*, by which Mexico recognizes new governments.

[4]Frank Billings Kellogg, United States secretary of state from 1925 to 1929; ambassador to Great Britain from 1924 to 1925; co-recipient of the Nobel Peace Prize in 1929.

[5]Augustín Castrejón, major in the Mexican army air service.

[6]Emilio Carranza, known as "Mexico's Lindy," set several Mexican aeronautical records. In 1928 he flew nonstop from Mexico City to Washington, D. C., thereby repaying Lindbergh's good will trip and helping to ameliorate Mexican-American relations. He perished, however, when his plane crashed on the return flight.

[7]Andréa, Audomaro, and Antonio Becerril, Mexican roping specialists.

[8]The Republican National Convention of 1928 was held in Kansas City, Missouri.

[9]John I. Moore, captain in the United States Army Air Service; veteran flier of World War I; based at Kelly Air Field in San Antonio, Texas.

[10]Will and Betty Rogers had three children living in 1928: William Vann "Bill, Jr.," Mary Amelia, and James Blake "Jimmy." A fourth child, Fred Stone Rogers, died in infancy in 1920.

[11]James Couzens, United States senator from Michigan from 1922 until his death in 1936; wealthy industrialist and former mayor of Detroit. A progressive Republican, Couzens proved a constant critic of the conservative monetary policies of Andrew Mellon.

[12]Charles Curtis, Republican United States senator from Kansas from 1907 to 1913 and 1915 to 1929; vice president of the United States from 1929 to 1933; claimed part Kansa and Osage Indian ancestry.

[13]Charles Dewey Hilles, New York insurance executive, corporate director, and political figure; member of the Republican National Committee from 1912 to 1938; adviser to Coolidge.

[14]The Democratic National Convention met in Houston in 1928.

LETTERS OF A SELF-MADE DIPLOMAT TO SENATOR BORAH (February 27, 1932)

[1]George Woodward Wickersham, American corporation lawyer who served as United States attorney general from 1909 to 1913. In 1929 he chaired a presidential commission that surveyed the enforcement of the Eighteenth Amendment. The commission concluded, in its voluminous report of 1931, that the federal machinery for enforcing prohibition was inadequate.

[2]Smedley Darlington Butler, major general in the United States Marine Corps; commander of the Marine Expeditionary Force in China from 1927 to 1929. Butler retired from active duty in October of 1931 after failing to be named commandant of the Marine Corps.

[3]Charles Spencer "Charlie" Chaplin, English-born comedian who starred in several classic American and British films. A near-legendary figure, Chaplin achieved universal fame for his portrayal of the "Little Tramp."

[4]Alfonso XIII, king of Spain from 1886 to 1931. After the municipal elections of 1931 showed an overwhelming republican majority and with discontent against his rule running high, Alfonso "suspended the exercise of royal power" and went into exile in Rome in April of 1931.

[5]Edward Albert, prince of Wales from 1911 until his succession to the British throne in 1936; briefly reigned as Edward VIII; extremely popular as a bachelor prince.

[6]Dino Grandi, Italian diplomat and statesman; minister of foreign affairs from 1929 to 1932.

[7]Franklin Delano Roosevelt, Democratic governor of New York from 1929 to 1933; president of the United States from 1933 until his death in 1945.

Newton Diehl Baker, American attorney and statesman; United States secretary of war from 1916 to 1921; member of the Permanent Court of Arbitration.

[8]Pierre Laval, French premier and minister of foreign affairs from 1931 to 1932.

[9]Dawes chaired an international war reparations committee in 1923-1924 that advanced the so-called Dawes Plan as a means of stabilizing postwar German finances.

[10]Edward Mandell House, Texas politician and United States diplomat; close friend and confidant of Woodrow Wilson; Wilson's personal peace envoy to Europe during World War I.

[11]Godfrey Rathbone Benson, Baron Charnwood, English politician, writer, and editor; author of a widely known and respected biography of Abraham Lincoln (1916).

Carl Sandburg, American poet and biographer. Sandburg's most ambitious work was a six-volume biography of Lincoln (1926-1939) for which he won a Pulitzer prize.

Once in a Lifetime (1930), a satiric play about Hollywood during the transition from silent films to "talkies"; written by American dramatists Moss Hart and George Simon Kaufman.

[12]Calvin Cobb, editor and publisher of the *Idaho Statesman* from 1889 until his death in 1928. A stalwart Republican, Cobb helped to establish Borah politically.

[13]Margaret Cobb, only daughter of Calvin Cobb.

[14]James Ramsay MacDonald, prime minister of Great Britain in 1924 and from 1929 to 1931 and 1931 to 1935.

Mohandas Karamchand Gandhi, Indian political and spiritual leader known as the Mahatma, or Great Soul; principal leader of the Indian struggle for independence from Great Britain, a goal finally attained in 1947.

[15]Henry Ford, American automotive pioneer and manufacturer; founder and president of Ford Motor Company.

[16]Dwight Morrow died in October of 1931 after serving only five months in the United States Senate.

[17]Alphonse "Scarface Al" Capone, infamous Chicago gang leader who became

a symbol of lawlessness in the 1920s and early 1930s. His notoriety prompted several accounts of his life, including Fred D. Pasley's *Al Capone; the Biography of a Self-Made Man* (1931).

[18]James Cannon, Jr., bishop in the Methodist Episcopal Church, South, from 1918 until his death in 1944; an ardent and active prohibitionist.

[19]Raphael Floyd Phillips Gibbons, American journalist, author, and radio commentator; an internationally-known, roving reporter; the leading war correspondent of his generation.

[20]China was embroiled for more than twenty years in a deeply-devisive and bloody civil war between Nationalists and Communists. In 1931 Japan, taking advantage of the civil strife in China, occupied Manchuria, where a year later it established the puppet state of Manchukuo.

[21]Henry Lewis Stimson, United States secretary of state from 1929 to 1933.

[22]John Nance "Jack" Garner, Democratic United States representative from Texas from 1903 to 1933; Speaker of the House from 1931 to 1933; vice president of the United States from 1933 to 1941.

LETTERS OF A SELF-MADE DIPLOMAT TO SENATOR BORAH
(March 5, 1932)

[1]Harry Carey, American motion picture actor and leading man of silent films. Although star of scores of westerns from 1908 until his death in 1947, Carey gained wide fame for his leading role in the 1929 *Trader Horn*.

[2]David Sinton Ingalls, United States assistant secretary of the navy for aeronautics from 1929 to 1932. A Republican, Ingalls ran unsuccessfully for governor of Ohio in 1932.

[3]George Selwyn Walden, general manager of the Indonesian affiliate of Standard Oil Company of New Jersey from 1929 to 1934.

[4]John Davison Rockefeller, Jr., son and namesake of the Standard Oil Company magnate; manager of the family philanthropies.

[5]Robert Pierce "Bob" Shuler, fundamentalist clergyman, lecturer, and author; pastor of Trinity Church in Los Angeles.

William Ralph Inge, British Anglican cleric and scholar; dean of Saint Paul's from 1911 to 1934.

[6]Robert Andrews Millikan, American physicist; director of the Norman Bridge Laboratory of Physics at the California Institute of Technology at Pasadena from 1921 until his death in 1953; recipient of the Nobel Prize in physics in 1923.

Albert Einstein, noted German physicist who received a Nobel prize in 1921 for his work in theoretical physics, notably on the photoelectric effect. He served as a visiting professor at the California Institute of Technology during the winter of 1930-1931.

[7]David Aiken Reed, Republican United States senator from Pennsylvania from 1922 to 1935.

[8]Hiram Bingham, Republican United States senator from Connecticut from 1924 to 1933; licensed pilot and promoter of military and civil aviation. Bingham had seven sons.

[9]William Cameron Forbes, American banker, special presidential commissioner, and diplomat; ambassador to Japan from 1930 to 1932.

[10]Dwight Filley Davis, United States governor general of the Philippine Islands from 1929 to 1932. Davis was visiting Japan with his eldest daughter, Alice Brooks Davis.

[11]Kikugoro Onoe VI, Japanese actor and dancer, renown for his performances in plays of plebian life; member of a distinguished family of *kabuki* actors.

[12]Mei Lan-fang, Peking opera star who was the outstanding figure in the Chinese theater during the first half of the twentieth century. Mei and his troupe made an unprecedented tour of the United States in 1930.

[13]Hiram Warren Johnson, United States senator from California from 1917 until his death in 1945; a maverick Republican progressive.

George Higgins Moses, Republican United States senator from New Hampshire from 1918 to 1933; president pro tempore of the Senate from 1925 to 1933; staunch supporter of the Coolidge and Hoover administrations.

[14]Eugenie Marie de Montijo de Guzman, Spanish-born empress of the French from 1853 to 1871 and wife of Emperor Louis Napoleon. A leader in international fashion, she contributed much to the brilliancy of the French court.

[15]Maurice Auguste Chevalier, French entertainer who gained an international reputation in the music halls of Paris in the 1920s. He also achieved fame as a star of American films, beginning with his appearance in *The Love Parade* in 1930.

[16]Jiro Minami, Japanese general and military leader; minister of war in 1931.

[17]Ann Pennington, American dancer who often performed in the *Ziegfeld Follies* and who won fame as the dancer with the "dimpled knees."

[18]Fanny Brice, American comedienne who was a master of comic awkwardness; star of burlesque, vaudeville, legitimate theater, radio, and motion pictures.

[19]William Sidney Graves, American army officer; commander of the American Expeditionary Force in Siberia from 1918 to 1920; author of *America's Siberian Adventures* (1931). A major general, Graves retired from the service in 1928.

[20]James Leo "One-Eyed" Connelly, heavyweight boxer of the late 1800s who was widely noted for his ingenious and successful schemes at gate-crashing and self-promotion.

LETTERS OF A SELF-MADE DIPLOMAT TO SENATOR BORAH
(March 12, 1932)

[1]Joseph Ridgway Grundy, American textile industrialist and banker; president of the Pennsylvania Manufacturers' Association from 1909 to 1930. A stalwart Republican and a leading protectionist, Grundy served in the United States Senate from 1929 to 1930.

[2]Japan blamed Chinese dissidents for the destruction in 1931 of the Japanese-owned South Manchurian Railway near Mukden. The mysterious bombing, known historically as the Manchurian Incident, gave Japan the impetus to establish a puppet government in Manchuria.

[3]Chang Hsueh-liang, Chinese war lord of Manchuria from 1928 until his

ouster by the Japanese in 1931; known as the "Young Marshal"; self-proclaimed emperor of Manchuria.

[4]Edward Grey, Viscount Grey of Fallodon, British statesman who served as minister of foreign affairs of Great Britain from 1905 to 1916; author of *Twenty-five Years, 1892-1916*. Grey played a crucial role in the events leading to World War I.

[5]Feng Yu-hsiang, Chinese military leader, known as the "Christian General"; made field marshal in 1923; held various positions in the Nationalist government from 1928 to 1933.

[6]George Herman "Babe" Ruth, popular professional baseball player who won fame as a home run slugger with the New York Yankees from 1920 to 1935; inducted into the Baseball Hall of Fame in 1936.

[7]John Joseph Pershing, American military officer, known as "Black Jack"; commanded the Allied Expeditionary Force in Europe during World War I; Army chief of staff from 1921 to 1924.

[8]William Jennings Bryan, prominent Democratic politician, known as the "Great Commoner"; unsuccessful Democratic candidate for the presidency in 1896, 1900, and 1908; United States secretary of state from 1913 to 1915. Bryan died in 1925.

[9]Japan tried to seize the Liao-tung peninsula of Manchuria in 1895 but was forestalled by the Triple Intervention.

[10]Chang Tso-lin, Chinese military leader who secured control of three Manchurian provinces in 1918 and occupied the northeastern provinces of China in 1926. While retreating from Peking in 1928, Chang died when the train he was riding was bombed by the Japanese army.

[11]William McKinley, Republican president of the United States from 1897 to 1901.

Marcus Alonzo "Mark" Hanna, capitalist and politician who, by 1890, was the ruling power in the Ohio Republican party; United States senator from 1897 to 1904; close adviser to McKinley and the major force behind the nomination of McKinley for the presidency in 1896.

[12]When the Japanese formally annexed Korea in 1910, they changed the name of the country to the old name, Choson.

LETTERS OF A SELF-MADE DIPLOMAT TO SENATOR BORAH
(March 19, 1932)

[1]The Treaty of Portsmouth of 1905 ended the Russo-Japanese War. It was signed at Portsmouth Naval Base, New Hampshire, after President Theodore Roosevelt had prevailed on the warring powers to end the conflict and to negotiate a peace agreement.

[2]George Charles Hanson, American foreign service officer and Far Eastern specialist who served as consul general at Harbin, Manchuria, from 1931 to 1933.

[3]The Lytton Commission, chaired by Lord Lytton of Great Britain, was sent by the League of Nations in 1932 to investigate the Manchurian situation. Its report, recommending in effect economic sanctions against Japan, prompted that nation to withdraw from the League in 1933.

[4]Ma Chan-shan, Chinese general who led military opposition to the Japanese

presence in Manchuria and who served as governor of Hejlungkiang province in northern Manchuria.

⁵William Randolph Hearst, powerful American publishing tycoon and Democratic politician; owner of a large chain of newspapers and magazines.

⁶Arthur Capper, Republican United States senator from Kansas from 1919 to 1949; owner and publisher of the *Topeka Daily Capital, Capper's Weekly, Capper's Farmer*, and other publications.

⁷Henry W. Kinney, American teacher and newspaperman who worked as a publicity agent for the Japanese-controlled South Manchurian Railway.

⁸Sao-ke Alfred Sze, Chinese minister to the United States from 1921 to 1929 and 1932 to 1935; delegate to the League of Nations Assembly in 1931; ambassador to the United States from 1935 to 1937.

⁹George Gorman, Irish newspaperman who was a correspondent in China for the *London Daily Telegraph* and an editor of Japanese newspapers in Peking.

¹⁰Clara Bow, American motion picture actress who symbolized the flapper age and the "Roaring 20s" as the "It" girl of the decade.

¹¹Greta Garbo, Swedish motion picture actress. Garbo, noted for her haunting beauty and sultry sexuality, arrived in Hollywood in 1926, where she soon became one of the highest paid performers in films.

¹²Fifi D'orsay, French-Canadian leading lady of Hollywood films in the early 1930s. She made her American film debut in 1929 with Rogers in *They Had to See Paris*.

¹³Huey Pierce Long, Democratic governor of Louisiana from 1928 to 1932; United States senator from 1932 until his death in 1935; creator of the "Long Machine," which dominated Louisiana politics after 1928.

¹⁴William Henry "Alfalfa Bill" Murray, Democratic governor of Oklahoma from 1931 to 1935.

LETTERS OF A SELF-MADE DIPLOMAT TO SENATOR BORAH
(April 2, 1932)

¹Francis Monroe "Frank" Hawks, American aviator who established numerous transcontinental and point-to-point speed records in the 1920s and 1930s.

²Simeon Davison Fess, Republican United States senator from Ohio from 1923 to 1935.

³Smith Wildman Brookhart, United States senator from Iowa from 1922 to 1926 and 1927 to 1933; member of the maverick progressive faction of the Republican party.

⁴Sun Yat-sen, Chinese statesman and revolutionary leader, called the "father of the Chinese Revolution"; provisional president of the Chinese Republic from 1911 to 1912; president of the Southern Chinese Republic from 1921 to 1922. A powerful force in Canton, Sun died of cancer in 1925.

⁵Chiang Kai-shek, Chinese general and political leader, president of the Chinese Nationalist government from 1928 and 1931, 1948 to 1949, and 1950 until his death in 1975.

⁶Elbert Hubbard, American author and publisher. An ardent believer in rugged individualism, Hubbard edited the inspirational magazine *Philistine* and was the author of the essay "A Message to Garcia" (1899).

Henry Louis Mencken, American editor, author, and publisher; a social and political critic, well-known for his acid pen.

[7]William Holmes McGuffey, American educator; professor of moral philosophy at the University of Virginia from 1845 to 1873; remembered chiefly as the compiler of the *McGuffey Eclectic Readers* (1836-1857).

[8]Cecil John Rhodes, British administrator and financier in South Africa who left much of his large fortune to provide scholarships to Oxford University for students from throughout the world.

[9]Tzu Hsi, Chinese dowager empress who served as regent from 1862 to 1873, 1875 to 1889, and 1898 until her death in 1908.

A LETTER TO THE PHILIPPINES (April 30, 1932)

[1]Boies Penrose, longtime Republican "boss" of Pennsylvania; United States senator from 1897 until his death in 1921.

[2]Tommy Lee, unidentified; possibly an Americanized spelling of a Chinese name.

[3]William Henry Donald, Australian journalist, known as "Donald of China"; adviser to Chang Hsueh-liang from 1928 to 1934 and, later, adviser to and close friend of Chiang Kai-shek.

[4]Hutton, unidentified.

[5]Hutchinson, unidentified.

[6]Victor Sassoon, British baronet who headed a vast financial empire in the Far East during the 1920s, including large banking interests and real estate investments in China.

[7]Hallett Edward Abend, American newspaperman, lecturer, and author; China correspondent for the *New York Times* from 1927 to 1942.

[8]Douglas Robertson, *New York Times* correspondent in Shanghai; assistant to bureau chief in China.

[9]Robert Tyre "Bobby" Jones, American amateur golfer who was one of the all-time great players of the sport; winner of four United States Open championships, three British Open crowns, and five United States amateur titles.

[10]Manuel Luis Quezon y Molina, Philippine statesman and leader in the struggle for national independence; president of the Philippine Senate from 1916 to 1935; president of the Commonwealth of the Philippines from 1935 until his death in 1944.

[11]Patrick Jay "Pat" Hurley, United States secretary of war from 1929 to 1933; Tulsa attorney and oilman. Hurley made an inspection tour of the Philippine Islands in the fall of 1931.

[12]Harry Barstow Hawes, Democratic United States senator from Missouri from 1927 to 1933. Hawes, long an advocate of independence for the American-owned Philippine Islands, coauthored the Hawes-Cutting bill in 1930 that called for independence five years after acceptance of a Philippine constitution. Hawes visited the islands in July of 1931 and assured the inhabitants that he would continue to work for their freedom. The United States granted independence in 1946.

[13]Reed Smoot, Republican United States senator from Utah from 1903 to 1933; Mormon Church official and Utah sugar beet producer; proponent of high tariffs, especially on imported sugar.

Notes

¹⁴Emilio Aguinaldo, Filipino revolutionary leader who led a costly and bloody insurrection against American authority from 1899 until his capture by United States forces in 1901. He was briefly imprisoned and then retired to private life.

INDEX

Chicago, Ill.: 56-58, 63, 101, 142; crime in, 29, 57-58, 77; waterway in, 44

Ch'i-ch'i-ha-erh, China: *see* Tsitsihar

chickens: 47

chili con carne: 44, 46, 68

China: war with Japan, 107, 108, 116, 120-21, 124-31, 132-34, 136, 138, 142, 143, 146, 147, 149, 161, 162, 172-73; military in, 125; people of, 125, 128, 130-31, 153, 154, 156, 157, 158-60; Rogers in, 126-30, 131, 146, 147-69, 171; army of, 128, 129-30, 134; lack of leadership in, 128, 129-30; civil war in, 129, 156; history of, 135; banditry in, 143, 156; war lords in, 143, 145, 164; humor in, 150; art in, 151; population control in, 153; foreigners, 155-57; government of, 155, 165; politics in, 155-56, 157; tradition in, 157; corruption in, 158; education in, 158; honesty in, 158; crises in, 160; food in, 163-64; aviation in, 164; starvation in, 164; railroads in, 165

China, Great Wall of: 98, 155

Chinchow, China: 131, 143, 166

Chinese Eastern Railroad: 141

Chinese language: 155

chopsticks: 119, 120, 149, 159, 163

Chosen: *see* Korea

Christian General: *see* Feng Yu-hsiang

Christianity: 130

Christians: 166

Christmas: 166-67, 168

church buildings, in Mexico: 33, 75, 77

cigarettes: 81

civilization: 23, 47, 106, 134, 137, 147, 151, 152, 163

Claremore, Okla.: 9, 36, 125, 143; Indian hospital at, 13

Claremore (Oklahoma) *Progress:* 6

Cleveland, Ohio: 16, 91

coal: 70, 110

Cobb, Calvin: 101

Cobb, Margaret: 101

cockfighting: 47

cocktails: 137

colleges and universities: 25; diplomas from, 40; students at, 40, 54, 165; graduates of, 54; professors at, 106; degrees from, 159

Colorado River: 44

Columbia River: 97

Columbus, Christopher: 82, 89

comedians: 5, 43, 65, 67, 143, 147, 152

comedy, in U. S. Congress: 108

commercial clubs: 24; *see also* luncheon clubs

commissions, presidential: 29-30, 70, 95-97, 100, 134, 153, 172

"common people": 5, 38

common sense: 26

communism and Communists: 142

Coney Island, N. Y.: 115

conferences, international: 11, 22, 44, 99, 107-108, 111, 125, 137, 138

confidence: 106; in Mexico, 82

Confucius: 110, 130, 135, 153, 158; sayings of, 157

Congressional Record: 161

Connelly, James L. (One-Eyed): 123

Constantine, _____: 68, 69

consular service, of U. S.: 73

conventions, political: delegates to, 91, 92

Coolidge, Calvin: 3-17, 21, 23, 25-26, 29, 31, 34, 35, 36, 37-38, 40, 42, 45, 49, 50, 52-53, 57, 58, 62-63, 64, 65, 69, 70, 72, 73, 81, 82, 90-92, 95, 97, 98, 105, 109-10, 119, 124, 134, 153, 160, 162; vacation of, 9, 35, 42, 62-63; cabinet of, 15; speeches of, 16; humor of, 17; dogs of, 7-8, 10, 13; farm of, 31; pet raccoon of, 35, 42

Coolidge, Grace A. G.: 4-7, 8-9, 10, 12-13, 14, 15, 16, 17; humor of, 7, 13

coonskin caps: 90

cooperatives, agricultural: in Mexico, 52

golf pants: 25, 26
Goodrich, James P.: 12, 13
Gorman, George: 147
government: of U.S., 3; economy in, 21, 31
governors, in Mexico: 69
graft: 75; in Mexico, 78-79; *see also* corruption
Grand Canyon National Park: 168
Grandi, Dino: 97, 101
Grant, Ulysses S.: 149
Graves, William S.: 122-23, 139
Great Sphinx: 98
Grey, Edward: memoirs of, 127
Grundy, Joseph R.: 126, 135
Guadalupe Day: 77
Guggenheim Foundation: 71
guitars: 63; playing of, 82
gunboats, of U. S.: 11, 23, 148

The Hague, Netherlands: peace conference at, 135
Haiti: 26, 57
Hamilton, Alexander: 21
Hankow, China: 129-30
Hanna, Marcus A. (Mark): 135
Hanson, George C.: 141-42
Harbin, China: 125, 136, 137, 138, 140-42, 143, 147
Harding, Warren G.: 8
Hart, Moss: 101
Harvard University: 74, 154
Harvey, George B. M.: 8
hash: 10, 15
hats: 114
Hawes, Harry B.: 169, 173
Hawks, Francis M. (Frank): 153
Hays, William H. (Will): 6
Healy, Patricio F.: 42
Hearst, William Randolph: 143
Heflin, J. Thomas (Tom): 29
Henry, Patrick: 71
heroism: 130
highways: 95
Hilles, Charles D.: 91
historians: 151
history: 89, 135, 138, 139, 158; study of, 25; of U. S., 105; of China, 135; of Korea, 135; of

Japan, 135
Holland: *see* Netherlands
Hollywood, Calif.: 82, 101, 107-108, 142, 162
honesty: 158; in China, 158
Hong Kong: 151
honor: 138; among nations, 23, 55
Hoover, Herbert C.: 5, 90, 91, 95-96, 98, 100, 105, 108, 109, 110, 119, 125, 148, 161, 169, 172, 173; presidential commissions of, 95-97, 153, 172
Hoover, Irwin H. (Ike): 5, 15
Hoover (Boulder) Dam: 37, 44, 54, 70
hors d'oeuvres: 40
horsemanship: 124
horses: 124-25; in Mexico, 47; Mongolian breed, 124, 149-50
hotels, Japanese-owned: 131
House, Edward M.: 98, 135; writings of, 127
Houston, Texas: 92
Hubbard, Elbert: 157
Hughes, Antoinette C. (Mrs. Charles E.): 9
Hughes, Charles Evans: 9, 44, 82, 83
Humane Society: 47, 139
humanitarianism: 91, 111, 133, 139, 140, 142
humor: 6, 7, 13, 17, 24, 96; of Coolidge, 17; in Mexico, 41, 42, 46; in foreign languages, 42; of Rogers, 42, 43-44; in Ireland, 46; in China, 150
hunger: 103, 106; *see also* starvation
hunting: 73
Hurley, Patrick J. (Pat): 169-70, 174
husbands: 34, 107
Hutchinson, _____: 165
Hutton, _____: 164

Idaho: 98, 101, 131
illiteracy: 5
imperialism: 131-34, 136, 171
independence: 23, 138
India: 125, 128-29, 133, 166, 172
Indiana: 12; politics in, 49, 109; spa in, 49